A FRAMEWORK FOR THE DEVELOPMENT OF ACCOUNTING EDUCATION RESEARCH

Copyright, American Accounting Association, 1988,
All rights reserved.
Library of Congress Catalog Card Number 88-071315
ISBN 0-86539-067-3
Printed in the United States of America

American Accounting Association
5717 Bessie Drive
Sarasota, Florida 34233

Foreword

As Director of Education in 1981–1983, my Education Advisory Committee and I became convinced that the education literature of disciplines related to accounting was frequently ignored by those engaged in accounting education research. A consequence was to reduce the quality of accounting education research. The decision was made to commission a research project to search out such literature and report on it for the benefit of accounting education researchers. I am pleased to report that the project has been completed most successfully with product being a monograph, a user manual and a diskette data base.

My deep appreciation is extended first to the researchers Professors Jan R. Williams, James H. Scheiner and Hartwell C. Herring III, all of the University of Tennessee and Professor Mikel G. Tiller, Indiana University. Second, I am most grateful to those individuals who helped in offering advice to the researchers both those in accounting: Professor Andrew D. Bailey, Jr., The Ohio State University, Professor E. Joe DeMaris, North Texas State University, Professor Douglas A. Snowball, University of Florida and Mr. Salvatore Luiso, Coopers & Lybrand and those from other disciplines: Economics Professor Bruce Dalgard, University of Minnesota; Psychology Professor Richard J. Klimoski, The Ohio State University, Education Professor Robert J. Menges, Northwestern University; and Psychology Professor Emeritus Marvin E. Shaw, University of Florida. Finally I extend my thanks to Coopers & Lybrand for their generosity in funding this project.

Thomas J. Burns
Chairman of Advisory Committee

December, 1987

Acknowledgements

This project was organized based on the assumption that a taxonomy of education research of interest to accountants could be developed from a review of empirical research of both accounting and non-accounting literature. Given the volume of potential sources, a computerized data search was employed to facilitate identification of the topics to be reviewed. Based upon the initial data retrieved, an outline was prepared that ultimately became the five main chapters of the monograph. Completion of the entire project thus required that the work be allocated to the authors in somewhat unique ways.

As project director, Jan R. Williams was responsible for maintaining communications with the AAA Committee, and contributed much in the way of organization of the monograph. He was the co-author with Hartwell C. Herring III on Chapter 3, "Research Related to Students," and with Hartwell C. Herring III and James H. Scheiner on Chapter 6, "Research Related to Administration and Constituents." He also co-authored Chapter 1, "Introduction to the Framework" and Appendix A, "Summary of Accounting Education Research Opportunities" with Mikel G. Tiller.

Developing the computerized data base was the responsibility of James H. Scheiner. Given the volume of potential sources, several assumptions and limitations were employed to keep the number of references within manageable proportions. Of particular importance was the limitation of the computerized search to published empirical studies. James H. Scheiner was the author of Appendix B, "Description of the Data Base," which describes the data base of references used in the study, and the co-author with Hartwell C. Herring III and Jan R. Williams of Chapter 6. He also wrote the data base manual which accompanies this monograph.

Mikel G. Tiller and Hartwell C. Herring III were the principal authors on the main body of the monograph. Mikel G. Tiller authored Chapter 2, "Empirical Research Methods in Education"; Chapter 4, "Research Related to Faculty"; and Chapter 7, "Outcomes." He also co-authored Chapter 1 and Appendix A with Jan R. Williams. Hartwell C. Herring III authored Chapter 5, "Research Related to the Educational Process," co-authored Chapter 3 with Jan R. Williams, and co-authored Chapter 6 with Jan R. Williams and James H. Scheiner. Since many of the books, and the accounting literature cited, were not found through the computerized data search, Professors Tiller and Herring contributed many references to the data base through their individual research efforts and were instrumental in determining the final organization of this monograph. In addition to writing major portions of the manuscript, Professor Tiller played a leading role in establishing the organization of this project. He provided direction and structure for the literature review as well as for the final form of the monograph.

Many individuals contributed significantly to the successful completion of this project. Financial support provided by the Coopers & Lybrand Foundation made it possible for the American Accounting Association to sponsor a project of this magnitude.

Thomas J. Burns of The Ohio State University was AAA Director of Education when this project was authorized, and then Chairman of the project's advisory committee. Professor Burns was particularly helpful in bringing together and coordinating the efforts of many talented individuals who provided valuable encouragement, suggestions, and critiques of this monograph at various stages of its development. Salvatore Luiso of Coopers and Lybrand ably represented the practicing profession on the AAA advisory committee. Other advisory committee members were Douglas A. Snowball of the University of Florida and Andrew D. Bailey Jr. of Ohio State. Both were extremely helpful as critical, supportive evaluators of our work.

We also appreciate the efforts of Donald L. Madden (University of Kentucky) and

Loren A. Nikolai (University of Missouri), who provided support for the project through their respective terms as AAA Directors of Education. The current Director of Education, Gary J. Previts (Case Western Reserve University) has also provided enthusiastic encouragement and assistance.

We benefited a great deal from the considerable expertise of reviewers from other disciplines. These were Robert J. Menges of the Center for the Teaching Professions, Northwestern University; Bruce R. Dalgaard, Director of the Center for Economic Education of the University of Minnesota; Marvin E. Shaw, Professor of Psychology of the University of Florida; and Richard Kilmoski, Professor of Psychology, The Ohio State University. Gerald L. Salamon and Earl A. Spiller Jr. (both of Indiana University) also provided helpful comments on the research methods chapter.

We are grateful to Donna Street, Cynthia Norwood, Dorothy Jones, and Richard Ellis for providing valuable research and library assistance for the project. We appreciate Evelyn Cherry's untiring maintenance of control over numerous manuscript drafts and many other administrative matters, as well as the additional assistance of Angela Rule, Bridget Graham, and Tracy Ashley for many patient hours of word processing. Final editing of the manuscript by Jean McDonald significantly enhanced the monograph's readability.

Finally, we would like to recognize the contribution of our families to this project. Their encouragement and support were invaluable to all of us.

Jan R. Williams, Project Director
Mikel G. Tiller
Hartwell C. Herring III
James H. Scheiner

Table of Contents

CHAPTER 1   INTRODUCTION TO THE FRAMEWORK

Research Approach Employed 2
The Framework 3
Organization of Specific Topic Area Discussions 3
Conclusion 5

CHAPTER 2   EMPIRICAL RESEARCH METHODS IN EDUCATION

Introduction 7
Reporting Empirical Findings 9
True Experiments 12
Field Experiments 17
Field Studies and Surveys 25
Measurement Issues and Problems 31
Conclusion 38

CHAPTER 3   RESEARCH RELATED TO STUDENTS

Student Attitudes and Beliefs 43
Communication Skills of Students 50
Academic Achievement 55

CHAPTER 4   RESEARCH RELATED TO FACULTY

Student Evaluation of Teachers 68
Faculty Performance Evaluation 74
Research 78
Teaching 80
Faculty Development 83

The Status of Women and Minority Faculty 86
Conclusion 90

CHAPTER 5 RESEARCH RELATED TO THE EDUCATIONAL PROCESS

Testing and Grading 99
Teaching Methods..108
Learning 121
Contextual Issues 123

CHAPTER 6 RESEARCH RELATED TO ADMINISTRATION AND CONSTITUENTS

Administrative Structure and Five-Year Programs 131
Accreditation of Programs 137
Faculty Vitality..140
Financing of Programs...143
Academic Program Ratings..144
Continuing Professional Education...148

CHAPTER 7 OUTCOMES

Identifying and Evaluating Outcomes 157
Outcome Specification in Higher Education.......................................162
Outcome Specification in Accounting Education 164

APPENDIX A

SUMMARY OF ACCOUNTING EDUCATION RESEARCH OPPORTUNITIES 169

APPENDIX B

DESCRIPTION OF THE DATABASE..183

CHAPTER 1

Introduction to the Framework

The primary purpose of this study, *A Framework for the Development of Accounting Education Research,* is to encourage and facilitate the continuing development of quality accounting education research. Although accounting education has been the subject of examination for many years, research on the topic has expanded rapidly in recent years, probably for a number of reasons. One of the most compelling reasons for the increased interest is that the practice of accounting is adapting to the challenges of a business environment that is changing at a dramatic pace. Innovations in financial markets, important advances in communications and computer technology, and the general movement toward a service-oriented economy combine to create an information-rich environment in which the accounting profession must continually reassess its role. Accounting educators must also react to these changes with unending textbook revisions, constant curricular changes, implementation of alternative educational delivery systems and technology-based innovations, and, increasingly, research.

Much of this monograph summarizes the results of a broad search of higher education literature as well as accounting education literature. One objective of this literature review is to discover what accounting educators and education researchers might learn from the extensive work of others in different areas of higher education. A second is to find, or create, a logical structure that might bring some sense of order and continuity to accounting education research endeavors, and a third objective is to provide guidance concerning the direction of future accounting education research, both in terms of the issues in need of exploration and the application of available research methods.

We found that the higher education literature offers a wealth of knowledge that is of vital importance to accounting educators, researchers, and the accounting profession. Many of the fundamental questions that we face in higher education are important regardless of our particular academic or professional disciplines. Perhaps the most basic problem is determining how we can best induce or encourage our students to learn in a meaningful fashion. What should we be doing in the classroom? How should we test knowledge acquisition, or the development of higher-order mental skills? What learning outcomes, in addition to knowledge acquisition, should we cultivate?

We also found that accounting education is, in many respects, quite different from many of the disciplines included in the higher education literature. Unlike many of the traditional academic branches, accounting academia serves a reasonably well-defined profession. Education programs in the field are responsive to the profession's continuing growth and cognizant of the changing demands placed on accounting professionals. Examples of academia's concern with professional issues abound. For example, information systems and statistical sampling are major topics covered in every undergraduate accounting curriculum, whereas fifteen years ago, they hardly existed. In addition, while only a decade ago we debated whether to allow students to use calculators during examinations, today we seek ways to encourage our students to use microcomputers as learning tools in order to prepare themselves for professional practice. More than many other disciplines, accounting education must be alert to the dynamics of the profession and business community it serves. The academic arm of the profession must maintain a relentlessly developmental orientation in order to help safeguard the professional integrity of the field. The important issue is assessing the profession's direction in order to be prepared for the future.

Accounting academia also must contend with some rather difficult problems that few other disciplines face. Accounting programs are embedded in political and educational institutions that must allocate scarce resources in a manner that achieves diverse educational goals. The demand for accounting education has exceeded the supply of limited educational resources which is not the case with most other disciplines. For example, while other fields seem to have overproduced Ph.D.s, they are in perpetual short supply in accounting. At the same time, the "body of knowledge" that comprises accounting has been expanding rapidly, further taxing the rational limits of its resources. Many accounting programs have gained a reasonable degree of autonomy from the traditional institutional structure and its economic constraints.

What is the most appropriate organizational structure for accounting programs? How many years' education should be necessary in order to prepare our students as professionals? What are the effects of economic reliance on the profession?

Our search of the general education literature and the accounting education literature also indicated that the transfer of knowledge between the two need not be unilateral. We can learn much from the education literature, but we can also provide a significant return. To some extent, our potential contribution is due to the relative uniqueness of the accounting discipline and profession. But it also should be attributable to the fact that we have begun to build on the base of knowledge already established in the rich literatures of higher education in psychology, engineering, law, communications, economics, and many other disciplines. This study is intended to build a foundation from which accounting education research may achieve its potential contribution to the profession and to the growing body of knowledge it builds upon. Although the foundation itself is incomplete, we hope that it is sufficient to provide the serious accounting education researcher a fruitful place to begin the task.

Accounting education research has progressed to its present state largely through the individual efforts of researchers responding to their own perceptions of what issues and problems need to be addressed. Many of these efforts have addressed important research questions with sound methodologies; many have not. The accounting education literature, though improving qualitatively in recent years, is marked by a lack of continuity. Indeed, some of the more consistent lines of research in accounting education have been in response to changes in the business and professional environment. We have failed to examine many important questions directed toward learning more about how our students should be educated.

Research Approach Employed

The initial stages of this research project entailed a thorough search of the accounting education literature and a preliminary, but very broad, search of the general education literature which was conducted largely through the Educational Resources Information Center (ERIC) system maintained by Dialog Information Retrieval Service. ERIC provides a basis for an organized search of the educational literatures of many disciplines via a keyword selection and retrieval process. We recreated the hierarchical structure of keywords in the *Thesaurus of ERIC Descriptors* essentially by arranging them according to which keywords were subsumed under other, broader keywords. After an examination of the citations appearing under various keywords, we chose the keywords "higher education" and "research" to begin our search. The search yielded over 4,000 references dating from 1975, of which about 1,500 were published articles and books. The remaining references—conference papers, working paper series, position papers, dissertations, etc.—we eliminated under the assumption that the most significant of these studies would have been published as articles or books. Thus, these 1,500 references, augmented by subsequent searches of current issues of leading education journals, were used to guide us through the higher education literature.

Based on our work with ERIC's keyword structure, preliminary reviews of major topical areas in education, and our search of the accounting education research literature, we began to organize our efforts by creating a tentative taxonomy of education research issues. As we further explored the literature, the "framework" began to emerge. It is not comprehensive in breadth, nor are all the topics and issues it addresses covered in the same depth. The end product is perhaps less a well-knit taxonomy than a frame of reference. At its most general level, it is a broad descriptive model of education and its environment, tailored to fit the needs of accounting education researchers.

The Framework

Figure 1 presents the major classifications of the framework in terms of the functional relationships among its four major components: students, faculty, administration and constituents, and the educational process. In essence, the framework presents faculty and students as "inputs" to the educational process. We view administration and constituents as sources of the structure in which the educational process takes place. Major research domains within these four classifications are listed below each of them. Chapters 3 through 7 of this monograph are devoted to the framework's four major components: students, faculty, the educational process, and administration and constituents, respectively. The research domains listed in Figure 1 are the major sections of each of these chapters. The third level of the framework is comprised of the specific topical areas that we explored within each research domain. These, and more specific subtopic areas, are shown in the figures at the beginning of Chapters 3 through 6.

An important objective of this study, and the framework, is to assist researchers in planning and conducting accounting education research that:

1. addresses substantive issues in accounting education,
2. builds logically on previous research efforts in accounting, education, and other disciplines, and
3. meets standards of research expected by leading accounting journals.

The discussions of the framework's issues and topics in Chapters 3 through 7 are intended to aid the researcher in achieving the first two goals. Chapter 2, a discussion of research methods as applied in education research, is designed to provide guidance to the researcher with respect to the third goal.

Organization of Specific Topic Area Discussions

Discussions of each topic area we explored are presented by first summarizing and analyzing education research from disciplines other than accounting, reviewing some of the related research in the accounting education literature, and identifying research opportunities in accounting education. The analysis of non-accounting literature by topic is intended to provide a point of entry into the relevant literatures of other fields. It is not comprehensive in the sense of covering all the literature in a given topical area, but rather represents the integration and summarization of major empirical findings with the citations of major works and indications of the research methods and tools typically applied. In planning research, the serious researcher should not limit his or her literature review to the references cited, but should use them as a point of departure for further

FIGURE 1
ACCOUNTING EDUCATION RESEARCH FRAMEWORK

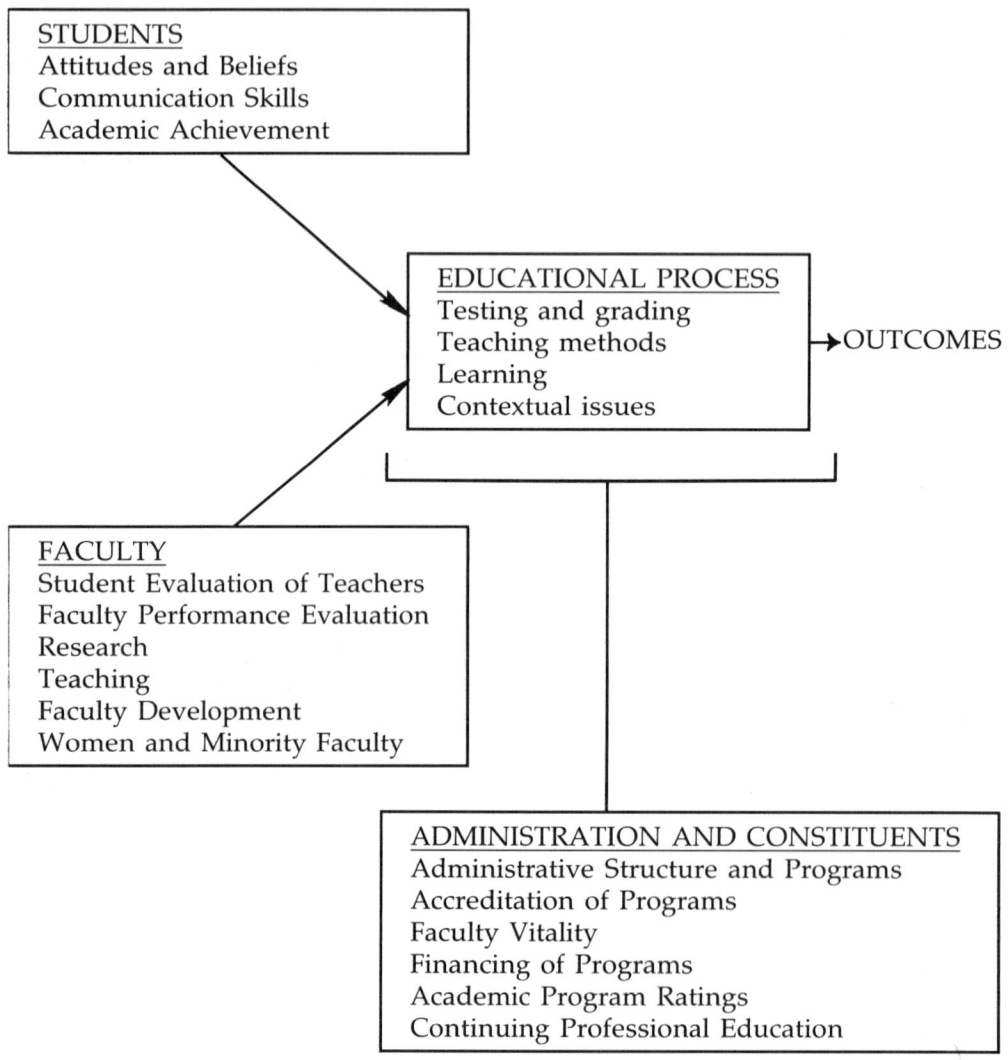

investigation. The data base described in Appendix B is also designed to assist the researcher in further explorations of the literature.

The summaries of accounting education research within each topic area, while important for the completeness of this study, do not represent its major contribution. As with the non-accounting literature, only selected studies that are related to the topic under consideration are included. Studies from the accounting literature are presented primarily to establish relationships among existing work and to help identify missing elements that require future research efforts.

INTRODUCTION TO THE FRAMEWORK

The research opportunities in accounting identified within each topic area are intended to suggest issues that appear worthy of further investigation, but we recognize that many other important researchable issues certainly exist. Appendix A contains an extensive list of specific research topics that might be addressed within each topic area.

In our search of the accounting literature, we identified certain studies and collections of studies which apply broadly to many areas of accounting education research. Several of these are included in the bibliography of this chapter; some of these are referred to specifically in later chapters. These studies provide valuable insight into many of the areas of accounting education which we recommend as fertile for future research; they are also an appropriate starting point for one beginning a program of accounting education research. We also encourage accounting education researchers to investigate the many previous AAA education research monographs and published committee reports that may have implications for their current research projects.

CONCLUSION

A definition of the elements comprising accounting education research, or even a general framework identifying their parameters, does not exist or at least has not been clearly articulated. One result of the absence of an identifiable framework for accounting education research is a literature that is quite diverse in terms of issues addressed and methodologies employed. Although this diversity may have been a necessary early stage in the continuing development of accounting education research, the resulting body of knowledge is, at best, highly fragmentary. Consistent lines of research that build upon prior work to provide a better understanding of education issues and solutions to problems are rare. Moreover, articles that have been published under the general heading of accounting education research represent a miniscule portion of the accounting literature. The foundation of accounting education research must be critically assessed and its growth carefully grounded in existing knowledge, so that a framework for a cogent body of knowledge may begin to emerge. Only after such an assessment is made, may accounting education research achieve a stature that is congruent with its importance to the profession.

CHAPTER 1 BIBLIOGRAPHY

AICPA, *Report of the Committee on Education and Experience Requirements for CPAs* (New York: AICPA, 1969).

American Accounting Association Committee on the Future Structure, Content, and Scope of Accounting Education, N. Bedford, Chairman, "Future Accounting Education: Preparing for the Expanding Profession," *Issues in Accounting Education* (Spring, 1986), pp. 168–190.

Committee to Prepare a Revised Accounting Teacher's Guide, *AAA Guide to Accounting Instruction: Concepts and Practices* (Cincinnati: South-Western Publishing Co., 1968).

Edwards, J. D., ed., et al., *Accounting Education: Problems and Prospects* (Sarasota, Florida: American Accounting Association, 1974).

Ferrara, W. L., ed., et al., *Researching the Accounting Curriculum: Strategies for Change* (Sarasota, Florida: American Accounting Association, 1975).

Gross, B., and R. Gross, *A Review of Innovative Approaches to College Teaching* (Sarasota, Florida: American Accounting Association, 1980).

Ijiri, Y., *Accounting Structured in APL* (Sarasota, Florida: American Accounting Association, 1984).

Rebele, J. E., and M. G. Tiller, "Empirical Research in Accounting Education: A Review and Evaluation," in Bishop, A. C., E. K. St. Pierre, and R. L. Benke, eds., *Research in Accounting Education* (Harrisonburg, VA: Center for Research in Accounting Education, James Madison University, 1986).

Roy, R. H., and MacNeill, J. H., *Horizons for a Profession* (New York: AICPA, 1967).

CHAPTER 2

Empirical Research Methods in Education

A chapter of this monograph is devoted to research methods in order to enhance the accessibility of education research and its reported findings. As the object of research, education presents a unique set of methodological problems and opportunities. An understanding of the major methodological issues with which education research must contend is obviously very important to accounting education researchers. Awareness of these issues is also important to those interested in understanding what has been and what is still to be learned from education research endeavors.

This chapter is about empirical research methods with a focus on problems likely to confront researchers as they apply research techniques (true experiments, field experiments, field studies, and surveys) widely used in education. The chapter does not provide a comprehensive coverage of research design and methodology. Research that does not directly involve data obtained from firsthand, controlled observation (e.g., nonempirical research such as model building and theory construction) is excluded. This omission is a pragmatic one and does not reflect the relative importance of empirical vs. nonempirical research. Reeve (1983) provides a good example of nonempirical accounting education research, and many other examples of analytic research methods in education are found in the *Journal of Economic Education*.

Most of the more comprehensive works that deal with the broader topic of the "scientific method" present theory-based empiricism as a methodological model of good science or as an ideal to be eventually attained within each discipline or developing research domain. Assertions that underlie this conception of science, as well as many opposing views, lead to epistemological issues that are continuously debated in the philosophy of science. Theory development and model building cannot be adequately addressed within the scope of this monograph. Selected references are presented in the conclusion of this chapter.

INTRODUCTION

The configurations of methodological problems confronted in much education research differ from those typically encountered in many other disciplines. The nature of many major education issues and the institutional settings in which they are addressed contribute to this relatively unique set of problems. Many education studies attempt to assess "learning" or some component of learning—knowledge acquisition, mental skills development, affective refinements, behavioral adjustments, etc. The focus on learning inevitably leads to research grounded in cognitive, social, and developmental psychology. In addition to the difficulties of appropriately applying theories and constructs from these disciplines, the associated problems of meaningfully measuring and interpreting cognitive, affective, and behavioral phenomena are often overlooked in education research. Attention to fundamental aspects of psychometrics and attitude measurement techniques is necessary as researchers continue to explore constructs developed in the behavioral sciences. Many of these are discussed in the "measurement" section of this chapter.

The institutional setting in which much education research is conducted affects the types of serious methodological issues that are encountered most often. For example, many studies involve direct intervention in "live" classes in order to examine the effects of various manipulations on learning outcomes. If a manipulation is clearly salient to the classes (as is often the case with truly innovative teaching/learning techniques), the "Hawthorne effect" is likely to take its toll on the interpretability of results. If an innovative teaching technique does yield more student learning than a conventional technique in similar classes, is the incremental learning attributable to the new technique itself, to the relative uniqueness of the technique (which, if it is adopted, may be short-lived), or to the subjects reacting to their being "observed" in some systematic, out-of-the-ordinary manner? The Hawthorne effect limits the researcher's ability to disentangle experimental effects from subject reaction to the perceived uniqueness of the experimental manipulations and the obtrusiveness of many research procedures. In many instances in the education literature, the Hawthorne effect is clearly the most plausible rival explanation for reported results. Several methodological problems, like the Hawthorne effect, derive from elements of the classroom setting in which so much education research is carried out. The methodological issues most often encountered in education research are the focus of this chapter.

The institutional setting for much education research also has significant practical and methodological advantages. Academic institutions generally maintain excruciatingly detailed records; thus, potentially useful archival data abound in academic departments, alumni relations offices, admissions and placement offices, and academic records systems. The subjects for many studies are easily drawn from the population of most interest—students—so that subject surrogation is rarely a problem. Indeed, the classroom is an almost ideal natural laboratory. Because the laboratory is "real," the impacts of effective experimental manipulations are more likely to be equally real. Unlike "laboratory studies" in the usual sense, the manipulations often involve aspects of the educational process that probably play an important part in student subjects' lives. Experimentation involving direct intervention into the educational process must be approached very cautiously. The researcher bears ultimate responsibility for protecting the integrity of the educational process and the well-being of the people involved in education research endeavors.

In the following chapters, the discussions of education research are often framed in terms of the developed language of research methods. Although we attempt to avoid using its obscure elements, we found that trying to summarize education research without at least some reliance on the accepted jargon of the social scientist was rather cumbersome, and perhaps misleading. The clumsiness of trying to express researchers' work without the elegance of the language may be illustrated by examining a researcher's assertion that, for example, faculty rank and age are "confounded" variables in a study exploring the effects of rank attainment on certain attitudes. The meaning of the statement is clear to the researcher and the research-initiate, but may not be at all clear to those practitioners, professionals, and policy makers who wish to learn what the researcher has found. The researcher could have said that the effects of faculty rank attainment, being observed as a possible cause of some interesting phenomenon, could not be separated from the effects of faculty age in the study because those faculty members involved in the study who had high rank also happened to be older than the study's lower-ranking faculty members. Thus, the results may be attributable to either rank, age, or both. The phrase "confounded variables" captures this lengthy explanation for the researcher.

We also felt that our discussions should capture the dual nature of education as both an applied discipline and also as the object of serious scientific endeavor. The education literature outside accounting represents a well-established research domain with a rich history of theoretical, practical, and methodological advances extending over several decades. As is the case with other social sciences, education researchers usually present their findings in language that has developed around the theories and research methods applied. For example, when a researcher summarizes his demonstration of some hypothesized relationship in terms of "causes" and/or "effects," the intended meaning of the cause-effect inference being made is usually quite restricted. Because causality cannot be empirically proved, the researcher intends to communicate the discovery of evidence that is supportive of a presumed causal relationship. The strength of the evidence is largely determined by the particular configuration of experimental setting, measurement tools, and research techniques applied in a particular study. An empirical researcher's causal assertions are always restricted endorsements that are circumscribed by the choice of theoretical constructs and the limitations imposed by alternative research techniques and statistical inference processes. The assertion, "A causes B," in an ordinary sense, conveys a sense of inevitability and sufficiency. In its specialized research usage, "A causes B" means that evidence (with an implicit caveat about the strength of that evidence) has been generated in support of a causal assertion. The specialized meaning of causality derives from the nature of evidence-generating activities of researchers. The language of research is intended to interpret and convey evidence generated in a research environment where knowledge of widely accepted research techniques, research procedures, etc. is taken for granted. Some basic understanding of the major methodological issues in education research is necessary in order to understand just what a researcher is reporting.

This chapter is organized around discussions of the research techniques used most often in education research—surveys and field studies, field experiments, and true experiments. The first section presents discussions of several research disclosure issues that we found to be problematic in our review of the empirical education literature. The following three sections address the methodological issues and problems often encountered in education research with each of the research techniques. The fifth section is a discussion of several measurement issues commonly confronted in education research, regardless of the research technique used.

REPORTING EMPIRICAL FINDINGS

Published research should provide the reader with enough information to properly evaluate its merits and limitations and understand its contribution to knowledge. Unfortunately, the reporting of research and its results in the accounting and general education literature is often incomplete. Particular areas of concern are the comprehensiveness of the literature review, the completeness of the discussion of the study's rationale and potential contribution, and the precision of the authors' delineation of limitations.

A study's incremental contribution is rather difficult to assess unless the related literature is discussed in enough detail to direct the reader's attention to the importance of the questions addressed. Adequate reviews are rare in the accounting education literature; although many authors present a cursory review of some of the accounting education literature, most ignore the richer general education literature. Quite often, the unsuspecting reader is left with an incomplete representation of the phenomena under examination. Most recent accounting education research endeavors can be assigned a place in a continuing stream of research in the general education literature. Unfortunately, reported findings of accounting education studies are usually not discussed in light of the existing, developed knowledge about the phenomena examined. To the extent that the education literature has not been properly explicated, accounting education research is too isolated from the general core of education knowledge to achieve its potential contribution.

A second, perhaps related, disclosure concern involves the researcher's discussions of the reasons for and contributions of the research presented. All too often, the underlying rationale of a study, in terms of its potential practical or theoretical significance, is underdeveloped. Having examined available evidence about the topic addressed and dealt with the practical problems of designing a meaningful study, the researcher must be concerned that his research report includes an adequate defense of the research endeavor. For example, some of the earlier studies in education used student responses to the global instructor evaluation item (e.g., "Rate your instructor's overall teaching effectiveness") as the dependent variable in evaluating the impact of several variables of interest. The implicit assumption in many of these studies seems to be that improving student evaluations of instructors is, in itself, a desirable primary outcome of the educational process. The assumed linkages between the student evaluation responses, student learning, and instructional effectiveness were often not clearly drawn in the reported research results. The readers, presumably with less knowledge of the subject area than the researchers, may not have enough information to assess the underlying rationale of the research. Thus, readers may dismiss the research as trivial, believing that enhancing student evaluations of instructors is not a legitimate educational objective. Or they may accept the results as important, believing that higher student evaluations are the result of greater instructional effectiveness, which is a generally accepted educational objective. The researcher is in the best position to assess and report his study's rationale and potential contributions, as well as its limitations.

The third area of weak disclosure that we noted in the education literature is concerned with discussions of the limitations of the research and its findings. Although research limitations may be discussed in a variety of ways, many authors speak in terms of the internal and external validity of their research (Campbell and Stanley, 1963). Internal validity is the logical strength of the arguments that researchers make as they move from the controlled observation of phenomena to the interpretation of their findings. In experimental research, internal validity is often presented as the extent to which an observed change in some phenomenon can be attributed to an experimental manipulation (e.g., alternative teaching techniques). Some minimum degree of internal validity is necessary in order for most experimental research to be meaningfully interpretable. External validity refers to the generalizability of the research results. It defines the extent to which similar results may reasonably be expected to occur outside the specific research reported. (We discuss internal and external validity in more detail throughout this chapter. Our concern here is with the extent and manner of disclosure of internal and external validity weaknesses and limitations in published research.)

Authors' discussions of internal validity issues are sometimes couched in terms of the developed language of the "threats to internal validity" (e.g., history, maturation, testing, etc., Campbell and Stanley, 1963; Cook and Campbell, 1979). Although the jargon is widely accepted among researchers in the social sciences, its use in published articles seems to be partially determined by the research orientation and audience of the journals in which the articles appear. At one extreme, articles in journals that are oriented toward methodological rigor and precision sometimes include a simple statement about the "usual limitations" that accompany the specific experimental design used. Other authors clearly delineate rival hypotheses (typically arising because of internal validity weaknesses) and fully discuss their plausibility in light of previous research and/or other evidence from outside the study being presented. Far too many authors in the more applied and professionally-oriented literature fail to explicitly recognize their internal validity limitations or to carefully discuss the factors that might have tainted the results.

For example, many studies involve the introduction of some "experimental" treatment in an existing section or class, with a similar section identified as a control group. Among other possible threats to internal validity, subject selection creates a serious potential problem that is often not disclosed or discussed. Students are actually assigned to sections via whatever registration procedures are used at the particular institution in which the research is conducted. Although some registration procedures may randomly assign students to sections (and therefore to experimental and control groups), many allow easily identifiable groups of students, often defined by class standing, number of hours earned toward degrees, or full- vs. part-time status, to register earlier than others. Sections taught at "popular" class times (e.g., mid-morning) are more likely to contain a much higher proportion of the groups of students who were allowed to register early. Thus, results obtained from simply comparing these sections with other sections may be attributable to the experimental treatment or to other differences arising through non-random subject selection. If the researcher becomes aware of this potential confound (e.g., by discovering that the experimental group was comprised largely of seniors, versus a control group of sophomores) too late to bring the confounded factor under statistical control, the apparent threat to internal validity must obviously be disclosed. Moreover, the author may help the reader understand the effect of the confound on the interpretability of obtained results. In our example, the authors should acknowledge (based on the literature review, from internally generated reports, etc.) that seniors typically earn higher grades than sophomores, and indicate the anticipated impact: grades in the section comprised mostly of seniors are probably inflated due to the experimental confound. Reviewers, editors, and perhaps other readers are then able to better assess the extent of loss of internal validity and interpretability.

Regarding external validity limitations, authors often warn us that the results are, of course, only generalizable to the institution from which subjects are drawn. Such restrictive caveats are seldom warranted. Researchers must be more precise in setting the generalizability boundaries of their findings. Because the author is in a better position than the reader to observe those boundaries, he should mark them carefully and clearly. For example, results of a study involving students at a single institution may be more or less generalizable to other contexts based on the representativeness of the research setting, the students involved, and the measurement techniques used. Most authors provide some information about their sample (typically types and sizes of classes involved, sometimes student demographics) so that a limited basis for generalizability inferences is presented. Even so, many authors could significantly improve the extent and precision of disclosure of those samples and other characteristics of their research that determine the degree of generalizability of results. An author's disclosure that the research was conducted in auditing courses at a large state university does not tell the reader enough about the research setting. More complete discussions of those characteristics of the research setting that might affect generalizability (e.g., the impact of an existing restrictive admissions policy on the available sample of students) should be presented.

In addition to the more accurate specification of the reasonable realm of generalizability, the more precise disclosure of those characteristics affecting generalizability should increase the value of replication across various populations and research settings. Confirming replications expand the boundaries of previous research findings to the different populations and/or settings under investigation. Disconfirming replications may indicate the rational limits of the construct extended to "new" populations or research settings.

For example, failure to successfully extend findings about the value of direct student-teacher interaction in doctoral programs to undergraduate programs at large universities may indicate that the construct "student-teacher interaction" has lost its essential meaning in the undergraduate population. Disconfirming replications may also suggest important theoretical revisions and measurement refinements as researchers attempt to discover why the replication failed.

Accounting education research can improve significantly as authors focus on the adequate disclosure of related research findings and the rationale for the research, as well as on its limitations. The next three sections discuss some common research techniques—true experiments, field experiments, and surveys and field studies. Our discussions are largely oriented toward those methodological pitfalls, limitations, and problems most often associated with each technique as it is applied in education research.

TRUE EXPERIMENTS

Of the three research techniques discussed, true experiments are the least widely used in higher education research. Given the alternatives presented by available archival data and student subjects in well-defined classes, true (or "laboratory") experiments are often comparatively costly and difficult to perform. Even so, their use appears to be increasing. For achieving many, but not all, research objectives, the true experiment is the most potent available tool. The distinguishing feature of a true experiment, as opposed to a quasi-experiment or field experiment, is the extent and nature of control that the researcher exerts over both observed and unobserved phenomena. Generally, as effective experimental control increases, the strength of the causal assertions examined in the research—its internal validity—is enhanced.

The primary objective of experimentation is the empirical examination of the presumed causal relationships among theoretically and/or practically significant phenomena. The strength of the causal assertions is largely determined by the degree and types of influence the researcher chooses to exercise in the experiment. Four of the major areas that may be under the researcher's influence are: — 1) subject assignment to treatments, 2) the variables manipulated in the study, 3) the variables "controlled" in the study, and 4) dependent variable specification and measurement. A true experiment is marked by a great deal of control in all these areas.

SUBJECT ASSIGNMENT

Frequently, the distinction between a true experiment and a field experiment is made in terms of the manner by which subjects are typically assigned to treatments. True experiments gain a high degree of control by random assignment of subjects to treatment groups. Consider the example of a study designed to evaluate the effect of two competing modes of videotaped instruction (treatments) on student learning. The researcher may select two sections of a class, with each viewing one of the one-hour videotapes, and then taking a brief examination covering the videotape material. By not using random subject assignment, the researcher makes his design susceptible to several uncontrolled influences, many of which engender rival explanations for obtained results. Systematic differences between the two sections prior to their receiving experimental treatments may influence or acccount for the results obtained.

For example, if the two sections are taught by different instructors, the groups' motivation to learn or some other unobserved variable differentially influenced by the two instructors may affect the interpretability of research findings. Even if no obvious alternative causal factors present themselves, nonrandom subject assignment diminishes the ability of the evidence generated to reveal the desired causal inference (e.g., videotape A is more effective than videotape B in inducing student learning). Reasonable alternative explanations for obtained results have not been ruled out, and the results are limited in internal validity. Videotape A may be more effective than videotape B, or it may not, depending on the effects of distortions introduced by unobserved pre-existing treatment group differences.

In our videotape comparison study, if students were randomly selected from all available sections of the course and randomly assigned to the two treatments, the likelihood of a confounding effect of "motivation to learn" is diminished considerably. Random assignment to our two treatments yields groups that are comparable, on average, because the many possible dimensions along which subjects can differ (including motivation to learn) are randomly distributed across the two groups.

True experiments allow random subject assignment and thereby provide significant control over several extraneous variables that may adversely affect internal validity. We will further explore their effects in our discussion of field experiments, in which alternative controls are often used to re-establish the internal validity lost when randomization is not possible.

INDEPENDENT VARIABLES

The second area in which the researcher may exert control is in the specification and manipulation of independent variables. In experimental research, whatever the design, independent variables are systematically manipulated by the researcher in order to observe any associated changes in relevant dependent variables. In a true experiment, the researcher is relatively free to choose the independent variables. For many experiments in education, the choice is largely determined by hypothesized relationships among theoretical constructs and/or reasonable expectations about relationships among numerous phenomena of practical interest (e.g., videotape A vs. B). Experiments based on reasonably well-developed theories or models are usually less susceptible to experimental confounding than intuitively-generated studies. To the extent that established theories specify important causal relationships, potent "nuisance" variables may be controlled so that the effect of the independent variable may be more clearly observable.

Internal validity is seriously undermined if the strength of the treatment (manipulation of the independent variable) is not sufficiently captured by changes in the dependent variable. Independent variables must be powerful enough potential causes of change in the dependent variable that the effect of their manipulation is not obscured by random variability of the latter. Assume that videotapes A and B are treatments of the independent variable "amount of audio/visual repetition" and that student learning is the dependent variable in a randomized experimental design. The objective of the research is to determine if the larger amount of repetition in videotape A will enhance learning more than the amount in videotape B. If the researcher has only two videotapes representing two "levels" of the treatment, the tapes must be sufficiently different in terms of the amount of repetition to reveal any resulting differences in student learning. In essence, the researcher should have reasonable cause to expect that the independent variables do indeed have an important effect on the dependent variable.

DEPENDENT VARIABLES

The third area in which the experimenter should assert significant control is in the identification and measurement of dependent variable(s). In a true experiment, the researcher has a great deal of freedom in specifying dependent variables, because he is not constrained by some of the practical considerations encountered in many field experiments. For example, inadvertent, perhaps psychologically threatening, evaluation apprehension may be aroused in the classroom if standardized psychological instruments (such as personality inventories) are used to measure dependent variables. The true experiment's (usually contrived) context may be less psychologically threatening because of the relative isolation of the laboratory from the "real" value-laden educational process. The choice of dependent variables is probably influenced by the researchers' interests, knowledge, concern about some specific problem, and many other practical considerations. Even so, the most important criteria for choosing the dependent variables should be their theoretical, practical, or social significance. The reasons for choosing student learning, teaching effectiveness, faculty research productivity, etc., as dependent variables in much of the education literature are readily apparent.

Many of the issues discussed in the measurement section are concerned with dependent variables. However, a brief discussion of one general concern, somewhat analogous to the strength of manipulation issue for independent variables, illustrates the advantage of control in true experiments. In many experiments, dependent variables, as operationalized and measured, are sensitive neither to changes in independent variables, nor to changes in the underlying construct that is being observed. In our randomized experiment comparing videotapes, the researcher compares the two groups' scores on an examination covering the videotape material. While fulfilling other objectives of sound measurement, the examination must measure knowledge acquisition over a range within which learning may be expected to be affected by the two videotapes. For example, if the examination is not difficult (discriminating) enough, it may not be able to reveal knowledge differences between the treatment groups. Very high average scores on the examination in both groups may indicate that the measurement range of the dependent variable is too low. Similarly, little variability in the scores of both groups may indicate that the achieved measurement range is too small relative to the theoretical learning range. Differential learning between the two groups is not captured by the examination, yet it may exist within a different measurement range. In a true experiment, dependent variable measurement, including measurement range specification, must be carefully controlled by the researcher. Dependent variable control is often an important source of internal validity in experimental research.

CONTROL VARIABLES

Finally, the true experiment allows the researcher to control the effects of potentially confounding factors (often called nuisance, external, or confounding variables before being controlled; control variables, blocking variables, or covariates afterwards) on the results. One of the advantages of randomization is that it obviates many potential confounds, whether observable or not, that could damage the interpretability of research results. The use of control variables, unlike randomization, requires that the possible sources of experimental confounding be identified, measured, and included in the experimental design and/or analysis of results. In some cases, research evidence is more precisely explicated via the use of control variables and randomization. The two need not be seen as alternative means of control, but a simple comparison of the results of control by randomization versus a control variable reveals the fundamentally different type of control exerted by the latter.

Let's assume that a researcher is interested in comparing the effect of two methods of teaching the cash flows statement to intermediate accounting students. Students are randomly selected from available sections of intermediate accounting, exposed to one of the two-hour lectures, and given an examination over the lecture material. With random assignment to treatments, existing differences between individual students are likely to be represented about equally in the two groups assigned to the two treatments. The proportion of students with previous knowledge of the topic, more effective instructors, etc. is roughly the same in the groups. Yet, if observable differences between individual students may reasonably be expected to significantly influence the dependent variable (learning, as measured by the examination score), allowing them to vary randomly across the two treatments may obscure the effect of the treatment. In our example, assume that the two factors that most influence performance on the examination are the teaching method to which the student was exposed (assume that method one is most effective) and the amount of pre-existing knowledge each student has about the cash flows statement. Our statistical analyses and inferences in this randomized experiment are based on examining differences in examination scores between groups (and therefore attributable to the teaching method), as compared to differences in examination scores within groups (and therefore attributable to numerous unknown possible factors, including pre-existing knowledge in our example). If the differences in exam scores between treatment groups are large enough, as compared to the differences within the two groups (frequently called error variance), statistical analysis will show that the group assigned to method one will have higher scores. Note that random assignment spreads the error variance across the two groups, but does nothing to control its magnitude. Yet the relative magnitude of the error variance partially determines the statistical inferences we can make about the effectiveness of the teaching methods.

A carefully chosen control variable will often enhance the interpretability of results by increasing the precision of the statistical inferences that are possible. In our example, the researcher might attempt to identify the students with prior knowledge about the statement of cash flows and divide the two treatments according to some observable indicant of prior knowledge. Let's assume that the researcher learns that those students who transferred from the state community college system do not study the cash flows statement in the first year of accounting coursework, while most other students do. Available student records may allow the researcher to identify two "groups" of students within each of the two treatments—"prior learning" and "no prior learning" students (as identified by transfer status). Inclusion of prior learning as a control variable has two important effects. First, the differences in examination scores attributable to the teaching method and those attributable to prior learning are separately estimable, as is their interaction if one exists. For example, method one's most positive effect on learning might be within the "prior learning" group, while method two's most positive effect is within the "no prior learning" group, so that prior learning is said to "interact" with the lecture method in determining the amount learned.

The second potential benefit of including a control variable is the increased power and precision of our statistical inference techniques. Up to this point in our discussions of control in a true experiment, we have discussed control by random assignment and experimental control (i.e., the experimenter's active role in identifying, manipulating, and measuring variables of interest). The increased statistical power from having added the control variable provides another type of control, often designated as statistical control. Note that statistical control is achieved in our example because a practically important, observable factor (prior knowledge) "accounts for" much of the error variance (within-treatment exam score differences). As before, our statistical inference techniques may examine differences in examination scores between the two lecture groups (and attributable to the teaching method), as compared to the error variance. To the extent that the control variable "explains" otherwise inexplicable within-group exam score differences, the magnitude of the error variance is reduced, and the probability of detecting differences attributable to the teaching method is increased.

We have discussed true experiments in terms of four areas of possible experimenter controls: 1) subject assignment to treatments, 2) independent variables, 3) dependent variables, and 4) control variables. Most experimental research is preceded by extensive pre-testing in order to fine-tune manipulations and refine measurements. Many researchers also perform one or more pilot tests in order to develop experimenter "scripts" and discover unanticipated implementation problems. Because of the importance of experimental control to internal validity, these pre-experimental adjustments are often crucial to the success of experiments. Because true experiments allow so much control, internal validity is often very high, while external validity is quite limited. Indeed, the laboratory is often chosen in those situations where theories are being rigorously tested. Important variables have been identified, and their expected relationships have been specified in rather precise theoretical terms. External validity is often not the primary concern when the research objective centers on tests of theories.

AN EXAMPLE FROM ACCOUNTING EDUCATION

Koch and Karlinsky (1984) performed one of the few true experiments reported in the accounting education literature. One objective of the experiment was the evaluation of alternative modes of presentation of educational materials to accounting students. Subjects were 89 junior and senior students enrolled in upper-division accounting courses at three universities. The primary independent variable was the mode of presentation of the content of an Internal Revenue Code section. Students were randomly assigned to read either IRC section 179 or a Research Institute of America commentary on the section. Dependent variables were student scores on an examination covering section 179, the amount of time students used in responding to the exam questions, and student perceptions of reading complexity. The study's findings were that the commentary readers performed better on the examination in less time and perceived the reading material to be less complex than the IRC section's readers.

The researchers took advantage of several controls available in a laboratory experiment and carefully noted most of the study's limitations. Subjects were selected from the population of students with no prior coursework covering section 179 and were randomly assigned to treatment groups. Two widely-used readability indices were applied to the code section and commentary before the experiment to demonstrate that they were comparable (a second experimental objective was a test of their validity). A pilot study was used to determine how much reading time subjects needed to complete the reading during the experiment, and sufficient time for the longer of the two readings was allotted. The examination consisted of 15 questions that were answerable from either of the two readings, so that dependent variable measurement should not have favored one over the other. The possibly confounding effects of an obtrusive reading complexity measure was controlled by including before-examination and after-examination measures of perceived reading complexity in the experimental design itself.

Internal validity in this study is reasonably strong, while, as noted by the authors, external validity is, by design, quite limited. The experimental task involved reading a specific code section (or its commentary), which may or may not be representative of many other alternative presentational modes for educational materials. However, section 179 was chosen partially because it has been shown to be a code section that is not extremely complex, so that its potential representativeness to other IRC sections is enhanced (under the assumption that the bulk of the code can be described as lacking complexity). Also, student subjects volunteered for the study, reducing external validity in some unknown manner. The extent of loss of external validity cannot be specified because the subject recruitment strategy was not disclosed. Possible self-selection criteria that may have induced some more- or less-representative sample to participate in the study cannot be evaluated. The mix of strong internal validity and limited external validity in Koch and Karlinsky's study is typical of most experimental research in education, where internal validity is the primary concern of the research design.

COMMON PROBLEMS IN TRUE EXPERIMENTS

Given the high degree of internal validity in most true experiments, only a few general problems typically arise in experimental education research. However, questionable construct validity (and measurement) of independent, dependent, and control variables often blurs the interpretability of findings. Generally, construct validity is low when the phenomena measured (e.g., examination scores) do not faithfully represent the theoretical construct under examination (e.g., student learning). When this is the case with the dependent variable, the researcher may fail to detect the real effect of the independent variables, or he may "discover" an effect in some measure that has no known theoretical or practical analogue. Poor construct validity of independent variables affects interpretability in a similar manner. Construct validity of control variables, a much more common concern in field experiments than true experiments, is illustrated in the next section.

Random assignment does not control all possible threats to internal validity. For example, if subjects drop out of an experiment after being randomly assigned to some treatment, randomization as a control technique is threatened. Although different dropout rates between treatments may sometimes be viewed as meaningful dependent variables themselves, any significant dropout behavior diminishes the effectiveness of control by randomization and makes the design susceptible to many of the internal validity weaknesses associated with field experiments. Further, if randomly-appointed experimental groups become aware that their treatment is different from that of other groups, the effect of their reactions may disguise true underlying relationships among the constructs examined in a variety of ways (Cook and Campbell, 1979).

Finally, note that true experiments in education often fail to fully exploit the advantages of gaining statistical control through observable control variables. If control variables can be properly specified and measured, the increase in the power of statistical inference will usually allow more precise interpretation of results. The use of a control variable in an otherwise "true experiment" may be necessary because of a loss of the experimental control that defines a true experiment (randomization) in favor of statistical control, which is most used in field experiments and field studies. Control variables combined with randomization often provide a maximum degree of internal validity. The discussion of field experiments focuses largely on overcoming internal validity weaknesses most likely to arise in experiments that do not achieve random subject assignment.

FIELD EXPERIMENTS

Field experiments are, for obvious reasons, widely used in education research. Experimental treatments may easily be applied to relatively well-defined groups of students (classes) in the environmental context of most interest. The real classroom settings used in many education studies, besides providing a reasonably representative environment from which generalizations might be made, include certain beneficial attributes usually associated with laboratory research. Control of the educational process resides largely with the instructor, just as control of most events in the experimental laboratory is managed by the researcher. Unlike field experiments in many disciplines, control over important aspects of the research setting is concentrated in a single individual exercising legitimate authority over most of the variables of interest. The researcher's intervention into the educational process is often less obtrusive and artificial than in the laboratory because it is implemented through the instructors' ordinary exercise of control. Also, evaluative measures of many dependent variables of interest (e.g., examination scores to measure learning, student evaluation ratings to measure teaching effectiveness) are often available without researcher intervention.

Like true experiments, field experiments allow the experimenter to manipulate independent variables in order to observe their effects on some important dependent variable. The most common difference between true experiments and field experiments is nonrandom assignment of subjects to treatments in the latter. The resulting loss of control by randomization has important internal validity implications as well as indirect effects on the researcher's use of other experimental and statistical controls. As in the last section, we discuss the effects of the degree and type of researcher controls on internal and external validity.

SUBJECT ASSIGNMENT

Most field experiments in education have minimal control over subject assignment to treatments. Instead, treatments are often assigned to existing classes whose members may be in those classes as a result of a number of underlying selection processes. The interpretability of research that simply compares two treatments (e.g., lecture methods) separately applied to two different sections of students suffers severe internal validity weaknesses. The research does not distinguish between the effects of the lecture methods and the effects of other between-group differences that are not "randomized out."

The researcher may attempt to assess the likelihood of systematic differences in the groups. By identifying the most likely outcomes of the selection process that assigns students to their sections (treatments), the researcher may choose to initiate additional statistical and experimental control. For example, suppose that a researcher wishes to investigate suspected negative outcomes of televised intermediate accounting instruction (TVI; cf. Snowball and Collins, 1980). One research question addressed is whether students in "live" classes develop more positive attitudes toward accounting than TVI students. Two similar intermediate accounting sections are chosen for the experiment. One is taught "live" by the same instructor, and as far as possible, in the same manner, as it was recorded for the TVI students.

If subjects are free to self-select into (and out of) the TVI section based on the knowledge that it is televised, the most obvious threat to internal validity is that some unknown variable influencing their choice of TVI might also influence their attitude toward accounting. In the case of subject self-selection, identifying the possible causes of initial group differences is often rather difficult. For example, would TVI more likely be chosen by nonaccounting majors seeking light exposure to intermediate accounting, by students planning to attend class very little, or by those hoping to take advantage of available videotape "replays" in order to enhance their learning? Quite probably, these and many other criteria influence the choices of individual students. If any of these self-selection criteria are operating in sufficient numbers of subjects, and if they are meaningfully associated with "attitudes toward accounting," they will probably obscure the results of between-group comparisons.

In our example, the researcher might compare the two groups in terms of available demographic and other measures (e.g., sex, academic class, major, etc.) in order to identify any unanticipated group differences that may differentially affect attitudes toward accounting. This approach may suggest some underlying selection rationale and criteria, but not necessarily.

If subject selection criteria are not observable, or if their effects are not directly measurable, a pretest may still be used to gain statistical control over some possible sources of selection bias. In our TVI study, the researcher could measure student attitudes toward accounting in both the TVI and control group at the beginning of the academic term. If existing pretest differences are not found, internal validity is strengthened somewhat. If pretest differences do exist, analysis of covariance (or its regression analysis counterpart) often provides a reasonable means of removing some of the effects of pre-existing group differences from the comparison of post-test scores (the dependent variable). As is the case when control variables are used, these statistical techniques may also reduce the error variance, increasing the power of statistical inferences about the treatment effect (see Kerlinger, 1973, chapter 21, for an interpretative discussion of analysis of covariance).

Whether our TVI groups were equal on the pretest, or adjusted statistically so that they could be compared, nonrandom selection processes may still influence the results. TVI and control groups may be different due to the indirect effects of selection criteria not directly related to the pretest. Moreover, the pretest/post-test (or repeated measures) design may be vulnerable to several internal validity threats, especially if the time lapse between pre- and post-tests is long.

Without random assignment, our TVI group may be different from the control group in some unknown manner not captured by the pretest. For example, suppose that, because of the selection process, subjects in the TVI group are, in reality, more "intellectually rigid" than their counterparts in the control group. If rigidity implies extreme attitude entrenchment or nonresponsiveness to the mode of lecture presentation, it may suppress any attitude change due to the TVI treatment. Other underlying selection-generated variables and aspects of the research setting, measures, manipulations, etc., may also interact in a manner that may affect the results, reducing internal validity.

The net effect of the loss of control over subject assignment in field experiments is a loss of some degree of internal validity. The loss due to nonrandom selection is typically offset somewhat by using some type of pretest/post-test control group design and more powerful statistical techniques. This rather straightforward design warrants special attention because it is so widely used in education research. Some of the important potential limitations of the design and data analysis are presented in the discussion of common problems encountered in field experiments.

INDEPENDENT VARIABLES

In many field experiments, the researcher exercises significant control over the independent variables. The distinction between a field study and a field experiment is the presence of experimenter-initiated intervention in the research setting. As in true experiments, the field experimenter's purpose is to systematically manipulate theoretically or practically important independent variables in order to effect changes in the dependent variable. More than in most true experiments, the independent variable in a field experiment is chosen because of its practical significance in the research environment. Field experiments often focus on manipulating "real" phenomena, rather than constructs that surrogate those phenomena. Thus, generalizability is often a more important research objective in field experiments than in true experiments.

In a field experiment, two areas that are often carefully scrutinized and controlled are the range of independent variable manipulation and its obtrusiveness in the real research environment. The available range of independent variable manipulation is sometimes restricted in field experiments for practical reasons. A study exploring the effects of large versus small class size on student achievement of educational outcomes (e.g., Buehlmann and Techavichit, 1984) should ideally include "treatments" that cover the reasonable range of possible sizes. If the research setting includes practical restrictions such that no classes smaller than 40 or larger than 100 can be created, possible effects of class size on achievement outside this range are not explored. Although the restricted range has internal validity implications, the external validity restriction is apparent; results may not be generalizable outside of the range explored.

The obtrusiveness of the experimental manipulation (independent variable) is an issue in most field experiments. In laboratory experiments, the researcher often disguises the research purpose and takes steps to obscure the salience of manipulations to subjects. By doing so, (s)he is attempting to avoid subject reactions to the purpose of the manipulation, experimenter, or measurement techniques as opposed to the manipulation itself (cf. testing, hypothesis guessing, evaluation apprehension, and experimenter expectancies in Cook and Campbell, 1979). Most field experiments also retain some control by limiting disclosures to subjects. Limiting subject knowledge of experimental manipulations, though very important to the success of much research, is fraught with ethical hazards in field experiments. For example, if a researcher examines the relative discriminability of different systematic orderings of examination questions, the manipulation is probably nonobtrusive and avoids many potential threats to internal validity. Suppose that the sequencing of examination questions is varied according to the difficulty of the questions. Obviously, the manipulation will not be salient to students unless the experimenter discloses the manipulation to them, at least not before the examination is graded and returned. If the different orderings are expected to affect student examination performance, the researcher faces an ethical problem by not disclosing the manipulation. Paretta and Chadwick (1975) performed just such an experiment in an intermediate accounting course. They mitigated the negative effects of the undisclosed manipulation by adjusting examination scores for those students adversely affected by the experimental examination. Researchers working within the classroom must carefully weigh the potential scientific benefits of their efforts against the potential negative effects on students, and on the perceived integrity of the educational process itself.

DEPENDENT VARIABLES

Field experiments in education often take advantage of well-defined measures freely existing in the research setting. Although the researcher is still concerned with the theoretical, practical, or social significance of dependent variables, their measurement is quite often an existing aspect of the research setting. For example, student achievement of educational objectives is measured by exam scores, grades, and success after graduation; teaching effectiveness is measured by standardized student and peer evaluations of teachers. In choosing these measures as dependent variables, the researcher may lose some advantages of more precise measurement. The available dependent variables are certainly too coarse to register the effects of many theoretically interesting independent variables. However, these measures are available because they measure practically significant phenomena. Hence, the importance of generalizability of findings about such measures is enhanced.

CONTROL VARIABLES

The issues surrounding control variable specification and measurement in field experiments are about the same as those in true experiments. A control variable allows the researcher to strengthen internal validity by extracting the control variable's effect from the treatment effect and by increasing the power of statistical inference. A common control variable in field experiments is student grade point average, especially in studies using student examination scores or grades as dependent variables. Suppose that a researcher administers some treatment to his morning class and another to his afternoon class and gives a brief examination over the material presented (at the end of each period). Besides other concerns he has about the design, the researcher should be concerned about the effects of the nonrandom selection processes that assigned students to the two classes. A pretest may be very artificial or otherwise unreasonable in this situation whereas a well-specified control variable may serve roughly the same control purpose. In our example, the researcher might use student GPA as a control variable. Grade point average, and other measures like it, are used as covariates in analyzing such nonequivalent group designs with some success. GPA is significantly correlated with many important dependent variables and often discriminates between nonrandomly selected treatment groups, as do entrance examination scores and other standard evaluative measures of student quality or ability.

Field experiments typically have less internal validity and more external validity than true experiments in education. The loss of experimenter control over subject assignment to treatments may create severe potential confounds in field experiments. Nonrandom subject assignment may obscure the observation of treatment effects or create artificial effects. Without random subject assignment, the treatment effects cannot be easily disentangled from the effects of other systematic differences between the groups. Pretests and control variables may be used to establish limited control over these between-group differences. Even so, field experiments, conducted in a rather rich environment instead of in a laboratory, are generally weaker in internal validity than most true experiments.

EXAMPLES FROM ACCOUNTING EDUCATION

Several field experiments in the accounting literature have appropriately controlled various aspects of the classroom research environment, although the controls exercised are virtually never as strong as those used in true experiments. The studies summarized below illustrate some reasonably sound researcher-initiated controls. As is the case with all field experiments, they also demonstrate that some planned controls are likely to fail.

Battista's (1978) field experiment examined the impact of self-paced instruction versus conventional instruction in an introductory accounting course at Rider College. The research results indicated that, as operationalized in this study, conventional instruction yielded more favorable learning outcomes than self-paced instruction. A pilot test of the self-paced instruction technique was conducted during the semester preceding the experiment in order to introduce the technique to the instructors and the student population, perhaps reducing the impact of the Hawthorne effect. Because the experimental manipulation was administered to intact classes during the semester, a pretest - posttest design was chosen, and several other aspects of the experiment were well controlled.

Four sections of the course were included in the study, with each of two instructors teaching one conventional and one self-paced section. Students in the conventional sections were not allowed access to self-paced learning materials. An achievement test was administered during the first (pretest) and last (post-test) weeks of class, and included 50 multiple choice questions that were extensively reviewed, pilot-tested, and tested for construct validity and reliability. Because pretest scores were not significantly different across the experimental groups, analysis of covariance (with the pretest as the covariate or "control variable") was not deemed necessary. As the author recognized, some control was lost by allowing the two instructors to design their own examinations and grading policies during the experimental semester. Thus, different examination/student study strategies, grading/feedback effects, and instructor/treatment interactions between the four sections may have affected the study's results. Analyses of the effects of these potential confounds were not reported in the study.

As in Battista's study, Dickens and Harper (1986) found that their pretest was not a useful covariate. They created an interesting alternative that had an important effect on their results. Dickens & Harper designed a pretest - post-test control group field experiment to evaluate the impact of limited computer-assisted instruction (CAI) on student learning of two rather difficult intermediate accounting topics. Subjects were randomly assigned from four sections of an intermediate accounting course to one of two experimental groups, each of which reworked assigned homework problems covering one of the two topics in a well-controlled microcomputer laboratory using specially developed tutorial-type software. The laboratory provided good control over independent variable manipulation, except that, as the authors noted, poor timing of the microcomputer exercise as compared to the classroom topical coverage may have diminished the impact of the exercise on learning in one of the groups. The authors also acknowledged that dependent variable construct validity may have been weak, perhaps contributing to the finding of no between-group differences on the dependent variable (learning, as measured by student scores on multiple choice questions covering the two topic areas on the course's first major examination). Even though subjects were randomly assigned to experimental groups, the authors tested for and found no instructor effects. Two pretests were given to subjects, one to assess prior learning of the targeted topical areas, and one to obfuscate the experiment's purpose. The study's "real" pretest, intended to identify any pre-experimental knowledge about the topics that students possessed, was comprised of multiple choice questions drawn from the same source as the post-test. When the pretest was found to neither reduce error variance nor control for possible pre-existing group differences, an alternative control variable was created to parcel out the effect of "student quality" from the effect of the experimental manipulation. This control variable, entered as a covariate in the analysis, was a measure of student performance on examination questions other than those that were designed to measure learning on the two topic areas included in the experiment. Because some of these other topics were closely related to the experimental topics (e.g., accounting for long-term debt is closely related to understanding complex EPS computations), the chosen covariate may have inadvertently captured some of the variance attributable to the independent variable in addition to that attributable to the intended "student quality" construct. The authors appropriately disclosed results with and without the covariate and noted that use of the covariate removed the hypothesized learning effect of computer-assisted instruction.

In contrast to Battista's and Dickens and Harper's studies, Baldwin and Howe (1982) and Baldwin and Howard (1983) used control variables that yielded the control and enhanced findings usually intended in field experiments. For example, in the latter study the researchers examined the impact of intertopical examination question sequencing (random versus ordered by topic area) on final examination scores and time required to complete a multiple-choice examination. Students in both an introductory accounting course and a tax accounting course took either a randomly ordered examination or an examination ordered by topics. The control variable (cumulative GPA at the beginning of the course) was trichotomized so that it could serve as a blocking variable in an analysis of variance (ANOVA), thus removing its effect from the error term and providing for straightforward interpretation of interaction effects among independent variables. Results of the analyses demonstrated that students with higher GPAs outperformed those with lower GPAs, as would be expected, and that students taking the examination ordered by topic had higher examination scores than those taking the randomly ordered examination. The most important finding, however, was the interaction effect of GPA and examination question sequencing on final examination scores. Randomly ordered examinations had a significantly more negative effect on examination scores for students with higher GPAs than for those with lower GPAs. Findings regarding the time required to complete the examinations were inconclusive because, as the authors noted, control over this dependent variable was limited by the examination time available. Most students used the entire period to complete the examination.

In addition to illustrating how several controls may be properly applied, the three studies summarized above demonstrate that control variables, which are an extremely important source of control in experimental research, may be quite onerous. They are also as important as the independent and dependent variables in most education research. Most of the education research literature has long since progressed beyond the simple examination of group differences, especially in field-based research. Regardless of the other benefits of control variables, the complexity of most education research issues demands recognition that, practically and theoretically, virtually no important educational outcomes (dependent variables) are explicable in terms of a single "cause" (independent variable). Because of the relative ease of independent variable manipulation, the availability of interesting dependent variables, and, importantly, the potency of pretests and many available control variables, results of field experiments are often both interpretable and generalizable to reasonably well-defined subpopulations.

COMMON PROBLEMS IN FIELD EXPERIMENTS

In field experiments, the most severe internal validity limitations derive from the inability to randomly assign subjects to treatments. All too often, authors analyze and discuss their results as if subjects were randomly assigned, even though treatments are applied to separate, existing classes. A simple treatment-control group design with random assignment provides reasonable assurance that the two groups are, on average, quite similar. The same design, without the benefits of randomization, often serves as an example of uninterpretable, faulty, or weak designs in research methods and experimental design textbooks. As discussed earlier, nonrandom subject selection into treatment groups may yield nonequivalent groups, with their differences affecting the dependent variable.

Other problems are encountered when researchers attempt to control for possibly nonequivalent comparison groups. When a pretest is given, researchers sometimes use "matching" to force some equality on groups that are found to be different on the pretest. For example, if one class had a mean pretest score significantly higher than the other, the researcher would "match" all the scores in one group with similar scores in the other group and ignore those that did not match. Since the groups are different on the pretest, high scores in one group and low scores in the other are dropped from the experiment.

On average pretest scores, the remaining groups are about equal, but the increased control may be illusory because of a phenomenon known as statistical regression toward the mean.

Statistical regression may affect the measurement and interpretation of the post-test. In this case, it refers to the tendency for students with extreme pretest scores to score nearer the population mean on the post-test. The problem is most easily seen by noting that if either of our two classes were given the pretest, no treatment, and then given the post-test, the sample means of the group's scores should not change, but individual scores will change (unless instrument reliability is perfect). Moreover, the general tendency is for extreme pretest scorers to converge toward the population mean on the post-test. Assume that, in order to match the groups, the top pretest scorers of one of the groups are excluded from the sample; then the remaining subjects receive no treatment and take the post-test. The statistical regression effect causes the mean post-test score of the reduced sample to be higher than its pretest score because the expected downward trend in the excluded (top-scoring) subjects is removed from the group. Thus, the effect of matching on pretest scores in our example may be the artificial creation of group differences on the dependent variable. Statistical regression may create similar effects in experiments where subjects are assigned to groups based on extreme scores on control variables.

Analysis of pretest - post-test score differences (change scores) is sometimes used with the pretest - post-test control group design as well as other designs. The researcher attempts to control for pre-existing group differences on the pretest by ignoring them and treating the change score as the dependent variable. Unfortunately, change scores are not necessarily very precise or responsive to underlying changes in the measured construct. They are also very susceptible to statistical regression effects and several measurement problems. Change score analysis, besides being potentially biased, lacks the statistical power of ANCOVA and regression analysis, and is recommended only in very limited circumstances (see Reichardt, 1979).

In many pretest - post-test field experiments, internal validity is diminished considerably if the span of time between the tests is long. Inadvertent between-treatment differences may arise because of changes in the research setting, the subjects, or the measurement instrument itself (designated by Campbell and Stanley as history, maturation, and measurement effects). Often, the pretest - post-test design, when conducted over a long span of time, does not control contact between subjects in different treatment or control groups. If the differences in treatments or their effects are salient to students, they may react to perceived disparities or inequities by sharing knowledge with each other or consciously competing, thereby reducing the practical effectiveness of the independent variable manipulation. The Hawthorne effect also is more likely to be operating in a longer time frame, since between-group subject interaction or continued exposure to the treatment may increase the obtrusiveness of the experiment. These potential sources of confounds and decreased precision in simple pretest - post-test control group designs may severely restrict their internal validity, given a long enough experimental time frame.

With the wide range and types of options available to offset the loss of randomization and other controls in most field experiments, they vary a great deal in both internal and external validity, although external validity is often quite strong as compared to field experiments in other disciplines. Field studies and surveys, discussed in the next section, are rarely concerned with internal validity, because they do not generally attempt to demonstrate causal relationships. Surveys and field studies often have fundamentally different research objectives than experiments, resulting in a primary emphasis on the generalizability and clarity of findings.

FIELD STUDIES AND SURVEYS

In the last two sections, we discussed experiments in terms of the degree of researcher control over subject assignment to treatments, independent and dependent variables, and control variables. The degree of control exercised was the important issue because experimental research is oriented toward making observations from which causal inferences can be reasonably drawn. In experimental research, the researcher actively manipulates independent variables in order to capture their hypothesized effect(s) on dependent variables. Available "controls" include, among others, subject/task isolation in a laboratory or classroom, random subject assignment, control groups, control variables, manipulation checks, pretest - post-test designs, and nonobtrusive experiments. Their purpose is to allow the researcher to separate the effects of the independent variables from the potential effects of various other possible causal factors. The effectiveness of the various controls exercised is judged in terms of their contribution to internal validity.

In field studies and surveys, research objectives rarely include the examination of causal relationships. Rather, the purpose is usually to describe and/or compare well-defined populations. In higher education, the populations of most interest are the actors—students, faculty, alumni, and administrators; and institutions—academic disciplines, departments, schools, and universities—involved in the educational process. We characterize surveys and field studies as ex post facto research because the researcher observes, but does not manipulate, the variables of interest. Independent and dependent variables, because they are defined by experimenter manipulation or some notion of causal directionality, are not meaningful constructs in most ex post facto research. The internal validity benefits of random assignment are not sought. Instead, ex post facto research relies heavily on random selection in order to describe a population, or to compare attributes of different populations.

In field studies and surveys, researcher control is extended only over the selection and observation of variables and samples. The effectiveness of control is evaluated in terms of the objectives of ex post facto research, rather than the degree to which internal validity is attained. Control is typically exercised in surveys in order to assure that the description obtained from a sample is representative of (generalizable to) the population. Most people think of surveys as polls, although many academicians view them more narrowly as research involving the use of mailed questionnaires.

We discuss *surveys* as research that describes a population's attributes. Their chief purpose is descriptive, and descriptive accuracy is an important criterion by which they are evaluated. We discuss *field studies* as research that compares the attributes of different populations. Like surveys, field studies are descriptive of the populations compared, but they also examine differences in population attributes. Often, their primary objective is comparative, in order to enhance descriptive accuracy or suggest possible relationships between population membership and the distribution of attributes common to compared populations. Thus, the conceptual difference between surveys and field studies is drawn in terms of their respective primary purposes—description of population attributes versus comparison of populations' attributes.

Two modes of observing population attributes are common to both—the use of existing archival data bases, and the active measurement of variables of interest. Regarding the latter, surveys and field studies use a variety of data collection devices, including mailed and on-site questionnaires, and less often, personal and telephone interviews. Regardless of the data collection device, the extent of control over subject selection and variable specification and measurement largely determines the extent of generalizability of surveys and the validity of comparing population attributes in field studies.

SUBJECT SELECTION

In education research, mailed questionnaires are frequently used to measure a population's attributes. After the population of interest is specified (e.g., professors at AACSB-accredited schools, senior accounting majors, schools of accounting), a sample of its members is selected in some manner that yields a more or less representative sample. The usefulness of random subject selection from the population of interest in these studies is self-evident. The members of a randomly-selected sample of a given size are no more likely to be chosen than any others, so that all members of the population have an equal likelihood of being "represented" in the sample. Thus, a randomly-selected sample generally yields the best description of its population's attributes. The description of the sample's attributes is generalizable to the population because the sample is representative of the population.

For a variety of reasons, education researchers rarely achieve a random sample. Often the population of interest or its attributes may not be very accessible, or the cost of gaining access to a very broad sample may be prohibitive. Frequently, the solution is to restrict the scope of the research to the sample and attributes that are available, and focus on generalizing to similar subpopulations. For example, many of the studies that explore the possible correlates of academic success rely on data from a single institution. Even though the attributes examined (such as high school class rank, college entrance examination scores, and student demographics) are potentially important correlates across the entire population of college students, the researcher's sample is drawn from a population defined by institutional boundaries. Strictly speaking, the extent of generalizability of results is also limited to the students at the institution providing the sample. However, many researchers point to the representativeness of the sampled institution or students in terms of observable attributes that may define subpopulations. In the study of achievement correlates mentioned above, for example, the researcher may describe those institutional attributes (e.g., a specific four-year public institution with an open admissions policy, and students with mean ACT scores very near the national average) common to other (but not all) institutions, and suggest that similar findings are more likely to be attained with similar students/institutions.

The reasonableness of extending the findings drawn from a restricted, nonrandomly selected population is probably determined by the selection processes in effect and the nature of the variables (population attributes) examined. For example, survey research often begins with a randomly selected sample, but because of subject nonresponse or attrition and other self-selection processes, the representativeness of the sample actually examined is threatened. Researchers may attempt to detect or estimate the biasing effects of self-selection on the sample's representativeness (we discuss nonresponse bias and detection in the "common problems" section), but significant uncertainty about underlying systematic causes of self-selection often remains. For this reason, many researchers opt for a subpopulation (e.g., students from one or two institutions) in which they can control data availability and the response rate, rather than a broader population that is susceptible to selection bias. In either case, generalizability is limited, but its limits may be more well-defined in the case of a carefully chosen subpopulation, where the influences of unknown self-selection processes are less likely to operate.

In field studies, two or more samples are drawn in order to compare attributes of the populations represented. As with surveys, descriptive accuracy is important, and random selection yields the most representative samples and generalizable population descriptions. Quite often, however, the primary purpose of a field study is comparative, and the representativeness of descriptions to populations is less important than the generalizability of the results of the comparison. Suppose that a researcher wishes to examine differences between accounting student knowledge of international accounting in AACSB-accredited undergraduate programs versus nonaccredited programs. Knowledge of international accounting is measured by an examination given to selected accounting majors near the end of an academic term. If the researcher administers the examination to a sample of accounting students randomly selected from among all programs in each population, we can have reasonable confidence in generalizing that any observed examination score differences between samples are representative of existing population differences. If subject selection within the two types of accounting programs is not random, but is the same in both programs (e.g., students enrolled in auditing courses), generalizability is reduced, but the comparison is probably reasonable because the selection process should have the same effect in both types of programs. The reasonableness of the comparative inferences drawn in field studies is subject to the same kinds of weaknesses associated with treatment comparisons in experimental research, and the same solutions generally apply. Suspected comparison sample differences that are not randomized out may be controlled to some extent by using control groups and control variables to keep their effects from distorting the comparability of the groups, or limited matching may be used to create apparently equivalent groups.

VARIABLES EXAMINED

Surveys in the education literature quite often deal with variables of obvious practical significance in the population examined. Surveys addressing issues such as faculty productivity and faculty performance evaluation are interesting to faculty and journal editors for obvious reasons. The variables examined in many surveys are factual, as opposed to attitudinal, population attributes. For example, several studies in the general education and the accounting literature have surveyed various institutional populations in order to identify common course content and curricular requirements (e.g., Holder, 1978; Burns, 1979). These studies avoid some of the measurement and construct validity problems associated with attitudinal variables. Many measures of cognitive phenomena—attitudes, opinions, beliefs, intentions, etc.—may require a comparison population in order to be meaningful. Exceptions include Brown and Balke's (1983) survey of accounting department heads about their intentions to seek accounting accreditation, Addams' (1981) survey of entry-level Big-Eight accountants' perceptions of the importance of communications skills to career advancement, and Kyle and Williams' (1972) survey of accounting department chairmen regarding the importance of the CPA certificate to accounting faculty. The variables examined in these studies are population attributes that were widely held to be important in themselves at the time the research was done. The variables examined, though "attitudinal," have a readily apparent meaning (e.g., intentions to seek accreditation) and/or are taken to be important, in a practical sense, without external validation (e.g., accounting department chairmen's opinions).

Other variables studied in education surveys and field studies do not possess such straightforward interpretability, often due to the questionable construct validity of many attitudinal variables. For example, studies in several disciplines, including accounting, have attempted to assess the perceived importance of covering various substantive topics in a specific course or curriculum. Most have used mailed questionnaires to gather data in the form of respondent ratings, on likert-type scales, of the pool of possible topics. Many gain some degree of construct validity by demonstrating that the questionnaire items (topics) that should theoretically be about equally important are rated similarly by respondents, and/or by showing that item responses from different groups of respondents reflect anticipated differences or similarities in the groups' attitudes or opinions.

COMMON PROBLEMS IN SURVEYS AND FIELD STUDIES

Surveys and field studies in education frequently fail to achieve their legitimate research objectives for several reasons. Nonrepresentative or ill-defined samples often threaten generalizability to such an extent that the contribution of many surveys cannot be determined. The variables examined in many studies have so little demonstrated construct validity that conclusions drawn about them can have little practical or theoretical significance. The data generated by many education researchers are rarely described adequately by the limited statistical techniques usually applied. Even when these issues are properly addressed in surveys and field studies, authors are prone to draw inferences that cannot be supported by their research findings. Indeed, this problem area—drawing inferences that are outside the limits of the research design—may be partially responsible for the negative reactions many academicians and editors have toward surveys and field studies. We briefly discuss these issues (except the construct validity problem, which is discussed in the measurement section) and some possible solutions in the following paragraphs.

Given the importance of sample representativeness in surveys, and perhaps to a lesser extent, field studies, education researchers must assess and disclose the representativeness of their samples to the target populations as such in the opening paragraphs of their research reports. Instead, most discuss their initial sample in terms of its selection (random or nonrandom) and their attained sample in terms of various secondary attributes (e.g., demographics and response rate). As we noted earlier, many researchers choose a restricted but well-defined sample such as students at a single university instead of students from many universities, in order to gain some control over the response rate. This approach may or may not yield a more meaningful sample than a broader-based sampling technique, depending on the representativeness of the restricted sample. The selection processes that "assign" members to the chosen sampling frame and the known attributes of those sampled must be carefully considered with respect to the population attributes (variables) of direct interest. Clearly, a restricted sample is defensible if the variables examined are not likely to be unduly affected by factors specific to the restricted sample, or if the restricted sample is reasonably representative of some important subpopulation (e.g., students at major state universities with graduate programs). In either case, the adequate disclosure of known population attributes, as well as "discovered" sample attributes, is often necessary in order for the degree of generalizability to be properly assessed.

Serious errors of interpretation of results may be avoided with more complete disclosures of sample characteristics. Early studies exploring the status of women and minorities in higher education relied on surveys of faculty members' hiring, salary, promotion, and tenure decision experiences. However, the types of institutions surveyed were often not reported, and the results were overgeneralized, eventually finding their way into the professional education literature and the popular press. Recently, researchers have recognized that, among other things, the types of institutions surveyed is a very significant factor in explaining the magnitude of the inequalities reported in the earlier studies. The results of early studies did not detect or report that their samples were drawn from a bimodal distribution comprised of types of institutions that have systematically different hiring, salary, promotion, and tenure practices. Yet the institutional affiliation of respondents was not disclosed or considered in generating descriptive statistics. Subsequently, faulty generalizations were made about inequities in higher education in general, rather than more appropriate generalizations about across-institutional differences. The many benefits of adequate disclosure are discussed in the research disclosure issues section of this chapter.

Perhaps the most common problem encountered in surveys and field studies is that posed by subject self-selection through nonresponse to the research instrument. Nonresponse bias may arise when some portion of a study's intended subjects choose not to respond to the data-gathering technique or instrument. Because it is a special form of self-selection bias, its negative effects are similar to those we discussed earlier. Like self-selection bias in experimental research, nonresponse bias in surveys and field studies is a problem because it removes the significant benefits of randomization from the research endeavor. The loss of randomization due to subject self-selection was discussed earlier in terms of its internal validity implications in experimental research. Loss of randomization in surveys and field studies diminishes the researcher's ability to generalize and to clearly identify the population.

To the extent that the unspecified factors that induced nonresponse from subjects are systematically related to the population attributes measured in the study, the respondents may not be representative of the target population or even the sample from which they emerged. For example, assume that a questionnaire regarding the perceived benefits of an accounting program's accreditation is mailed to a randomly-selected sample of U.S. accounting faculty in both accredited and nonaccredited programs. One would expect that the highest response rates would be from those schools recently accredited or contemplating accreditation (cf. Brown and Balke, 1983). If the survey is not designed to distinguish between responses from accredited programs versus those from nonaccredited programs, the potential for nonresponse bias is rather high. One of the best-known apparent causes of nonresponse is a relative lack of active interest in the subject matter of the survey. Stated from the opposite perspective, the degree of respondent interest in the survey's subject matter is positively associated with the response rate achieved. Thus, the respondents to a survey regarding accounting accreditation would be expected to have more interest in the issue than those from the original sample. If their higher level of interest is associated with the attributes measured by the questionnaire, and a large portion of the sample fails to respond, then the reported results may not accurately portray the original sample's attributes, and the generalizability boundaries of the results are obscured.

Nonresponse in field studies may create an additional distortion of results involving inadvertent interaction between nonresponse and the population attributes sampled and compared. If the accounting accreditation study mentioned above draws two samples, one from accredited and the other from nonaccredited programs for comparative purposes, one would expect that the response rates of the two groups would differ. If they do, the likely nature of the bias within groups would have a predictable effect on their comparison. The comparison may degenerate into a comparison of the most interested respondents from accredited programs and a smaller, even less representative sample from nonaccredited programs. If the groups' respondents share a common reason for responding, such as interest in the issue, the most likely outcome of the comparison of the achieved samples is, intuitively, that the two groups will appear to be more similar than their underlying populations really are.

However, the likely causes of nonresponse may be different across samples, or the same causes may affect the measured attributes in different manners, so that the bias's effect on reported results cannot be specified, even intuitively. The unknown nature of the many possible causes of nonresponse and effects of nonresponse bias on results is particularly troublesome, given the relatively simple comparative purpose of most field studies and the large proportion of nonrespondents in most of them.

Many researchers attempt to test for the existence of nonresponse bias by designating a subset of the respondents as surrogates for nonrespondents and comparing them with the remaining respondents. Some empirical support for treating late respondents as surrogates for nonrespondents exists. The choice of an appropriate group of late respondents varies a great deal in the education literature. When a single mailing of a questionnaire is used, with no follow-up mailing(s), researchers choose the quartile or decile received last, the last "batch" received (indicating a naturally occurring break), or enough of the latest responses to lend statistical power to the comparison. Too often, this last criterion is not considered, and the last quartile, decile, or batch is too small to accomodate the statistical tests used to detect bias. On the other hand, if too large a subsample is chosen, perhaps the latest half of the respondents, any detectable differences in the surrogate nonrespondents and the remaining respondents may be hidden somewhere among the designated surrogates. When two or more mailings are used to elicit responses, second and/or third mailing respondents serve as surrogates for nonrespondents.

Most of the available evidence demonstrating the validity of comparing early and late respondents to test for nonresponse bias is based on multiple mailings. Those who respond to a second mailing have been shown to be more representative of the remaining nonrespondents, even though some form of residual nonresponse bias potentially remains as long as any significant portion of the original sample fails to respond. The most prudent applications of early-late tests are based on at least two mailings, and examine possible between-mailing differences in both questionnaire responses and along other available dimensions. Differences in early and late questionnaire responses indicate that the biasing effect of nonresponse resides in the attribute measures themselves. The achieved sample's measured attributes may be systematically different from those of the intended sample. Differences in early and late respondents along other dimensions not measured by the questionnaire itself may also be meaningful. Comparisons in terms of the demographic information included with the questionnaire, and of other archival information available, may indicate identifiable sample characteristics that allow the achieved sample to be more clearly identified.

In our accreditation study example, the researcher might compare early and late respondents on demographic measures such as respondent age, requested via the questionnaire, and measures such as respondent rank, available through Hasselback's directory, which serves as the sampling frame for most accounting education survey research. These comparisons might reveal, for example, that relatively higher ranking, older faculty in both sampled groups tended to respond to the questionnaire, or that the respondents from the nonaccredited programs tended to be higher ranking and older than those from accredited programs. Indeed, the faculty development literature suggests that extent of concern with institutional issues (and interest in the questionnaire?) is positively associated with faculty rank and age.

Whether the early-late response comparisons reveal differences or not, comparisons of faculty rank and age, across samples and as compared to known population parameters, may allow the potentially biased sample(s) to be recast in terms of the representativeness of the achieved samples. Both samples being compared might be redesignated as, for example, higher-ranking faculty, or one or both samples might be reconstituted by matching on these variables. Note that matching on such external variables is not particularly susceptible to statistical regression artifacts associated with matching on pretests in experimental research. The matching here creates comparable groups by omitting those sample-defining respondents (e.g., lower-ranking faculty) whose nonresponse largely creates the bias. The research focus narrows from comparing attributes of nonaccredited program faculty and accredited program faculty to a comparison of higher-ranking faculty attributes between the two types of programs. Given the importance of representativeness to generalizability in surveys and field studies, nonresponse bias must be carefully evaluated along many possible dimensions in order to avoid incorrect inferences about apparent sample attribute differences and about the samples actually examined.

A related problem in the survey and field study literature is the artificially limited examination and disclosure of the obtained data. Descriptive statistics representing sample attributes often include only the mean or median, ignoring the potential meaningfulness of the dispersion and shapes of their distributions. Because description is a fundamental objective of surveys and field studies, the descriptive summaries of the attributes described should be as complete as possible. Presentation of measures of central tendency without measures of dispersion of attributes may be misleading insofar as they lead the naive reader to comparative inferences that are properly made only with more complete knowledge of the distribution of responses. In most instances, the data aggregation rules that govern the calculation of means, medians, standard deviations, frequencies, etc. used to describe sample attributes are the same as those assumed by various inferential statistics. Most quantifiable data, if capable of being summarized into a meaningful description, can be further examined by appropriately matched inferential statistics techniques. Further, inferential statistics should not be limited to simple comparisons of group responses in terms of mean or median measures, but should often include direct comparisons of measured dispersions. In addition to guiding the choice of appropriate inferential statistics for comparing means, medians, or frequencies, dispersion comparisons may be meaningful indicators of within-group homogeneity, which may itself represent an interesting descriptive variable.

Finally, a significant problem in education surveys and field studies involves the drawing of inferences that are beyond the scope of the data collection technique and/or statistical analyses used. The education literature reveals an apparent researcher predisposition toward causal inferences, even though they are rarely warranted in ex post facto research. Survey researchers are generally limited to drawing descriptive inferences. Researchers engaged in field studies are similarly limited to descriptive and comparative inferences. The unfortunate tendency in much of the literature is for the findings to be discussed solely in terms of the suspected causal factors that influenced the choice of sample attributes examined in the study. For example, a field study might compare the work-oriented values of senior accounting majors with those of staff accountants because the researcher suspects that systematic shifts in these values occur as practical work experience is gained. Regardless of the outcome of the comparison, it does not suggest very much about shifts in values. Even so, researchers tend to discuss their findings in terms of shifts or changes rather than in terms of the simple differences actually observed. Internal validity issues are sometimes discussed, even though causality inferences, requiring the controlled observation of change, are not reasonable. Often, the descriptive and comparative inferences that can be fruitfully drawn from surveys and field studies are overshadowed by misdirected discussions of causality.

MEASUREMENT ISSUES AND PROBLEMS

Throughout our discussions of the problems most often associated with the various data-gathering techniques, we deferred discussion of certain measurement problems. The fundamental issues surrounding the measurement of independent, dependent, and control variables, and population attributes are similar across many research techniques. The measurement problems that arise in education research are crucial to the interpretability of most empirical work. The importance of these issues (e.g., validity, reliability, and measurement range), as well as the frequency with which they go unrecognized, suggests that a summary of common problems and their potential solutions might be useful to those interested in accounting education research. In the next two sections, we briefly overview some fundamental measurement issues and discuss the most commonly encountered problems in the following section.

MEASUREMENT RELIABILITY

The reliability of a measure, whether it is a single questionnaire item, an entire questionnaire, or a widely accepted, easily accessible measure such as grade point average, is the extent to which the obtained scores are invariant with respect to different possible conditions that might affect them. Reliabilities are presented in the testing manuals that accompany most widely-used standardized tests such as intelligence tests and personality inventories. They are usually reported as correlation coefficients indicating the extent of positive relationship between two administrations of the same instrument to the same subjects at different points in time (test-retest reliability), with the test-retest time spans depending on the theoretical stability of the measured constructs over time. In a sense, these reliabilities indicate the practical time span over which the attribute, as we are able to observe it, might be expected to remain stable in the absence of some intervening, attribute-altering events. For example, if an instrument has a moderate test-retest reliability at a two-month interval, the practical time frame within which manipulations and measurements must fall is prescribed. The instrument should be able to distinguish the often-hypothesized change in some attribute from random changes that might be expected to occur within a research time frame not longer than two months. Disclosure of reliability time spans, when available with standardized instruments, provides a reasonable basis for understanding the demonstrated stability of the attributes measured. The policy implications that are suggested by the findings of a study are likely to vary across different possible results/reliability combinations because these combinations may also suggest time spans within which policy action can be expected to effect its intended attribute change.

When standardized instruments are not used to measure attributes, reliabilities may also be calculated and presented. Although test-retest reliability cannot be directly assessed without at least two or more administrations of the instrument, other forms of reliability are usually calculable. Internal consistency is a dimension of reliability that captures the common content of questionnaire items that measure a common attribute. If two or more questionnaire items are intentionally included to measure the same attribute, split-half reliabilities may be presented by creating two subtests, each comprised of conceptually similar items, and calculating their response correlations. The well-known Kuder-Richardson test is often used to assess internal consistency among several conceptually similar questionnaire items. Like split-half reliabilities, KR reliabilities are based on the homogeneity of responses from a single administration of the instrument, and indicate the extent to which conceptually similar measures capture the same or related attributes. A factor analysis approach to identifying similar groups of item responses addresses this same reliability issue. These reliabilities tell us nothing about temporal stability. Instead, they assess the extent of agreement, or convergence, of multiple measures of a posited attribute.

The relationship between the questionnaire items and the attributes they are intended to examine (the instrument's construct validity, discussed below) is tenuously drawn when a researcher-developed questionnaire attempts to measure cognitive phenomena such as attitudes, opinions, beliefs, or intentions. High internal consistency among questionnaire items that are designed to measure the same attribute provide some assurance that the items measure the same or closely related phenomena. This type of reliability allows us to infer the existence of some underlying attribute, if not its exact nature. Because an instrument's reliability often varies across populations, presentation of reliabilities for compared samples may provide insights into the relative meaningfulness of the questionnaire across the two populations. If acceptable reliabilities are found in one sample, and low or uninterpretable reliabilities are found in a sample from a different population or treatment, the measured attribute is not stable across populations or treatments. Low reliabilities in either sample, for whatever reason (e.g., questionnaire items often contain language that is more familiar to one population than another; the substantive issues addressed by many attitudinal measures are better-understood in one population than another), significantly reduce the interpretability of sample comparisons. Different reliabilities across different populations may have significant implications for the meaning of the attributes being measured.

CONSTRUCT VALIDITY

A measured attribute's meaning, in its most fundamental sense, is referred to as its construct validity. The construct validity of a questionnaire item or instrument is the extent to which its responses are systematically related to other external indicants of the attribute being examined. Like most reliabilities, validity coefficients are usually expressed as correlations. They indicate a predictive or defining relationship between instrument responses and other phenomena that are taken to be valid indicators of the measured attribute or its effects. For example, every major standardized college entrance examination has been validated against various measures of academic success, such as grade point averages, attrition rates, graduate school attendance rates, and professional examination pass rates (including the CPA examination; see Leathers, 1972 and Dunn and Hall, 1984). These, in turn, have been validated against other, perhaps more concrete, "measures" that are viewed as socially significant phenomena, including career choice, professional success, and work performance. Moreover, these entrance examinations have been validated against each other and against numerous other socially significant phenomena.

The construct validity of these measures, as well as many others, such as standardized personality inventories, achievement tests, intelligence tests, and aptitude tests, is established by more than the correlations drawn from studies specifically designed to demonstrate their validities. They are successfully used as control variables in numerous studies involving a wide variety of independent and dependent variables across many populations. Other measures, such as grade point average, have also been shown, through use, to have construct validity, without the carefully controlled validation techniques applied to standardized measures. However established, the degree and extent of construct validity for many available measures is reasonably well specified. In essence, we may think of construct validity as addressing the question of what it is that we are describing or predicting with our measure.

As with reliabilities, validity coefficients may be calculated for most questionnaires and measurement instruments. Although several types of validity are discussed by various authors, most include content validity and criterion-related validity in their typologies. Although not all-inclusive, these two appear to be the most important and the most widely reported dimensions of construct validity.

Content Validity

Content validity is often the chief concern in the creation of a research instrument designed to measure a reasonably well-specified attribute. When an instructor attempts to design a final examination that is comprehensive, covering all the subject matter or major topics in the course, the focus on complete coverage of the measured attribute (course-specific knowledge) is driven by a desire for content validity. The same is true in the many studies that attempt to validate internally-developed instruments or techniques to predict academic persistence or achievement (e.g., Delaney et al., 1979; Hicks and Richardson, 1984). In the first case, the domain of the attribute "course-specific knowledge" as measured by the examination is specified by the instructor as he carefully selects examination questions that are representative of the substantive content of the entire course. Questions have content validity to the extent that the range of measured responses is sufficient to capture a meaningful portion of the attribute's domain. But the distribution of final examination scores should be partially explicable in terms of individual student attributes, such as ability and motivation, and other such individual differences. Often, GPA is used as a measure of ability/motivation, and correlations between examination scores and GPA are presented as content validity coefficients. To the extent that the examination scores are "explained" by that portion of ability/motivation reflected in GPA, final examination scores are expected to similarly reflect the underlying effects of this same ability/motivation as it was applied to the attainment of "course-specific knowledge." Content validity may also be represented by correlations between particular test examination scores and scores on relatively independent parts of the examination, using the same reasoning. A significant positive correlation between the examination scores and GPA lends content validity to the examination insofar as it demonstrates that the examination captures a potent, presumably causal attribute—student ability/motivation. Those researchers who include well-validated variables such as GPA as control variables (e.g., the covariate in many analyses of covariance, blocking variables in analyses of variance, the structural variables in regression analyses) are implicitly testing the content validity of their dependent variables. Note that content validity is not concerned primarily with *what* the instrument measures as much as with whether it measures a broad enough portion of the attribute's known domain.

Criterion-Related Validity

The criterion-related validity of a questionnaire or measurement instrument is its ability to predict or describe some other measure or behavior, whether or not the examined attribute's domain is well-known as the instrument is constructed. Most individual researcher-designed instruments are constructed without the examination preparer's knowledge of the attribute's domain. Because most researchers attempt to measure attitudes, opinions, beliefs, and intentions, their content validity is often an open question—these cognitive attributes "exist" in some domain whose dimensions are difficult to specify. Thus, concern over whether the measurement range of the instrument adequately covers the attribute's known domain (content validity) is not as pertinent as whether it meaningfully measures anything interesting or important.

The demonstration of a correlational or predictive relationship between the instrument's responses and some interesting, important external criterion is the purpose of most criterion-related validity coefficients. For example, "attitudes toward five-year accounting programs" might be measured in a field study. The existence of a positive association between the attitude measures and respondent affiliation with such programs indicates that the measures tap the domain of interest. The criterion in this case is institutional affiliation. It operationally defines the attribute "attitudes toward five-year accounting programs" in terms of institutional affiliation, which serves as an external indicant that might be deemed interesting in itself.

Criterion-related validity may also be presented by focusing on the predictive ability of the measure, as opposed to concurrent (defining) criteria. For example, a positive correlation between doctoral candidate affiliation with major state universities and subsequent professorial appointments with similar institutions suggests some underlying relationship. This type of criterion-related validity is based on the assumption that externally observable potential outcomes of the measured attributes (such as the type of likely institutional appointments for graduating Ph.D.s) represent interesting or important phenomena. The extreme example of an instrument designed for high predictive criterion-related validity is an aptitude test. Exactly what it measures is less important than how well it predicts important future outcomes, and this capability is reflected in the choice of the external criteria (subsequent performance, success, or satisfaction) typically used to demonstrate an aptitude test's criterion-related validity. Whether it defines the attribute or predicts its outcomes, along with content validity, criterion-related validity indicates that the instrument measures something that is interpretable in terms of some real-world phenomena. Construct validity coefficients, as well as other evidence bearing on the practical meaning of a research instrument's measures, are extremely useful disclosures in most empirical education research.

COMMON MEASUREMENT PROBLEMS

A few measurement problems and interpretation issues appear quite frequently in accounting education research, often severely limiting its interpretability. The single most common measurement oversight is the failure to assess construct validity and reliability. Too often, discussions of statistically significant relationships among variables offer little indication about the meaning of the constructs measured, perhaps under the assumption that questionnaire item responses, for example, should be taken at face value. This assumption may be warranted in some cases, but because so little is known about the conditions under which the assumption is correct, validity and reliability coefficients should be presented and interpreted when possible, and other external evidence that might enhance the interpretability of the measures should be considered.

The other, less general, measurement-related problems that often arise in education research include:

1. Viewing questionnaire responses as absolute measures existing along some well-specified continuum
2. Ignoring dependencies that exist among measured variables
3. Using, or failing to recognize, a too-restricted measurement range
4. Attaching too much meaning to measured variables and their relationships

We briefly describe the nature of each of these problems, along with some possible solutions, in the remainder of this section.

Unless the construct validity of a measurement instrument is established, as is the case with many standardized examinations and psychological inventories and instruments, the meaning of an X marked on a scale cannot necessarily be directly inferred from the questionnaire item itself or the verbal labels associated with the response. For example, suppose that a researcher is interested in evaluating various criteria that might be important in a faculty promotion or tenure decision context. A questionnaire comprised of several items intended to measure specific dimensions of faculty performance, including research, teaching, and service, is administered to a representative sample of department chairmen. For the sake of simplicity, assume that each questionnaire item requests a response on a five-point likert-type scale, with verbal labels at each point ranging from "not at all important" to "extremely important" at the endpoints. Mean responses are calculated for each questionnaire item, and, quite often, discussed in terms of the verbal labels that are nearest the mean response. For example, a mean item response between 3.5 and 4.5 is discussed as demonstrating that the respondents believed that the item is "very important" (the verbal label attached to "4" on the scale). The "very important" label has not been shown to be meaningful in any practical sense. Our researcher may try to address the issue by making within-questionnaire item comparisons. The assumption is that viewing each mean response along a continuum of mean responses to other (statistically significantly different) questionnaire items allows the degree of relative "importance" to be specified with reference to these other items. Yet the meaning of these responses—their construct validity—has not been established either. Perhaps more importantly, few questionnaires are constructed in a manner that allows reasonable within-questionnaire item comparisons because of potential dependencies among the item responses.

Dependencies among questionnaire item responses often arise because of potential questionnaire item ordering effects. Most accounting education researchers use one version of a questionnaire or instrument, with the items ordered in the same manner for all respondents. As the respondents move through the questionnaire, responses to later items are conditioned by responses to earlier items. The verbal labels are continuously redefined as the respondents associate them with each item response made. In our faculty promotion criteria example, the questionnaire might begin with a series of items about the importance of various faculty service activities, followed by several items assessing the importance of a number of research performance criteria. Assume that, apart from the questionnaire, research criteria actually are more important in the promotion/tenure process than service criteria. Even though the questionnaire instructions may request that the respondents evaluate each item independently, the verbal labels (or numbers) are associated with the service criteria and assigned some degree of importance by the respondents. As the respondents continue into the research section of the questionnaire, the response categories are, in essence, defined by their use in evaluating the importance of several less important criteria (cf. Chapter 4 discussion of faculty performance evaluation). The respondent may find that, in relation to the service criteria just evaluated, the research criteria should be "off the scale." Responses are, however, confined to a scale that has been shrunk by the subject's previous responses. A cluster of responses at the high end of the scale may indicate that the effective item response range is too restricted to capture the relative importance of research criteria. It probably also indicates that the potentially interesting variability among research criteria item responses is artificially truncated. Had the questionnaire items been arranged in the opposite order, service criteria item responses would have been conditioned by research criteria responses in a similar manner. In either case, within-questionnaire item comparisons are often inappropriate because of data dependencies attributable to the order of questionnaire items.

The obvious solution is to randomly order questionnaire items for each subject, so that no order effect can exist. This solution is rather costly and time-consuming, but would enhance the validity of making the desired within-questionnaire comparisons. It might also significantly increase the error variance in the responses to the extent that the random ordering would force the respondents to bounce among a heterogeneous set of questionnaire items (service, research, and teaching criteria, in our example). An alternative is to create alternative versions of the instrument, each uniquely ordered, so that the potential order effect can be estimated statistically. In our promotion/tenure criteria study, the researcher might create two versions of the questionnaire—one with research criteria listed first, the other with service criteria listed first. Or, the questionnaire might be reconstructed using a scaling technique that provides a more directly comparative response opportunity than the likert-type scale. Ranking, fixed-sum point allocations, magnitude scaling, and many other scaling techniques may be more appropriate than the likert-type scale in research where within-questionnaire item comparisons are desired.

The third measurement-related problem involves the use of an overly restrictive measurement range. The limitations imposed by measurement range restriction of independent and dependent variables were discussed earlier in this chapter, and the likely effect of a mis-specified range was illustrated above. Sometimes, careful pilot-testing of the research instrument can reveal measurement range restrictions so that the measures may be adjusted (e.g., the instrument's power to discriminate between responses at all points on the scale is enhanced) or the scaling technique may be changed to capture a broader range of possible responses. The detection of a restricted measurement range is occasionally reported in the literature by authors who note relatively compact item response distributions very near the end of the scale. Again, the utility of examining the distributions, as well as the scalar locations of responses, is apparent.

The final measurement concern that we noted in the education literature is the researcher's assumption that the measured variables and the relationships found among them are capturing practically important real-world phenomena. Research instruments and scaling techniques used in education research often do not establish the link between measured variables and their practically significant real-world outcomes. Ultimately, we would like to know if (or more probably, under what conditions) the items evaluated by the respondent to the research instrument will have a discernible effect on some important real-world phenomena. As discussed in the field studies and surveys section, the attributes measured by a research instrument may sometimes be accepted at face value with little concern over construct validity, as in the case where the researcher requires factual, as opposed to attitudinal, responses. More often, the attributes or variables under examination are not readily interpretable because the external validation criteria are so far removed from the attribute measured (attitudinal constructs).

In many instances, the measured attribute's apparent proximity to acceptable external validation criteria may be enhanced. For example, compare two modes of eliciting responses from subjects: having them judge the relative importance of several questionnaire items or having them make more realistic judgments involving the use of the variables under examination. A research instrument that encompasses important aspects of an actual, practically significant decision context (e.g., faculty promotion/tenure deliberations, student admission decisions, recruiting decisions, etc.), presented in a realistic manner, is more likely to capture a meaningful representation of the phenomena under investigation. In our faculty promotion/tenure criteria illustration, the instrument might have elicited promotion/tenure decisions and judgments from department chairmen evaluating several bogus faculty members' summarized vitae, where the configurations of performance criteria (research, teaching, and service) are systematically manipulated.

The construct validity of such judgments is not as important an issue in this case because we are partially replicating an important decision context rather than asking for evaluative judgments about the importance of various items thought to be important in that context. Indeed, the comparative importance of teaching, research, and service, as evaluated by questionnaire responses, is largely inconsistent with that demonstrated by research that examines relationships among actual performance measures of teaching, research, and service with important outcomes such as salary level and promotion/tenure attainment (see Chapter 4). The validity of comparing judgment outcomes, such as a yes or no vote on promotion/tenure, is often easier to establish than that of comparing evaluative judgments about aspects of the judgment context. A statistically significant difference in judgments with real-world analogues establishes some construct validity for the measurement instrument. A statistically significant difference in evaluative judgments about decision context variables may or may not reflect a difference that would affect the actual decision. Statistical significance is more likely to represent practical significance in the former case than the latter. When possible, researchers should attempt to measure the behaviors and/or attitudes for which construct validity indicants (i.e., important external behaviors or decision outcomes) are at least observable and ideally replicable in the research context.

CONCLUSION

Research in the general education literature reflects a continuing trend toward the more sophisticated use of research and measurement techniques. Methodological progress in the measurement area has kept pace with the general growth of the literature, as have the development of useful research paradigms and the rigorous application of the research techniques discussed in this chapter. In the introduction to this chapter, we noted some of its more significant omissions. Most of the topics that were omitted, or only introduced, may be further explored in the literatures of numerous disciplines. Some of the major works, and some of the more accessible, are suggested below.

In the accounting literature, Abdel-khalik and Ajinkya (1979) present a very helpful introduction to the relationships among theory/model development and empirical verification. The AAA Committee on the Relationship of Behavioral Science and Accounting (1974) presents an interesting, and perhaps extreme, position on the importance of models to empirical researchers. Other accounting treatments of research topics are included in Sterling (1972). More philosophical discussions of the issues affecting the role of theories and models in science are found in Poincare (1952), Toulmin (1960), Popper (1965), Simon (1977), and Nagel (1979). Heisenberg (1958) provides a readable illustration of theory development and modification, based on his own revolutionary contribution in physics. Related debate surrounding the "revolution vs. evolution" conceptions of theory development are in the well-known work by Kuhn (1962), and in Lakatos and Musgrave (1970), Popper (1972), and Kuhn (1977).

This chapter does not present a comprehensive coverage of experimental design. Several research designs are introduced and illustrated in the discussions of experimental research. The designs that are mentioned are those that are most widely used in education research, partially because they are relatively straightforward and easily interpretable. Perhaps the most well-known research design (and methodology) texts are Cook and Campbell (1979), Campbell and Stanley (1963), and Cochran and Cox (1957). More applied discussions of design implementation are found in Abdel-khalik and Ajinkya (1979), Ackoff (1962), Kerlinger (1973), and Kinney (1986).

Those interested in the measurement issues raised in this chapter will benefit from Nunnally (1978), a "traditional" treatment of psychometrics; Anastasi's (1982) comprehensive discussions of psychological testing and test construction; and the practical advice concerning questionnaire construction in Simon (1978) and Dillman (1978). A potentially valuable tool for behavioral researchers in education is Buros' series of available psychological tests and instruments (Buros, 1975 a, b, c; 1978), as well as sourcebooks by Comrey, Backer and Glaser (1973); Chun, Cobb and French (1976); Goldman and Saunders (1974), and Goldman and Busch (1978). Buros includes evaluative reviews of tests by experts in the field, as well as information concerning each test's applicability and availability.

Discussions of a broader range of research issues (other than experimentation, causality, and theory-testing) are included in Kerlinger (1973), Simon (1978), and Dillman (1978). Those research methods that involve what are loosely described as "qualitative techniques" (Simon, 1978), such as case studies, ethnographies, and participant observation, are introduced by Erickson and Schulman (in Whittrock, 1986). Certain hybrid "quantified" qualitative research methods are becoming increasingly popular in education research. They include content analysis (Kerlinger, 1973), protocol analysis (Newell and Simon, 1972; Nisbett and Wilson, 1977), and meta-analysis (Glass, 1976; 1978). These are important nonexperimental research techniques that are very useful in education research, primarily in exploratory or integrative investigations.

We hope that those interested in pursuing or appreciating accounting education research will benefit from discussions of the methodological issues in this chapter and the substantive issues addressed in the following chapters. Both sets of issues are our distillations of numerous, extremely heterogeneous configurations of research tools, objectives, and methodologies reported in the education literature. We are limited by our nonrandom, but, we hope, representative, literature sampling technique (described in chapter one), as well as whatever other biases we may have inadvertently brought with us as we explored the literature. We present an overview of the literature—a view that must necessarily be incomplete. Our hope is that we accurately portrayed the research that we reviewed, and that our samples are representative of fruitful, important research.

CHAPTER 2 BIBLIOGRAPHY

Abdel-khalik, A. R., and B. B. Ajinkya, *Empirical Research in Accounting: A Methodological Viewpoint* (Sarasota, Florida: American Accounting Association, 1979).

Ackoff, R., *Scientific Method: Optimizing Applied Research Decisions* (New York: John Wiley & Sons, 1962).

Addams, H. L., "Should the Big 8 Teach Communication Skills?" *Management Accounting* (May 1981), pp. 37–40.

American Accounting Association, "Report of the Committee on the Relationship of Behavioral Science and Accounting," *The Accounting Review* (supplement, 1974), (Sarasota, Florida: American Accounting Association, 1974), pp. 126–139.

Anastasi, A., *Psychological Testing* (New York: MacMillan, 1982).

Baldwin, B. A., and T. P. Howard, "Intertopical Sequencing of Examination Questions: An Empirical Evaluation," *Journal of Accounting Education* (Fall 1983), pp. 89–96.

———, and K. R. Howe, "Secondary-Level Study of Accounting and Subsequent Performance in the First College Course," *The Accounting Review* (July 1982), pp. 619–626.

Battista, M. S., "The Effect of Instructional Technology and Learner Characteristics on

Cognitive Achievement in College Accounting," *The Accounting Review* (April 1978), pp. 477–485.
Brown, J. F., and T. E. Balke, "Accounting Curriculum Comparison by Degree Program of Schools Intending to Seek AACSB Accreditation," *Issues in Accounting Education* (1983), pp. 50–59.
Buehlmann, D. M., and J. V. Techavichit, "Factors Influencing Final Examination Performance in Large Versus Small Sections of Accounting Principles," *Journal of Accounting Education* (Spring 1984), pp. 127–136.
Burns, J. O., "A Study of International Accounting Education in the United States," *International Journal of Accounting Education and Research* (Fall 1979), pp. 135–145.
Buros, O. K. (ed.), *Intelligence Tests and Reviews* (Lincoln, Nebraska: University of Nebraska, 1975(a)).
———, *Personality Tests and Reviews II* (Lincoln, Nebraska: University of Nebraska, 1975(b)).
———, *Vocational Tests and Reviews* (Lincoln, Nebraska: University of Nebraska, 1975(c)).
———, *The Eighth Mental Measurement Yearbook* (Lincoln, Nebraska: University of Nebraska, 1978).
Campbell, D. T., and J. C. Stanley, *Experimental and Quasi-Experimental Designs for Research* (Chicago: Rand McNally, 1963).
Chun, K., S. Cobb, and J. R. P. French, *Measures for Psychological Assessment* (Ann Arbor, Michigan: Institute for Social Research, 1976).
Cochran, W. G., and G. M. Cox, *Experimental Designs* (New York: John Wiley and Sons, 1957).
Comrey, A. L., T. E. Backer, and E. M. Glaser, *A Sourcebook for Mental Health Measures* (Los Angeles: Human Interaction Research Institute, 1973).
Cook, T. D., and D. T. Campbell, *Quasi-Experimentation: Design & Analysis Issues for Field Settings* (Boston: Houghton Mifflin, 1979).
Delaney, P. R., D. E. Keyes, C. L. Norton, and J. R. Simon, "An Admission Test for Intermediate Accounting," *The Accounting Review* (January 1979), pp. 155–162.
Dickens, T. L., and R. M. Harper, "The Use of Microcomputers in Intermediate Accounting: Effects on Student Achievement and Attitudes," *Journal of Accounting Education* (Spring 1986), pp. 127–146.
Dillman, D. A., *Mail and Telephone Surveys: The Total Design Method* (New York: John Wiley & Sons, 1978).
Dunn, W. M., and T. W. Hall, "An Empirical Analysis of the Relationships Between CPA Examination Candidate Performance," *The Accounting Review* (October 1984), pp. 674–689.
Glass, G. V., "Primary, Secondary, and Meta-analysis of Research," *Educational Researcher* (1976), pp. 3–8.
———, "Integrating Findings: The Meta-analysis of Research" in L. S. Shulman (ed.), *Review of Research in Education* (1978).
Goldman, B. A., and J. C. Busch (eds.), *Directory of Unpublished Experimental Measures*, Vol. 2 (New York: Human Sciences Press, 1978).
———, and J. L. Saunders (eds.), *Directory of Unpublished Experimental Measures*, Vol. 1 (New York: Human Sciences Press, 1974).
Heisenberg, W., *Physics and Philosophy: The Revolution in Modern Science* (New York: Harper and Row, 1958).
Hicks, D. W., and F. M. Richardson, "Predicting Early Success in Intermediate Accounting: The Influence of Entry Examination and GPA," *Issues in Accounting Education* (1984), pp. 61–67.

Holder, W. W., "Graduate-Level Public Sector Accounting: Status and Forecast," *The Accounting Review* (July 1978), pp. 746–751.

Kerlinger, F. N., *Foundations of Behavioral Research*, second edition (New York: Holt, Rinehart and Winston, 1973).

Kinney, W. R., "Empirical Accounting Research Design for Ph.D. Students," *The Accounting Review* (April 1986), pp. 338–350.

Koch, B. S., and S. S. Karlinsky, "The Effect of Federal Income Tax Law Reading Complexity on Students' Task Performance," *Issues in Accounting Education* (1984), pp. 98–110.

Kuhn, T. S., *The Structure of Scientific Revolutions* (Chicago: University of Chicago, 1962).

———, *The Essential Tension: Selected Studies in Scientific Tradition and Change* (Chicago: University of Chicago, 1977).

Kyle, D. L., and J. R. Williams, "The Significance of the CPA Certificate for Accounting Professors," *Journal of Accountancy* (May 1972), pp. 85–87.

Lakatos, I., and A. Musgrave (eds.), *Criticism and the Growth of Knowledge* (London: Cambridge University, 1970).

Leathers, P., "Relationship of Test Scores to CPA Examination Performance," *The Journal of Accountancy* (September 1972), pp. 101–103.

Nagel, E., *The Structure of Science: Problems in the Logic of Scientific Explanation* (Indianapolis: Hackett Publishing Company, 1979).

Newell, A., and H. A. Simon, *Human Problem Solving* (Englewood Cliffs, New Jersey: Prentice-Hall, 1972).

Nisbett, R. E., and T. D. Wilson, "Telling More Than We Can Know: Verbal Reports on Mental Processes," *Psychological Review* (May 1977), pp. 231–259.

Nunnally, J. C., *Psychometric Theory* (New York: McGraw-Hill, 1978).

Paretta, R. L., and L. W. Chadwick, "The Sequencing of Examination Questions and its Effects on Student Performance," *The Accounting Review* (July 1975), pp. 595–601.

Poincaré, H., *Science and Hypothesis* (New York: Dover Publications, 1952).

Popper, K. R., *Conjectures and Refutations: The Growth of Scientific Knowledge* (New York: Harper and Row, 1965).

———, *Objective Knowledge: An Evolutionary Approach* (London: Oxford University Press, 1972).

Reeve, J. M., "The 5-year Accounting Program as a Quality Signal," *The Accounting Review* (July 1983), pp. 639–646.

Reichardt, C. S., "The Statistical Analysis of Data from Nonequivalent Group Designs," in Cook and Campbell, *Quasi Experimentation: Design & Analysis Issues for Field Settings* (Boston: Houghton Mifflin, 1979), pp. 147–205.

Shulman, L. S., "Reconstruction of Educational Research," *Review of Educational Research* (1970), pp. 371–396.

Simon, H. A., *Models of Discovery* (Dordrecht, Holland: R. Reidel, 1977).

Simon, J. L., *Basic Research Methods in Social Science: The Art of Empirical Investigation*, second edition (New York: Random House, 1978).

Snowball, D., and W. A. Collins, "Televised Accounting Instruction, Attitudes and Performance: A Field Experiment," *The Accounting Review* (January 1980), pp. 123–133.

Sterling, R. R. (ed.), *Research Methodology in Accounting* (Lawrence, Kansas: Scholars Book Company, 1972).

Toulmin, S., *The Philosophy of Science* (New York: Harper and Row, 1960).

Whittrock, M. C. (ed.), *Handbook of Research on Teaching* (New York: McMillan, 1986).

CHAPTER 3

Research Related to Students

Education research on students seems to be generally divided into two distinct categories: student attitudes and achievement. The substantial research on student attitudes has been concerned with assessing how college changes student's attitudes and beliefs about the world and themselves. Most of these studies emphasize the importance of demographic variables and the extent to which these variables mitigate or accentuate the impact of college on students.

The second distinct category of education research on students is concerned with achievement and the variables which affect it. Much of this work seeks to find ways of predicting student achievement. A subset of achievement, communication skills, seems so important for accounting education that we have treated that topic separately within this chapter. The most significant subject of research within the area of communication skills is communication apprehension and the way it affects performance and choice of major. Accordingly, the subject of achievement is divided into two sections, communication skills and academic achievement. An overview of the topics contained in this chapter is shown in Figure 2.

STUDENT ATTITUDES AND BELIEFS

EDUCATION RESEARCH IN OTHER DISCIPLINES

Research on student attitudes and beliefs can be broadly categorized into studies about (1) the effect of college on student attitudes, (2) college destination and choice of major, and (3) student attitudes toward the institution and the instructor. A related topic, student attitudes toward instruction, is covered in Chapter 4, which addresses faculty issues. Most of this research employs survey techniques. In some studies the data were gathered directly from respondents, and in others they were obtained from institutional sources such as the American College Testing Program. A major problem in studying student attitudes is obtaining data which are both multi-institutional and longitudinal in nature, a prerequisite to broad generalization of the conclusions. In the gathering of multi-institutional data, care must be taken to assure that the intensity of the college experience is randomized. Simply randomizing across institutions may not accomplish this goal. It is also necessary to control for whether students live on or off campus and to gather data from individuals who never attended college at all. Another important consideration in longitudinal studies of changes in attitudes is controlling for systematic differences in the subjects such as race, age, and sex (Astin, 1977). Relatively few studies employ data from multiple institutions, but the statistical consideration of background variables is generally comprehensive.

An important book by Astin (1977) reports on a ten-year empirical study sponsored by the Cooperative Institutional Research Program (CIRP) of the American Council on Education and the University of California, Los Angeles. This study reports on a continuing project which is designed to measure the impact of college on students, and addresses all three of the attitudinal research areas mentioned above. Specifically, the study discusses changes in student attitudes, beliefs, self-concepts, patterns of behavior,

FIGURE 2

STUDENT ATTITUDES AND BELIEFS

Attitudes and Beliefs
  Effect of college
    Aspirations and goals
    Values and beliefs
  College destination and choice of major
    Institutional selectivity effects
    Prediction of college destination
    Choice of major
  Student attitudes about institutions and instruction
    Institutional characteristics
    Instruction

Communication Skills
  Communication apprehension
  Business communication and business English
  Communication skills and career success

Academic Achievement
  Predicting college success
  Anxiety effects
  Student responsibility for learning
  Professional examination outcomes
  Women and minorities
  Other factors affecting achievement

competency, achievement, career development, and satisfaction with the college environment.

The Effect of College on Student Attitudes

The study of student attitudes is important because student attitudes potentially affect decisions about choice of major, career goals, and other factors relevant to educational administration decisions. Substantial evidence exists which indicates that the aspirations and life goals of college students changed dramatically over the decade of the 1970's, particularly among women students. In an extensive study of students at the University of California at Davis, Regan and Roland (1982) found significant changes in the patterns of life goal aspirations and educational expectations of men and women who graduated in 1979 as compared with a group of 1968 graduates. Respondents were asked to select their first and second most important life goals from a list of six choices that included (1) career or occupation, (2) family relationships, and (3) leisure time and recreation. They were also asked to indicate their first and second most important career goals for their college careers from six choices which included (1) provide knowledge and techniques directly applicable to your career, (2) develop ability to get along with others, and (3) prepare for a happy marriage and family life. Regan and Roland, in using chi square tests to identify significant differences in the percent of men and women selecting the various choices for the 1968 graduates as compared with the 1979 graduates, noted a number of significant patterns. For women graduates, there was a notable increase in the importance of career as a life goal, coupled with a decrease in the importance of family relations. Male students indicated an increase in the importance of leisure and a decline in both the career and family categories. The analysis of educational goals revealed increases in the perceived importance of interpersonal skills and technical skills and marked declines in the importance of education as preparation for marriage and family for both men and women. The most notable change observed was in the educational goals of women, where there was a 100 percent increase in the percentage of respondents who indicated career knowledge as their most important objective. In analyzing a related question, the authors noted an approximately threefold increase, from 16 to 44 percent, in the number of women graduates choosing a professional career requiring advanced study.

To some extent, these trends are a manifestation of broad changes in the values of society. Increased societal emphasis on materialistic values has manifested itself in the choices that students make when they attend college. Thus we find dramatic increases in the numbers of students who choose to major in business, engineering, computer science, and other professional fields. There are corresponding decreases in the popularity of majors which emphasize more altruistic values, such as education, fine arts, social sciences, and the humanities (Astin, 1985).

This research constitutes a valuable contribution to our understanding of the changing attitudes of students. Whether these changing attitudes continue and manifest themselves in attitudes toward careers is a question that needs further study. To some extent such a manifestation depends on whether the attitude changes in students are a result of their college experiences or of changing societal attitudes in general. Such research would be of particular interest in the professional disciplines such as engineering, law, accounting, and medicine. Historically, these fields have had a high drop-out rate among women students (Fenske and Scott, 1973). As more and more women become members of these professions, it will also be important to study resulting changes in the professions themselves.

College attendance also has a significant impact on the values of students, who generally undergo a variety of changes in attitudes, beliefs, and self-concepts during the four years they are enrolled in college. Important changes which are identified include a more positive self-image, more liberal political views and social attitudes, and a decline in traditional religious affiliations. Definitive evidence on the nature of these changes is also provided by Astin (1977), who employed factor analysis to classify attitude, self concept, values, and belief variables obtained from subjects surveyed in the CIRP. Responses of the subjects, 1,966 freshmen, were compared with a follow up survey four years later. The research design incorporates procedures which control for differences in students when they first enter college and then identifies characteristics associated with the various outcomes. For example, Astin notes that sex, race, and academic ability are associated with a number of observed changes. Astin's research, as well as other theories concerned with the effects of the college experience, is reviewed by Parker and Schmidt (1982). Among these theories are models that predict the effects of higher education on society and models which measure the direct and indirect costs and benefits of higher education to individuals and society.

Theories of Cognitive Development

The intellectual changes that students undergo during their college years are dynamic. Cognitive development theories suggest that intellectual change occurs as the result of *cognitive conflict*. Students are exposed to more sophisticated thinking and reasoning, which causes a disequilibrium in the balance between their reasoning and experience. Repeated exposure to the cause of the conflict results first in acceptance or assimilation of the reality of the conflict and later in an alteration in the cognitive structure and reasoning process (Rogers, 1980). Perry (1970, 1981) employed protocol analysis techniques to model the processes of intellectual development of students during their undergraduate years. Students generally enter college with the view that knowledge can be compartmentalized into either of two categories—right or wrong. Perry calls this stage "dualism." He believes that students progress from dualism into three subsequent stages. In the "multiplicity" stage, students accept that there are alternative, legitimate ways of viewing problems. In the next stage, "relativism discovered," problems are viewed within specific contexts in which some solutions are superior to others. The final stage is termed "commitments in relativism." In this stage people understand that life is uncertain, that they must remain open to new ways of understanding, and that they must choose for themselves ways of knowing and understanding. Other researchers have developed theories of student development anchored in social, psychological, and moral principles. Extensive review of this literature is included in Chickering (1981) and Creamer (1980).

College Destination and Choice of Major

Two conflicting sociological theories exist concerning the effect of college destination on student aspirations. Relative-deprivation theory suggests that the choice of a selective institution will have a negative effect on aspirations because students will have greater difficulty obtaining good grades at a selective institution. In contrast, environmental press theory suggests that students will perform best and have higher aspirations in an environment where fellow students are academically superior and also have high aspirations. Drew and Astin (1972) used regression and correlation analysis to test the effects of selectivity on grades, self-concept, levels of aspiration, and changes in degree plans. They found that both theories seemed to operate interactively and that there are instances when both theories tend to demonstrate positive association between selectivity and the dependent variables. There were also instances when the two theories conflict.

A later study by Reitz (1975) reaches more definitive conclusions. Reitz reviews the Drew and Astin study as well as an earlier paper by Davis and uses the Davis data to further refine the relationship between college selectivity and career decision by differentiating between the concepts of career *aspirations* and career *field choice*. Reitz believes that the effect of selectivity on career aspirations is near zero because the negative effect of grades tends to be offset by a residual positive effect. With respect to career field choice, the effect of college selectivity is negative. Students with similar aspiration levels attending selective institutions will tend to gravitate toward the career fields in which they may expect to achieve the highest educational level within that field. This effect on career choice is not a result of relative deprivation but results from the fact that selective institutions reinforce preferences for educationally high careers within each given field.

Aspiration effects aside, college selectivity does affect economic well-being and career opportunity. These effects may be much more important than the aspiration effects. Hearn (1984) concluded that ability measures are more important determinants of college destination than are socioeconomic factors, but that both were significant. These conclusions reinforce the findings of earlier writers that the academically and socioeconomically advantaged tend to enroll at schools that provide greater intellectual and material resources than do less advantaged students. These results imply that the expansion of post-secondary educational opportunities in society do not necessarily result in greater equality and opportunity for the disadvantaged, particularly if they are channeled into lower-quality, lower-status institutions.

These conclusions are supported by Sewell and Hauser (1972), who have modeled status attainment in terms of education, occupation, and earnings. Employing regression techniques, they were able to build models which were highly predictive of educational and occupational attainment, but not of earnings. The principle variables in their models were measures of socioeconomic background, mental ability, personal goals, and aspirations of friends.

Finally, there is evidence that many students are uncertain about their career goals upon entering college, and this uncertainty results in their changing majors as well as educational aspirations in terms of years of study and degree goals. Fenske and Scott (1973) analyzed biographical data available from the American College Testing program regarding students' choices of major, education goals, and two other non-academic activities. After two years they conducted follow-up surveys for community college students and after four years they surveyed four-year college and university students to determine the extent to which students' expectations were fulfilled. Their results revealed that fewer than half of two- and four-year college students retained their original choices of college majors. Furthermore, students who originally aspired to only an Associate degree were highly likely to plan to obtain a four-year degree after two years of college. In the four-year follow-up, they observed that substantial numbers of students who initially planned only to obtain a Bachelor's degree had, by the time they were seniors, planned also to obtain a Master's degree. For students who had initially aspired to obtain advanced degrees there was a regression effect toward lower degrees observed in both the two- and four-year follow-ups. This tendency was particularly notable for students who had initially planned to obtain the Ph.D., M.D., J.D., or D.D.S.

Student Attitudes about Institutions and Instruction

About institutions. Traditional measures of faculty quality, including publications and interest in research, appear to be somewhat negatively associated with student attitudes. Bayer (1975) investigated the association between the INVENTORY OF COLLEGE ACTIVITIES (ICA) "concern for the individual student variable" and three categories of closely related variables: student characteristics, structural characteristics of the institution, and faculty characteristics. Employing a variety of regression techniques, Bayer identified a number of variables that are predictive of the dependent variable. Notably, he found that the traditional measures of faculty quality, including publications and interest in research, are negatively associated with concern for the individual student. Positive correlates were such factors as informal faculty/student contact. After controlling for a number of student characteristics, Bayer still found significant associations of the nature just described. When structural variables, such as institutional size, were controlled for, none of the faculty variables was significant. In large, impersonal institutions faculty contribute little, if anything, to the perception by students that the institution is other than an impersonal place where they are only numbers. Most importantly, the existence of a faculty with outstanding academic credentials has no impact on the perception that the school is concerned with individual student's needs. Since the concern factor is related to the learning process, this conclusion suggests that from the students' viewpoint growth beyond some optimal size has very little to recommend it.

About instruction. Student attitude toward instruction is a topic that has received much attention in education research. Most of our knowledge about the subject resulted from studies of student evaluations of teaching (SET hereinafter). At the outset it can be said that this research generally involves studies of the relationship of the overall SET score and other variables which may be related to that score. Principal factors identified as potentially related to SET score include expected/actual course grade, attitude toward instructor, self-concept, and instructor characteristics. The research does not lead the reader to clear conclusions about the impact of student attitudes on SET scores because conclusions of some studies have conflicted with others. The problem of modeling or predicting SET scores is complex and multifactorial in nature. Much work remains to be done before SET scores can be reliably modeled in all circumstances.

In Chapter 4 of this monograph, we review substantial literature on the validity and reliability of SET. The review which follows is concerned with research which provides additional information about student attitudes and beliefs as they relate to, or are impounded in, SET scores.

A major question in research on SET is whether a student's grade affects his or her attitude about the course. In particular, it is of interest to know if a higher grade contributes to a more positive attitude, which is in turn manifested in the evaluation. Extensive research has been conducted on the existence and nature of this association. Feldman (1976), who reviewed the literature up to about 1975, concludes that previous work generally shows that grades are positively correlated with course and teacher evaluations. Most correlation studies show small but significant correlations in the .10 to .30 range. Feldman defends the relevance of these almost miniscule coefficients by observing that they represent means from observations pooled across several classes and thus may significantly underestimate the strength of association in some courses. He also notes that correlation coefficients are based on the assumption of linear relationships, and nonlinearity of the actual data may provide further potential for underestimation of the strength of association. A regression study done by Mirus (1973) which modeled overall SET score using a number of independent variables found a significant and strong association between the students' expected grades and the SET scores. Mirus concluded that the existence of such a relationship contributes to the grade inflation problem. Similar conclusions are reached by Soper (1973), who cites a number of studies which imply that a positive correlation may exist between evaluations and grades. Soper suggests that the mere perception on the part of faculty of such an association may result in grade inflation. A study done at Central Michigan University where student evaluations were used in administrative decisions on merit pay, tenure, and promotion, provided evidence of such a relationship. We observe that this perceived association might also affect faculty behavior in other undesirable ways, including reinforcement of what might be called the groveling syndrome—statements or actions whose sole purpose is to boost the subsequent SET score. Soper also reviews other papers in which the correlations between grades and SET scores were either insignificant or negative. In a study of Principles of Economics students at the University of Missouri, no significant relationship was found between post-TUCE (Test of Understanding of College Economics) scores and SET.

Other writers have also concluded that student attitudes are not affected by the grades they receive. Greenwood, et al. (1973) surveyed both students and faculty to determine characteristics which were associated with good and bad teaching. The resulting responses were subjected to tests for variability of response, neutrality of response, and behavioral specificity. Items not meeting certain thresholds of criteria in these areas were eliminated. The items remaining constituted a 60-item set of characteristics which were deemed to be associated with either good or bad teaching. Separate factor analysis procedures for each response group produced seven factors for each group. There was a high degree of commonality between the items in the faculty response group as compared with the student group. The authors then performed a discriminant analysis on the student and faculty responses to the 60 items. The degree of similarity in the responses of the two groups leads to the conclusion that students and faculty are in general agreement as to what constitutes good teaching and that student attitudes about instruction are determined principally by the quality of the teaching effort. Greenwood's conclusions, however, suffer from the fact that students may not actually evaluate faculty in the way that questionnaire responses would indicate. Certainly we would not expect them to admit that their evaluations are affected by the grades they receive.

A paper by Seiver (1983) provides some explanation for the conflicting findings regarding the effect of grades on SET scores. He conducted a study to determine whether professors could buy good evaluations by giving good grades. The data employed were 1,702 SETs for all sections of introductory economics for the years 1979–80 at Miami University (Ohio). Seiver regressed SET scores on grades, GPA, and a number of other background variables. The regressions show that grade is a significant variable in the predictive model, a finding similar to that of earlier writers who used such models as a basis for concluding that professors are buying SETs with higher grades. Seiver argues that the above approach is methodologically invalid and states that two-stage least squares, whereby both SETs and grades are used as dependent variables in the two-stage model, is more appropriate. Using this approach, the grade variable is not significant when SET is the dependent variable whereas measures of instructional quality and instructor availability are significant. In the second model the coefficient for SET on grades was positive and highly significant. The implications of this paper are that better faculty provide the impetus to better student performance. Similar views are expressed by Rippey (1975). He argues that SET can provide useful information about student attitudes because (1) students spend more time with instructors than colleagues, and (2) students have the unique ability to judge whether the instructor responded to their level of understanding.

Thus the most plausible explanation for the SET/grade relationship is that instructional quality, not grade, is of paramount significance. The key factors in instructional quality are enthusiasm, clarity of presentation, and the existence of a positive relationship between the instructor and student (Lumsden, 1973; Cooper, Stewart, and Gudykunst, 1982). Another factor which is related to a positive teacher/student relationship is the existence of a positive self-concept on the part of the student. In particular, students with positive self-assessments in the area of academic ability are likely to have a positive attitude toward their teachers (Haslett, 1976; Cooper, Stewart, and Gudykunst, 1982).

Finally, there is evidence which suggests the existence of strong preconceived student attitudes about individual instructors. Work by Cundy (1982) employs path analysis to attempt to measure the indirect efforts of student background and attitude factors on SET scores. The subjects were 361 American Government students in eight different classes taught by five different instructors. Cundy collected a substantial amount of background and attitudinal data on each subject, each of whom was required to evaluate the course in several dimensions, including some first-day impressions collected after about 10–15 minutes of introduction to the course. The paper supports the work of earlier writers regarding the significance of instructor/student relationship, student self-concept, and student interest factors in predicting SET scores. But it also concludes that the subjects in the study were highly biased and formed much of their opinions before ever attending class or after the first few minutes of class.

ACCOUNTING EDUCATION RESEARCH

A very limited amount of work has been done in accounting literature on student attitudes and beliefs. These studies are typified by an approach that compares accounting students with students majoring in other subjects. They have generally found that accounting students differ from other students in that they are somewhat more conformist (Aranya, Meir, and Bar-Ilan, 1978) and more materialistic (Baker, 1976). Limited work also indicates that accounting students are concerned with solving social problems and have positive attitudes toward other people (Brenner, 1973). However, the quantity of work done in the accounting literature is not extensive enough to indicate conclusively that accounting students are different from other students in any significant fashion.

RESEARCH OPPORTUNITIES IN ACCOUNTING

The literature clearly shows that substantially greater numbers of women students currently express a desire to enter a career requiring professional education than is the case historically. This trend is evidenced in accounting programs by vastly increased numbers of women students. We suspect that the career orientation of women accountants is different from that of men and that their attitudes and beliefs as students and as professionals are also different. The attitudes of students, particularly women students, are undergoing changes, and the evidence suggests that attitudinal differences between male and female students are diminishing. There has been almost no research on the impact and implications of the almost revolutionary changes in the male/female mix of accounting students and accounting graduates on the career orientation, aspirations, and attitudes of accounting students.

The literature also reveals that substantial numbers of students change their majors during their college careers. Historically, there has been a tendency for women to abandon majors in traditionally male-dominated fields. We believe that this tendency has diminished, if not disappeared altogether, in accounting programs. Research is needed on this topic as well as on the subject of changing majors in general. This work would help us to understand what factors are significant in the decision to change majors and could play a significant role in development of curriculum and admission/retention standards.

Research on student attitudes about the institution reveals that learning is positively associated with an environment in which students perceive that the institution is concerned about the individual student. The research further shows that such an atmosphere is most likely to be absent in a large institution. Professional programs in general, including accounting programs, are frequently located in large institutions; therefore such issues as professional school designation, Beta Alpha Psi programs, and other activities which promote student/institutional identity and student/faculty contact are perceived as positive factors in the learning experience of students.

Research which provides new evidence regarding the many issues discussed above is certainly needed. Since most of the existing work is of a case-study nature, research which employs multi-institutional, longitudinal data would be of particular value. In addition, research is needed on the subject of evaluations of upper division courses, since most of the previous work has used students in survey courses.

COMMUNICATION SKILLS OF STUDENTS

The communication skills of accounting students has been a topic of much discussion among recruiters of accounting students as well as educators and others for many years. Lack of skill, particularly in the area of written communication, has frequently been cited as the single greatest deficiency of accounting graduates.

EDUCATION RESEARCH IN OTHER DISCIPLINES

Nonaccounting studies are found primarily in the education, psychology and communications literature. They tend to focus on two areas—communication apprehension and the content of business communication and business English courses.

Communication Apprehension

Theory suggests a person's perception of his or her own fear will affect verbal and nonverbal encoding and decoding capacities and behavior. Not only does the fear of communication affect communication behavior, but the fear of reporting or admitting this fear may be significant in the self-concept of individuals. On the other hand, if communication apprehension is as high as we have been led to believe in the past, admission of the fear may be socially acceptable, and disclosure of the fear may contribute little additional threat to one's self-concept. The fear of communication itself is probably the greatest threat to self-concept, not the disclosure of the fear.

Wheeless (1975), who studied communication apprehension among students and its impact on their communication ability, observed that the apprehension involved in sending information is different from the apprehension involved in receiving information. The former is probably related more to fear of social disapproval, while the latter is probably related more to fear of misinterpreting, inadequately processing, and/or not being able to adjust psychologically to messages sent by others. Communication fear also appears to vary with the context in which the communication exists (e.g., informal conversation vs. formal speaking).

Wheeless studied 324 students enrolled in the lower division interpersonal communications course at West Virginia University. At the beginning of the term, students were tested for communication apprehension; shortly after mid-semester, students completed a self-report instrument designed to test receiver apprehension. Both factor analysis and correlational analysis indicated that self-reported receiver apprehension varies independently from self-reported apprehension experienced by sources of communication. Further, Wheeless concluded that most of the subjects in the study experienced lower apprehension as receivers than as sources. A fairly substantial number of subjects, however, were classified as highly apprehensive sources and receivers.

Daly (1978) studied the "apprehension construct," which is a person's general tendencies to approach or avoid situations perceived to demand writing accompanied by some amount of evaluation. Theoretically, the apprehensive individual will avoid, if possible, situations where writing is perceived as required. Further, when unavoidably placed in a writing situation, this individual will experience more than normal amounts of anxiety and perform at lower quality levels.

Testing this theory on over 3,000 first-semester undergraduates at a large mid-western university, Daly used one instrument to categorize students in terms of their writing apprehensiveness and a second instrument to determine their writing competency several days later. The hypothesis that individuals with low writing apprehension would perform significantly better than those with high apprehension was confirmed for both overall tests and the majority of sub-tests. Daly demonstrated that high apprehensives not only write differently and with lower quality than low apprehensives, but they also fail to demonstrate as strong a knowledge of writing skills. He concluded that an individual who fails to exhibit appropriate and necessary writing skills is unlikely to find much success in writing. This, in turn, results in maintained apprehension and a continued avoidance of practice and evaluative feedback.

Daly and Miller (1975) studied the impact of writing apprehension on language intensity. Language intensity indicates the degree and direction of distance away from neutrality. Earlier research demonstrates that persons under more stress tend to write with a greater degree of ambivalence than those under less stress. At West Virginia University, where 98 students completed measures of language intensity and writing apprehension, those students with high apprehension of writing encoded less intense messages than did those with low apprehension, as hypothesized.

Daly and Shamo (1978) studied 181 students enrolled in the basic communications course at a large midwestern university. Subjects completed four questionnaires:

1. Writing apprehension instrument—Students were classified according to their degree of writing apprehension
2. Perceived writing demands—Students classified 28 college majors based on their perceived writing demands
3. Desirability of majors—Students categorized the 28 majors according to their perceived desirability
4. Actual major choice—Students indicated their individual majors

(Business administration was treated as a single major and was not included in either the ten highest or lowest in perceived writing requirements and was excluded from further study. Accounting was not listed as a separate major. High writing majors were general liberal arts majors; low writing majors were in sciences and engineering.)

Significant interaction between apprehension levels and writing requirements was observed in terms of the perceived desirability of majors. Also, actual major choices reflected the tendency for high apprehensive students to select majors perceived as having fewer writing requirements than those chosen by nonapprehensive students.

Hall (1982) explored the consequences of permitting more flexibility and choice in economics education. Two hundred and thirty-six first-year economics students at Kuring-gai College of Advanced Education (Australia) were allowed to make a constrained choice from a variety of assessment components. Specifically, students were required to complete an essay examination, a multiple-choice examination, and a take-home case study for 50 percent of their course grade. The remainder of the grade was based on several additional activities from which each student could choose, emphasizing written and oral communication skills. Students were also asked to evaluate their own competence in several skill areas and the significance of those skills for success in their chosen careers. Most of the students intended to become accountants or business administrators.

Students were found generally to adopt a learning and assessment strategy which made best use of their existing skills and which tended to ignore their perceived skill needs. Nevertheless, most students adopted a mixed strategy that involved them in some activities in which they did not have as much skill as they wished or as much as was needed in their chosen career fields. Furthermore, students tended to start with good intentions of adopting a strategy oriented toward increasing their learning and knowledge, but later gravitated toward a position which used their existing skills.

In some cases, students were found to assess their own skill levels incorrectly and to be unaware of specific skills needed in their chosen career fields (e.g., concise oral presentation and argument).

Business Communication and Business English

David (1982) reported a study of 253 business communication courses at colleges in the United States. Several conclusions were drawn, including the following:

1. Over half of the business communication courses are in business departments; less than 20 percent are in English departments.
2. Few schools offer laboratory hours. More frequently offered are testout examinations.
3. Most students take business communication because it is a required course.
4. Four-year schools assign fewer papers during the course than do two-year schools. Allowing students to rewrite to improve their grades is a policy occurring more often in two-year schools and schools with small enrollments than in larger universities.
5. Grading criteria for papers are, in descending order of importance: (1) content, (2) organization, (3) mechanics, (4) tone/audience, (5) style and format (tied).

Because enrollments in business schools have mushroomed, business communications courses are dealing with class size and staffing problems. The national trend of grade inflation appears in the data with a high percentage of A and B grades awarded in all college business communication courses.

Warner (1979) studied Business English students at the University of Akron. Four evaluative tools were used: an in-class writing sample, an edited exercise, a vocabulary test, and a questionnaire in which each student was asked about his/her background in English and attitude toward grammar and writing skills.

Despite the fact that 60 percent of the students had studied grammar in high school and 80 percent had studied grammar in junior high and elementary schools, only seven percent felt they understood grammar. Over 20 percent indicated virtually no understanding of grammar at all. The author observed that one of the most alarming problems in our educational system is the compartmentalized and fragmented manner in which students are taught. Many students in college have the idea that no one considers grammar, spelling and punctuation of any importance except the English teacher, "who is a little peculiar anyway."

Warner proposed ten suggestions for improving written communication skills of students based on her research summarized above. Two of these suggestions which appear particularly relevant are as follows:

1. We must find concrete ways to show our students the direct relationship between communication skill and job success.
2. In addition to the primary evaluation of content, students' written work in all business subjects should be marked and some grade deduction made for writing and grammar errors.

ACCOUNTING EDUCATION RESEARCH

Estes (1979) studied the present and future importance of selected knowledge and skills for success in professional careers in accounting. Specifically, he established rankings of 57 areas of knowledge and skills by surveying junior and senior level accountants with public accounting firms, corporations and governmental organizations and accountants in education. Oral and written communication skills were consistently ranked as very important for present and future success in accounting. In fact, only junior-level public accounting respondents ranked written and oral communications other than the two most important skills for successful careers in accounting.

Andrews and Koester (1979) were concerned by the apparent disparity between the communication instruction given in the classroom, accounting students' perceptions of what would be expected of them in the business world and the accounting profession's expectations of newly-hired employees in terms of communication skills. Professional accountants in industry, public accounting and government, senior accounting students and AACSB accounting educators were surveyed to determine the extent of agreement or disagreement among the groups concerning the significance of communication skills and how they should be taught. Accounting educators and accounting professionals were found to be in general agreement about the communications needs of accountants. Some disagreement, however, was found on how to achieve the necessary skills levels.

Ingram and Frazier (1980) surveyed professional accountants in public accounting and industry, as well as accounting educators, to identify the types of communication skills required by entry-level accountants. Also, they attempted to identify deficiencies perceived to exist in entry-level accountants. Those responding to their survey felt that all 20 of their identified communications skills were required by staff accountants. Deficiencies identified in staff accountants were believed to be greater in written communications than in oral communications. Accounting educators were not satisfied with the level of communication skills of their graduates, but generally felt that current accounting graduates were adequately prepared in terms of their communications skills.

Addams (1981) questioned whether CPA firms should teach communications skills to first-year accountants if they are as important as thought in the evaluation of those accountants. Based on a survey of first-year accountants in the Big-Eight CPA firms, he concludes that communication skills should be taught during the first year in practice. The major thrust of this training should be (1) narrative, accompanying audited or unaudited statements, (2) programs for conducting audits, and (3) letters.

Andrews and Sigband (1984) surveyed accounting department chairpersons at AACSB accredited universities and the managing partners of the 105 largest accounting firms in the United States. The purpose of their study was to determine the extent of satisfaction of communication skills of recent accounting graduates. They state that three "inescapable" conclusions can be reached from their research: (1) New accountants are not sufficiently skilled to handle job requirements in the areas of written, oral and interpersonal communications. (2) Universities are not preparing accounting students adequately in these areas. (3) More instructional time should be allocated to communications skills.

Rebele (1985) used the method of paired comparisons to study accounting students' opinions on the importance of written and oral communications skills for success in public accounting. His results indicate that accounting students perceive writing skills as relatively unimportant and oral communication skills as only moderately important.

Borthick and Clark (1987) studied the impact of a computer-implemented writing aid for language analysis on written assignments submitted by accounting students. The assignments studied were (1) documentation for beginning users of a microcomputer spreadsheet program and (2) a memorandum recommending a computer hardware upgrade plan for a company. Students who used the writing aid experienced improved performance, suggesting that the use of writing aids for language analysis has potential for improving accountants' written communication skills.

RESEARCH OPPORTUNITIES IN ACCOUNTING

The importance of communication skills for accounting students is well established. The subject of where these skills should be learned and in what manner or fashion they should be taught is not clear. Related questions are the extent to which communication skilis can be successfully integrated into accounting courses.

The literature on communication apprehension raises a number of questions concerning students' choices of accounting as a major and the impact on their success as accounting students. Specifically, research is needed on the way students view accounting as a career in terms of their own communication skills and those required for success. Students' attitudes toward the further development of both oral and written communication skills would contribute to our understanding of their attitudes toward specific course activities and our knowledge of how to best institute course requirements that foster the development of communication skills. Finally, research into appropriate ways of dealing with accounting students' varying levels of communication development and varying degrees of communication apprehension would contribute greatly to future curriculum development efforts.

ACADEMIC ACHIEVEMENT

EDUCATION RESEARCH IN OTHER DISCIPLINES

The most thoroughly researched topic in the area of student achievement centers around effort to determine what other cognitive or noncognitive characteristics can be associated with high levels of achievement. Since literally hundreds of articles have appeared on this subject, a discourse on the theory of achievement is beyond the scope of this monograph. However, a useful reference on this subject is Sewell, et al., eds. (1976) whose chapter on the theory of achievement presents a psychological model of intellective performance. The model attempts to explain how personality and environment interact to affect behavior and performance. The work differentiates between the antecedents of performance at immediate tasks as compared with long-range performance and takes into account students who are overmotivated and those who are underachievers.

Two classes of variables are correlated with achievement. Nonintellective correlates include personality, anxiety, attitude, habit, interest, and activity measures (Lenning, 1974). Intellective correlates include grades and standardized test scores. An established fact is that undergraduate grades can be fairly well predicted using high school grades and scores on college admissions tests, with high school grades almost always carrying more weight than test scores. The conclusion can also be reached that students who did well in certain secondary school subjects are likely to display skill in those same areas in college. Also, students who are high achievers will progress at a faster rate than will less talented students, will be more likely to complete a technical or scientific degree, and to publish original writing. Research in the area of achievement aspirations indicates that there are systematic differences between men and women students which must be controlled in conducting research in this area. A number of other environmental factors such as place of residence (on/off campus) and selectivity of the institution have also been found to have a systematic effect on student achievement (Astin, 1977).

In addition to the traditional measures of high school grades and test scores, a number of variables are important in predicting success in college, including attitudinal, psychometric, and demographic measures. Merante (1983), who reviewed a substantial number of papers which identify these variables, notes that some outcomes (such as scholarship winners) are extraordinarily difficult to predict. Merante also observes that a substantial amount of literature indicates that three variables—high school grades, SAT/ACT scores, and high school class rank—are good predictors of academic success in college. He then cites a number of studies which deal with socioeconomic and demographic variables, including age, sex, birth order, parent's education, income, and geographic factors.

A problem limiting the power of predictive models using intellective correlates is that high school grades and standardized test scores are themselves correlated. Adams, Higley, and Campbell (1976) employed regression analysis to compare the predictive power of the ACT and the SAT in predicting first-semester grade-point average. The sample consisted of 1,080 entering freshmen at Brigham Young University during the years 1969–1971. A variety of tests were run in which the authors controlled for geographic variation and sex of the population. When high school GPA was used as one of the independent variables, there was no difference in the capacity of the ACT as compared with the SAT to predict freshman grades. The authors also note that in equations where high school GPA is included, neither the ACT nor the SAT contributes more than .02 to the R square value of the prediction equation.

It must be strongly emphasized that the work which indicates that college grades can be predicted using the variables listed must be interpreted with great caution. The association between high school grades and the intellective correlates is not very high, thus, the use of admission standards which place great emphasis on such intellective measures could result in many misclassifications in terms of suitable students denied admission and unsuitable students admitted. It is also possible that the relationship between test scores and achievement is nonlinear, and thus test scores might serve particularly well as reference points in admission decisions, even though overall correlation with future grades is low. In addition, the strength of association between aptitude measures and achievement varies across career fields. Achievement is more closely related to measures of academic aptitude in fields which, by their very nature, demand such aptitude (Baird, 1985). This monograph addresses this issue more fully in Chapter 5 in the section on grades and grading.

In addition, academic ability does not necessarily translate into professional potential. Many students have talents which make them particularly well suited to certain kinds of careers, and these talents are not necessarily reflected in grades or achievement/aptitude test scores. Currently, we do not have efficient ways of incorporating these variables into achievement prediction models. Without consideration of both the intellective and nonintellective characteristics of applicants, the administration of admissions to selective programs will remain a very inefficient process.

Studies on graduate students are generally consistent with the conclusions for studies using undergraduates as subjects. Malstrom, Klecka, and Shell (1984) used discriminant analysis to predict successful completion of a Master's program in engineering at the University of Cincinnati, collecting data for nine variable groups. Two of these were numerical values for honors received and for undergraduate GPA. The remainder were dummy variables for several background and demographic characteristics. Since the university did not require the GRE exam for the subjects studied, it was not used in the study. The authors were able to achieve an overall prediction success ratio (where success was defined as a 3.0 GPA) of slightly less than 80 percent. The five most important variables in the discriminant function were number of honors, status (whether full- or part-time), work experience, undergraduate grades, and marital status.

Gough and Hall (1975) gathered data on 1014 graduates and 57 dropouts from The University of California Medical School for the years 1955 through 1971. The researchers ran regression analyses on a number of different combinations of cognitive and personality variables. The model with the greatest predictive power was a six-variable model of the quantitative score on the MCAT (Medical College Admissions Test), premedical school grades for the last two terms, and four personality inventory scales. This research emphasizes the importance of considering nonintellective variables in the admissions decision. Such considerations are particularly important where graduate programs are targeted toward students with substantial professional experience. In a study of Master of Public Administration students at Western Michigan University, Thompson and Kobrak

(1983) employed regression analysis to attempt to predict graduate grade-point average. Using as independent variables an English qualifying exam score, undergraduate grade-point average, a measure of relevant work experience, and a measure of time since receipt of the undergraduate degree, they were able to explain only 16 percent of the variance in graduate grade-point average. The GRE was not required of these students and was not included in the equations. The authors conclude that a two-stage admissions process which admits some students on a conditional basis would be one way of allowing for the substantial uncertainty which exists in predicting the suitability of some applicants.

Siegel and Schmitt (1976) conducted a study of 383 applicants to a medium-sized MBA program to determine if there was a relationship between GMAT score and years of interruption between the Bachelor's degree and graduate school. No linear relationship was noted, but the research did show that candidates with more than seven years of interruption had considerably lower scores than the four- to seven-year group. Whether these lower scores were the result of an absence of test validity or actually reflect a lower quality applicant was not a question addressed in the paper. In a similar study involving journalism students, Brown and Weaver (1979) reach essentially the same conclusions.

Responsibility and Achievement

Research suggests that students who accept responsibility for the learning process are likely to be high achievers. One important assumption of teacher evaluation use noted by Lehr (1983) is that classroom achievement is determined solely by the instructor's ability to assure that the material is mastered by the students. This approach to evaluation ignores the issue of whether students have some responsibility for their own learning and whether they have met those responsibilities. Lehr compared a self-evaluation questionnaire which was administered to one of his education classes with the examination results of the students in the class. The questionnaire asked respondents to evaluate their own efforts in terms of a number of variables including attitude, preparation, and willingness to accept responsibility for the learning process. The results of the comparison show a significant rank correlation between the results of the responsibility questionnaire and exam scores.

Achievement and Professional Examinations

Only a few fields exist where professional examinations are a prerequisite to practice. Our research revealed that little work has been published on any aspect of professional exams. One study of particular interest resulted from a rule adopted by the Supreme Court of the State of Indiana which conditioned eligibility for the bar exam after January 1, 1977 on successful completion of 54 semester hours in 14 specific subject areas. Cutright, Cutright, and Boshkoff (1975) conducted an empirical test of the justification for this rule by comparing the performance of successful and unsuccessful candidates who met or did not meet the proposed requirements. The data included 272 candidates and two different exams. The findings clearly indicated a significant association between cumulative grade-point average in law school and pass rates, but little if any association between specific courses and success on the exam. The authors concluded that the conditioning of bar exam eligibility on specific law school courses is unnecessarily restrictive and counterproductive to development of legal education.

Achievement of Women and Minorities

Women. Research reviewed by Trent and Cohen (1973) indicates that historically gender has been an important consideration in achievement prediction models. Women and men have traditionally been subjected to different social and parental influences and consequently manifest different patterns of achievement and aspirations. Historically, fewer women have attended college than men, although as children they tended to be better students in that they were better behaved and took their studies more seriously. Furthermore, women who have attended college have traditionally avoided male-dominated fields, including professional and graduate studies. Within the last decade, a greater percentage of women students have expressed interest in professional careers, and changes in Federal law have eliminated many of the discriminatory barriers facing females who aspired to these careers. These recent changes must be applauded, because they have facilitated the achievement of much on the part of those who have benefited from the changes. However, barriers remain to the career development and advancement of women. Those who choose to have children face the prospects of interruption in their advancement, often for several years. Research reviewed by Bernard (1981) indicates that there are a number of strategies available for career women to help them cope with these realities. In the long run, changes in the social structure offer the potential for greater equality of opportunity for women.

Two recent articles (Regan and Roland, 1982; 1985) report on the changing career aspirations of women as compared with men students. The most recent study employed log linear analysis to compare the structural relationships of lifestyles and career goals of seniors at the University of California at Davis in 1970 and again in about 1980. The findings show dramatic changes in the lifestyle commitments and career orientation of women students over the years. The percentage of women with family-oriented lifestyles has declined substantially, and the percentage of women choosing professional careers has approximately doubled. The comparative statistics for men show significantly less change.

Minorities. Virtually all of the research on minority achievement has used black students as subjects. Much attention in this literature is given to the differences between the achievement of black students and of the student population as a whole. Literature prior to 1973 on this subject has been reviewed by Trent and Cohen (1973). This research indicates that black students have lower-than-average SAT scores and lower-than-average college grades. These results can be attributed to substandard precollege education for black students. Thus, a significant recommendation made by writers concerned with improving college level achievement by black students is that the quality of their secondary school education must be improved (Thompson, et al., 1984; Keith and Page, 1985). More opportunities for black students to earn degrees at quality undergraduate and professional schools cannot be fully successful until those students have had access to elementary and secondary education of the same quality available to non-black students.

Even with greater opportunity in secondary schools, blacks face some additional barriers to academic achievement. Those from predominantly black environments attending predominantly white schools sometimes have difficulty adjusting to college life. If faced with overt racism and hostility, some of these students may develop a separatist attitude and withdraw into an all-black subculture (Fleming, 1981). Given blacks' potential for a wider range of social contacts, extracurricular activities, and other fulfillments, Fleming suggests that attendance at predominantly black institutions may better meet the needs of many black students in spite of the fact that these schools may not always have the best resources (Fleming, 1981, p. 293).

Allen (1985) conducted an extensive study of black students attending college at predominantly white campuses which clearly indicates this is a continuing trend. In the ten years ending in 1973, the proportion of black students attending predominantly black schools had declined from 60 percent to 25 percent. Furthermore, the percent of degrees awarded to students by predominantly black schools declined from 80 percent in 1968 to 56 percent in 1978–79. Allen's study reaches the inescapable conclusion that the issue of achievement by black students does not accommodate simple explanations. There are many social and psychological factors which must be considered in modeling achievement for these students. The study does reinforce the conclusion that students who are socially involved in campus life tend to have better interpersonal skills. Allen was not, however, able to establish a relationship between career aspirations and grades or between economic status and grades.

Hall, Mays, and Allen (1984) note that the statistics showing increased college enrollment by blacks are subject to overly optimistic interpretation. Many black college students attend only two-year colleges, and the withdrawal rates for blacks attending four-year schools are much higher than for whites. In fact, black enrollment in graduate and advanced professional schools has actually declined since 1975. This paper also reviews the relatively limited previous work on the subject of academic and career achievement by black students. As with white students, sex is a major predictor variable of attendance at professional schools. A substantially smaller percentage of black women than black men attend professional schools, although the percentage of each group expressing a desire to attend either graduate or professional school is approximately the same.

An interesting anomaly regarding achievement by black students is found in the data on the relationship between grades and choice of major. Much of the literature indicates that white students choosing technical majors such as science and engineering have better grades than students majoring in other subjects. The reverse has been found for minority students. Although no concrete evidence explains this finding, it is perhaps associated with the fact that black students tend to be less prepared in precollege education.

An important factor in attracting minority students is the presence of minority faculty. Much data support the conclusion that programs with black faculty members will be better able to attract black students. Other factors which must be present to encourage blacks to pursue nontraditional career goals are adequate funding and meaningful career counseling. Positive action in terms of funding, role models, and mentors is required to affect the aspirations of these minority students. Long-run achievement by minority students is not limited by factors inherent in race or sex, but by societal institutions and the people who control them.

The question of whether affirmative action programs have increased the educational opportunities and subsequent economic status of minorities is an important one. In spite of considerable study the evidence to date is inconclusive, with some writers noting positive effects and others concluding that education has not improved the economic status of blacks (Cohn, 1979, p. 121).

Other Factors Affecting Achievement

Paul (1982) employed regression analysis to assess the impact of outside employment on student performance in economics classes. The subjects were 836 students in macroeconomics principles during a seven-semester period. All respondents had the same instructor. Paul evaluated his data using three regression models. The dependent variable in all three models was total exam score on all exams. The first model was a simple linear regression on hours of outside employment. A second regression model included grade-point average as an additional variable. A final model added a measure of attitude toward the outside job, in addition to hours worked, and GPA. The regressions were significant in all three cases, with GPA the most significant variable. Hours worked were inversely related to examination scores, while GPA and attitudes toward the job were positively related to examination scores. The highest R square for any of the three models was .2543 for the three-variable model. Paul's work indicates that a statistically significant inverse relationship may exist between hours of outside employment and grades, but the paper does not demonstrate whether outside employment has an impact on long-term economic welfare. Working one's way through college may certainly be preferable to not going to college at all.

O'Connor, et al. (1980) employed correlation analysis to measure the association between hours of study and grades in introductory psychology. The subjects surveyed were 90 undergraduates at a four-year university. The results of the study show significant negative correlation between the two variables, even after controlling for SAT score, high school grades, and academic load. The authors suggest that the findings may be explained by the fact that the students receiving the lowest grades failed to study with the proper intensity, studied the wrong material, or used their time inefficiently due to a limited knowledge of study skills. Other research is cited which suggests that a fourth explanation is that the students did not use effective study skills, even though they were aware of the actions required to master the material in the course.

A related subject concerns the amount of time that a student might be expected to study. Davis and Heller (1976) surveyed the daily activities of 19 medical students at the University of Michigan Medical School for a 28-day period. The findings of the study were that, on the average, students may be expected to spend about 60 hours per week in academic pursuits. The amount of study time noted by the respondents tended to be above average in the week before an examination and below average in the week following an examination. The principle activity to decrease during the time of increased study was recreation. The authors cite studies at other schools which are consistent with their findings.

Winsberg and Ste-Marie (1976) employed correlation analysis to determine whether there is an association between achievement in physics and the motivation of individual students. According to Maslowian theory, there are three types of motivation: (1) motivation to satisfy need for security, (2) motivation to satisfy need for esteem, and (3) motivation to satisfy need for personal growth in such areas as cultural and intellectual dimensions. Winsberg and Ste-Marie hypothesized that the first type of motivation is negatively associated with achievement in physics, because Maslowian theory asserts that need for security is stronger than all other needs and would thus impede growth. The two other types of motivation were hypothesized to be positively associated with achievement in physics because the study of science involves development of creativity.

The correlations were measured between the Merritt College Motivation Inventory (MCMI) scores for the subjects and final grade in a required survey of physics course. The subjects were 85 students in the health science program at Ahuntic College d'Enseignement General et Professional in Montreal. The findings were that there were significant negative correlations between achievement and the need for security for the subjects. The correlation between achievement and the need for esteem and growth were not significant. The authors conclude that, alone, the desire to achieve is not sufficient to ensure success. They attribute the lack of correlation for the growth variable to the likelihood that the grading in the course under study was based on acquisition of knowledge rather than the development of intellectual processes and as such was not designed to reward innovative thinking.

Entwistle, Thompson, and Wilson (1974) reviewed the literature on the relationship between motivation and study habits and conducted an interview study of students at The University of Lancaster (England) in hope of providing additional evidence on the major issues. They found a remarkably consistent pattern of results. Different types of students are motivated by different circumstances. High levels of performance were observed by students who were confident and goal-oriented as well as by those who were uncertain of themselves and haunted by fear of failure. The authors found that students of differing personality and motivational types approached their studies in different ways and perceived their environment in different ways. This research suggests that a number of important questions about motivation and academic success are worthy of research. These questions include: (1) Can courses be adapted to suit students of differing personality types? (2) How can students be given more ready access to the faculty in a large university? (3) What can be done to help new students quickly adjust to the university environment? and (4) How can the curriculum be designed to maximize its personal relevance to students?

ACCOUNTING EDUCATION RESEARCH

The principal question of interest to accounting faculty about student achievement concerns ways of identifying the factors relevant to success in accounting classes or for success on professional examinations. Two studies have found an association between college entrance exam scores and performance on the uniform CPA exam. Leathers (1972) found positive relationships between SAT, ACT, and the AICPA Level II exam and scores on the May, 1970 CPA exam. On a more basic level, a study at Illinois State University (Buehlmann, 1975) indicates that the AICPA level I test score was predictive of success in Intermediate Accounting. In a more recent article, Dunn and Hall (1984) found that the SAT score was positively associated with the CPA exam score. Their regression analyses also established that GPA and accounting hours were significantly associated with the CPA exam score. This research confirms what one would expect from reviewing nonaccounting literature, that GPA tends to be a better predictor of achievement than admissions tests such as ACT and SAT. A number of other researchers, notably Hicks and Richardson (1984) and Eckel and Johnson (1983), report similar results. A study investigating the ability of achievement measures in introductory accounting to predict performance in intermediate accounting also supports these findings. While introductory grades are correlated with performance in intermediate, GPA and student demographic variables are much stronger predictors of success in intermediate accounting (Frakes, 1977).

In other research, Belkaoui (1975) conducted an experiment that tested accounting students' responses to stress when solving accounting problems. He reported that students will resort to the first learned technique when placed in a stressful situation. This reaction is consistent with research findings for other performance environments as reported by Weick (1983).

It seems unlikely that researchers will find it as easy to predict professional success as it is to predict academic achievement. In a study of staff accountants at a Big-Eight CPA firm, Ferris (1982) was unable to find a relationship between college grades and compensation. He did note that an initial salary differential existed for holders of Master's degrees and that the quality of the institution attended had some impact on starting salary. Both these factors appear to decline in significance as the subjects advanced toward the rank of senior accountant and were insignificant for persons at that rank. When the dependent variable was changed to performance rating, no relationship was found between performance and GPA, institutional quality, or level of advancement.

Research does indicate that professional achievement may be linked to individual motivation. Belkaoui (1986) has studied the relationship between need for achievement and career aspirations. In an experiment involving male and female intermediate accounting students, Belkaoui measured the subjects' need for achievement using the Mehrabian need for achievement scale and compared the results with career aspirations using chi square tests. His findings indicate a strong association between need for achievement and a desire to advance toward higher status positions in professional accounting. In addition, Belkaoui found that female respondents with a low need for achievement tended to have unrealistic long-term expectations about their career goals.

RESEARCH OPPORTUNITIES IN ACCOUNTING

The research cited above points to a number of different types of studies which would be of particular interest to accounting educators. Work which examines both the intellective and nonintellective correlates of achievement of accounting students is needed. In particular, this research should control for age, sex, and demographic variables to be of maximum value. In addition, data which are both multi-institutional and longitudinal would contribute much to the external validity of the research.

Very little is currently known from a scientific perspective about the qualities and qualifications which are predictive of success in accounting. Research which assists in the establishment of admission and retention standards would increase the effectiveness of accounting programs by making them more efficient, particularly from an advising viewpoint. Such research is particularly pertinent for graduate admissions, since work done in other professional fields tends to suggest that undergraduate grades may be very poor predictors of the level of achievement that may be attained by graduate students.

While some work has been done in the area of professional examinations, we believe that there are a number of areas which are of particular interest. Research is needed in determining what the educational levels for CPA exam candidacy should be. A few states have increased the requirement for sitting for the exam, but there has been little work which indicates whether pass rates have been affected by these requirements. Work which measures the relevance of the CPA exam to the common body of knowledge would also be of value.

Finally, much additional work should be done in the area of student demographics, particularly on the ways that women and minorities can become fully integrated into the accounting profession. Research is needed in the area of recruitment of minority students as well, and on the professional advancement of women and minorities, and education and placement of older students.

CHAPTER 3 BIBLIOGRAPHY

Adams, L., H. B. Higley, and L. H. Campbell, "Statistical Comparison of Entrance Prediction Equations Using ACT or SAT Scores or Both," *College and University* (Winter 1976), pp. 174–182.

Addams, H. L., "Should the Big 8 Teach Communication Skills?" *Management Accounting* (May 1981), pp. 37–40.

Allen, W. R., "Black Student, White Campus: Structural, Interpersonal, and Psychological Correlates of Success," *Journal of Negro Education* (Spring 1985), pp. 134–147.

Andrews, J. D., and N. B. Sigband, "How Effectively Does the 'New' Accountant Communicate? Perceptions by Practitioners and Academics," *The Journal of Business Communications* (Spring 1984), pp. 15–24.

———, and R. J. Koester, "Communication Difficulties as Perceived by the Accounting Profession and Professors of Accounting," *The Journal of Business Communications* (Winter 1979), pp. 33–42.

Aranya, N., E. I. Meir, and A. Bar-Ilan, "An Empirical Examination of the Stereotype Accountant Based on Holland's Theory," *Journal of Occupational Psychology* (1978), pp. 139–145.

Astin, A. W., *Four Critical Years: Effects of College on Beliefs, Attitudes and Knowledge* (San Francisco: Jossey-Bass Publishers, Inc., 1977).

———, *Achieving Educational Excellence* (San Francisco: Jossey-Bass Publishers, Inc., 1985).

Baird, L. L., "Do Grades and Tests Predict Adult Accomplishment?" *Research in Higher Education*, Vol. 23 (1985), pp. 3–85.

Baker, C. R., "An Investigation of Differences in Values: Accounting Majors vs. Non-Accounting Majors," *The Accounting Review* (October 1976), pp. 886–893.

Bayer, A. E., "Faculty Composition, Institutional Structure, and Students' College Environment," *Journal of Higher Education* (September/October 1975), pp. 549–565.

Belkaoui, A., "Learning Order and Acceptance of Accounting Techniques," *The Accounting Review* (October 1975), pp. 897–899.

———, "The Accounting Students' Need for Achievement and Career Aspirations: An Experiment," *Issues in Accounting Education* (Fall 1986), pp. 197–206.

Bernard, J., "Women's Educational Needs," in Chickering, A. W., ed., *The Modern American College* (San Francisco: Jossey-Bass Publishers, 1981), pp. 256–278.

Borthick, A. F., and R. L. Clark, "Improving Accounting Majors' Writing Quality: The Role of Language Analysis in Attention Directing," *Issues in Accounting Education* (Spring 1987), pp. 13–27.

Brenner, V. C., "Some Observations on Student Values and Their Implications for Accounting Education," *The Accounting Review* (July 1973), pp. 605–608.

Brown, T. R., and D. H. Weaver, "More Than Scores Needed to Predict Graduate Success," *Journalism Educator* (July 1979), pp. 13–15.

Buehlmann, D. M., "ISU's Use of the AICPA's College Testing Program," *The Journal of Accountancy* (May 1975), pp. 93–96.

Chickering, A. W., ed., *The Modern American College* (San Francisco: Jossey-Bass Publishers, 1981).

Cohn, E., *The Economics of Education* (Cambridge, MA: Ballinger Publishing Company, 1979).

Cooper, P. J., L. P. Stewart, and W. B. Gudykunst, "Relationship with Instructor and Other Variables Affecting Student Evaluations of Instruction," *Communications Quarterly* (Fall 1982), pp. 308–315.

Creamer, D. G., ed., *Student Development in Higher Education* (Washington: American College Personnel Association, 1980).

Cundy, D. T., "Teacher Effectiveness and Course Popularity: Patterns in Student Evaluations," *Teaching Political Science* (Summer 1982), pp. 164–173.

Cutright, P., K. Cutright, and D. G. Boshkoff, "Course Selection, Student Characteristics and Bar Examination Performance: The Indiana Law School Experience," *Journal of Legal Education* (1975), pp. 127–137.

Daly, J. A., "Writing Apprehension and Writing Competency," *The Journal of Educational Research* (Sept–Oct 1978), pp. 10–14.

———, and M. D. Miller, "Apprehension of Writing as a Predictor of Message Intensity," *Journal of Psychology* (1975), pp. 175–177.

———, and W. Shamo, "Academic Decisions as a Function of Writing Apprehension," *Research in the Teaching of English* (May 1978), pp. 119–126.

David, C., "Report on Standards for a Business Communication Composition Course: Results of a Study," *The ABCA Bulletin* (March 1982), pp. 21–29.

Davis, W., and L. E. Heller, "The Effects of a Demanding Curriculum on Student Allocation of Time," *Journal of Medical Education* (June 1976), pp. 506–507.

Drew, D., and A. W. Astin, "Undergraduate Aspirations: A Test of Several Theories," *American Journal of Sociology* (May 1972), pp. 1151–1164.

Dunn, W. M., and T. W. Hall, "An Empirical Analysis of the Relationships Between CPA Examination Candidate Attributes and Candidate Performance," *The Accounting Review* (October 1984), pp. 674–689.

Eckel, N., and W. A. Johnson, "A Model for Screening and Classifying Potential Accounting Majors," *Journal of Accounting Education* (Fall 1983), pp. 57–65.

Entwistle, N. J., J. Thompson, and J. D. Wilson, "Motivation and Study Habits," *Higher Education* (November 1974), pp. 379–396.

Estes, R., "The Profession's Changing Horizons: A Survey of Practitioners on the Present and Future Importance of Selected Knowledge and Skills," *The International Journal of Accounting Education and Research* (Spring 1979), pp. 47–50.

Feldman, K., "Grades and College Students Evaluations of their Courses and Teachers," *Research in Higher Education* (1976), pp. 69–111.

Fenske, R. H., and C. S. Scott, "College Students' Goals, Plans, and Background Characteristics: A Synthesis of Three Empirical Studies," *Research in Higher Education* (1973), pp. 101–118.

Ferris, K. R., "Educational Predictors of Professional Pay and Performance," *Accounting, Organizations and Society*, Vol. 7, No. 3 (1982), pp. 225–230.

Fleming, J., "Special Needs of Blacks and Other Minorities," in Chickering, A. W., ed., *The Modern American College* (San Francisco: Jossey-Bass Publishers, 1981), pp. 279–295.

Frakes, A. H., "Introductory Accounting Objectives and Intermediate Accounting Performance," *The Accounting Review* (January 1977), pp. 200–210.

Gough, H. G., and W. B. Hall, "An Attempt to Predict Graduation from Medical School," *Journal of Medical Education* (October 1975), pp. 940–950.

Greenwood, G. E., C. M. Bridges, W. E. Ware, and J. M. Mclean, "Student Evaluation of College Teaching Behaviors Instrument: A Factor Analysis," *Journal of Higher Education* (November 1973), pp. 596–604.

Hall, C., "Giving More Choice to Students in Economic Education: Results and Evaluation," *Journal of Economic Education* (Winter 1982), pp. 19–31.

Hall, M. L., A. F. Mays, and W. R. Allen, "Dreams Deferred: Black Student Career Goals and Fields of Study in Graduate/Professional Schools," *Phylon*, Vol. 45, No. 4 (1984), pp. 271–283.

Haslett, B., "Attitudes Toward Teachers as a Function of Student Academic Self-Concept," *Research in Higher Education* (1976), pp. 41–58.

Hearn, J. C., "The Relative Roles of Academic, Ascribed, and Socioeconomic Characteristics in College Destinations," *Sociology of Education* (January 1984), pp. 22–30.

Hicks, D. W., and F. M. Richardson, "Predicting Early Success in Intermediate Accounting: The Influence of Entry Examination and GPA," *Issues in Accounting Education* (1984), pp. 61–67.

Ingram, R. W., and C. R. Frazier, *Developing Communication Skills for the Accounting Profession* (Sarasota, Florida: American Accounting Association, 1980).

Keith, T. Z., and E. B. Page, "Do Catholic High Schools Improve Minority Student Achievement?" *American Education Research Journal* (Fall 1985), pp. 337–349.

Leathers, P., "Relationship of Test Scores to CPA Examination Performance," *The Journal of Accountancy* (September 1972), pp. 101–103.

Lehr, M., "Student Responsibility as a Factor in Determining Learning Achievement," *Clearing House* (February 1983), pp. 245–247.

Lenning, O. T., *Nonintellective Correlates of Grades, Persistence, and Academic Learning: The*

Published Literature Through the Decade of the Sixties (Iowa City: American College Testing Program, 1974).

Lumsden, K. G., "Summary of an Analysis of Student Evaluations of Faculty and Courses," *Journal of Economic Education* (Fall 1973), pp. 54–56.

Malstrom, E. M., W. R. Klecka, and R. L. Shell, "Findings: Predicting Academic Success in Engineering Graduate Programs," *Engineering Education* (January 1984), pp. 232–234.

Merante, J., "Predicting Student Success in College: What Does the Research Say?" *NASSP Bulletin* (February 1983), pp. 41–46.

Mirus, R., "Some Implications of Student Evaluation of Teachers," *Journal of Economic Education* (Fall 1973), pp. 35–37.

O'Connor, E. J., M. B. Chassie, and F. Walther, "Expended Effort and Academic Performance," *Teaching of Psychology* (December 1980), pp. 231–233.

Parker, C. A., and J. A. Schmidt, "Effects of College Experience," in H. E. Mitzel, ed., *Encyclopedia of Educational Research*, 5th. ed. (New York: Free Press, 1982).

Paul, H., "The Impact of Outside Employment on Student Achievement in Macroeconomic Principles," *Journal of Economic Education* (Summer 1982), pp. 51–56.

Perry, W. G., *Intellectual and Ethical Development* (New York: Holt, Rinehart, and Winston, 1970).

———, "Cognitive and Ethical Growth: The Making of Meaning," in A. W. Chickering, ed., *The Modern American College* (San Francisco: Jossey-Bass Publishers, 1981).

Rebele, J. E., "An Examination of Accounting Students' Perceptions of the Importance of Communications Skills in Accounting," *Issues in Accounting Education* (1985), pp. 41–50.

Regan, M. C., and H. E. Roland, "University Students: A Change in Expectations and Aspirations Over the Decade," *Sociology of Education* (October 1982), pp. 223–228.

———, "Rearranging Family and Career Priorities: Professional Women and Men of the Eighties," *Journal of Marriage and the Family* (November 1985), pp. 985–992.

Reitz, J. G., "Undergraduate Aspirations and Career Choice: Effects of College Selectivity," *Sociology of Education* (Summer 1975), pp. 308–323.

Rippey, R. M., "Student Evaluation of Professors: Are They of Value?" *Journal of Medical Education* (October 1975), pp. 951–958.

Rogers, R. F., "Theories Underlying Student Development," in Creamer, D. G., ed., *Student Development in Higher Education* (Washington: American College Personnel Association, 1980), pp. 10–95.

Seiver, D. A., "Evaluation and Grades: A Simultaneous Framework," *Journal of Economic Education* (Summer 1983), pp. 32–38.

Sewell, W. H., R. M. Hauser and D. L. Featherman, eds. *Schooling and Achievement in American Society* (New York: Academic Press, 1976).

———, and ———, "Causes and Consequences of Higher Education: Models of the Status Attainment Process," *Journal of Agricultural Economics* (December 1972), pp. 851–861.

Siegel, S. R., and E. W. Schmitt, "The Effects of Years of Interruption on ATGSB Scores for Applicants to MBA Programs," *College and University* (Winter 1976), pp. 193–199.

Soper, J. C., "Soft Research on a Hard Subject: Student Evaluations Reconsidered," *Journal of Economic Education* (Fall 1973), pp. 22–26.

Thompson, L., and P. Kobrak, "Predicting the Success of Students in an MPA Program," *Teaching Political Science* (Summer 1983), pp. 182–193.

Thompson, W. A., et al., "Enhancing Career Opportunities in Medicine and the Sciences for Minority Students," *Journal of Medical Education* (August 1984), pp. 675–677.

Trent, J. W., and A. M. Cohen, "Research in Teaching in Higher Education," in R. M. W. Travers, ed., *Second Handbook of Research on Teaching* (Chicago: Rand McNally College Publishing Company, 1973), pp. 997–1071.

Warner, J. E., "Where Has All the Syntax Gone?" *The ABCA Bulletin* (March 1979), pp. 17–21.

Weick, K. E., "Stress in Accounting Systems," *The Accounting Review* (April 1983), pp. 350–369.

Wheeless, L. R., "An Investigation of Receiver Apprehension and Social Context Dimensions of Communication Apprehension," *The Speech Teacher* (September 1975), pp. 261–268.

Winsberg, S., and L. Ste-Marie, "The Correlation of Motivation and Academic Achievement in Physics," *Journal of Research in Science Teaching* (July 1976), pp. 325–329.

CHAPTER 4

Research Related to Faculty

As our education framework indicates, faculty, as well as students, are viewed as "inputs" into the educational process. Much research that focuses on teaching and learning activities involving faculty is discussed under the heading "Educational Process" in Chapter 5, but several other significant areas of research into issues that directly affect faculty are discussed in this chapter (Figure 3). The most extensive literature explored is that concerning student evaluation of teachers, which clearly represents one of the largest bodies of empirical work in the education literature. Among the issues most often addressed are the validity and reliability of student evaluation of teachers, its impact on teaching effectiveness, and the potential effect of nuisance variables. Faculty performance evaluation and the related topics of research and teaching have become significant issues in higher education in recent years, and this significance is reflected by the recent research in these areas. Faculty performance evaluation research has focused primarily on the relative importance and measurement of the various dimensions of faculty work in salary, promotion, and tenure decisions. The literature devoted to research and teaching is largely concerned with the nature of the relationship between the two. Several studies have explored the determinants of research productivity and teaching activities. The empirical faculty development literature is much smaller, perhaps reflecting its comparatively underdeveloped status as a well-defined research area. Finally, the research examining the status of women and minorities in higher education appears to be among the most rapidly expanding bodies of literature in higher education.

These major topic areas in the higher education literature are only beginning to be developed in accounting education research. Many important accounting research issues in each topic area are likely to require a slightly different focus than in other academic disciplines. For example, the activities that comprise faculty work in higher education—research, teaching, and service—are influenced by the constituents of each academic discipline. In accounting, as in medicine and law, the academic discipline must provide an education that prepares students for professional practice. The task seems to dictate that the academic disciplines keep abreast of current practice, and ideally, anticipate and initiate future developments. The important relationship between professional practice and education has significant implications for accounting faculty and their work.

In varying degrees, accounting faculty research and publishing activities deal with issues of direct interest to the accounting profession. Much of this work can be characterized as applied research in that it is rarely very far removed from some practical problem or issue faced by the profession. The methodological issues, problems, and solutions typically encountered in applied research appear to be more complex than in "pure" research (cf. Campbell and Stanley, 1963; Cook and Campbell, 1979). Teaching, too, may be a somewhat more demanding activity for accounting faculty to the extent that it involves the development of professional values among students, in addition to teaching technical skills. Service requirements for accounting faculty also appear to be broader than in many other academic disciplines. Accounting faculty may be much more heavily involved in activities facilitating academic/practitioner interaction than in other disciplines. Active participation in professional and student organizations, student placement activities, and continuing professional education are necessary "service" functions that, although not peculiar to accounting, seem to comprise a larger portion of the faculty workload than in most other disciplines.

FIGURE 3
FACULTY

Student Evaluation of Teachers
    Validity issues
    Reliability issues
    Effects on instructor performance
    Nuisance variables

Faculty Performance Evaluation
    Relative importance of evaluative criteria
    Faculty performance measurement

Research
    Perceptions of the causes of poor productivity
    Rewards and correlates of productivity

Teaching
    Rewards and determinants of effective teaching

Faculty Development
    Faculty maturation and developmental models
    Faculty demography and developmental models

The Status of Women and Minority Faculty
    Women
    Minorities

Other factors, notably AACSB accreditation guidelines regarding professional experience and professional certification and the continuing imbalance in the marketplace for accounting faculty, may also influence the allocation of faculty effort to research, teaching, and service. Faculty work in accounting is likely to differ from that of the academic disciplines typically studied in the higher education literature. These differences must be carefully considered as researchers begin to pursue topics related to faculty work and evaluation in accounting.

The first section of this chapter presents a discussion of the extensive literature on student evaluation of teachers. Sections two, three, and four cover the related topics of faculty performance evaluation, research, and teaching. Section five is devoted to the faculty development literature, and the last section presents an exploration of the burgeoning literature on the status of women and minorities in higher education.

STUDENT EVALUATION OF TEACHERS

EDUCATION RESEARCH FROM OTHER DISCIPLINES

Student evaluation of teachers (SET), the most extensively studied topic in the higher education literature, is also one of the most controversial areas of concern for teachers. The literature is saturated with educators' strongly-held opinions about the utility of SET, as well as considerable debate over the validity of reported empirical findings. Fortunately, this line of research is so well developed that many methodologically sound research efforts have clearly sharpened the focus of reasonable debate about SET. Recent research focuses less on whether SET is appropriate for faculty performance evaluation and more on the conditions under which it might be used to achieve a variety of goals.

McKeachie (1979) identifies four purposes for which SET can be useful: improving teaching effectiveness, providing data from which judgments about teaching effectiveness may be made, aiding students in their choices of courses and instructors, and stimulating students to think about their educational experience. The bulk of SET research has explored the first two of these purposes, and researchers in these two areas have faced the significant methodological problem of measuring teacher effectiveness while recognizing its fundamental multidimensional nature. Many have broadly defined teaching effectiveness as the extent to which the teacher facilitates student achievement of educational goals (Cohen, 1982).

Although more than 25 criteria have been suggested to gauge student achievement of educational goals (Elliott, 1950), three have received the most attention: student learning of substantive course content, student development of basic cognitive processes, and student motivation to continue learning. Student learning of course content, as measured by examination scores and final course grades, typically serves as the criterion by which student achievement of educational goals and, by surrogation, teaching effectiveness is judged (Dowell and Neal, 1982). The obvious assumption here is that students' examination scores and grades measure their learning of course content.

Validity Studies

The validity issue is the fundamental problem addressed by education researchers examining SET. Having accepted student examination and course grades as reasonable measures of achievement, researchers often assess the validity of SET by examining the relationships among student ratings of teachers and students' grades. Theoretically, a positive causal relationship exists: more effective teaching (measured by SET) yields greater student learning (measured by grades). Many of the early validity studies therefore used some form of correlation analysis to explore the degree of association between SET ratings and grades. Although most of these studies reported the expected positive relationship, the failure to examine the direction of causality, as well as the absence of control over many "nuisance" variables (discussed below), abrogated their credibility (Howard and Maxwell, 1980; Marsh, 1980a,b). Cohen (1982, 1983), who conducted meta-analyses to synthesize findings on the relationship between SET ratings and grades, reported that the typical study correlated mean instructor ratings with mean class grades in a multisection course, using a common rating instrument and examination/grading procedures. Many of the studies he reviewed provided for experimental or statistical control over several nuisance variables. Cohen concluded that the available empirical evidence supports the hypothesized positive, causal relationship between SET ratings and grades.

SET validity has also been studied by researchers using criteria other than student learning of course content. Several studies have examined the relationship between student rating of teachers and student motivation to continue learning in the teacher's discipline. For example, McKeachie and Solomon (1958), Sullivan and Skanes (1974), and Bolton, Bonge, and Marr (1979) reported that students of highly rated introductory psychology instructors were more likely to enroll in upper-division psychology courses. Some researchers have explored convergent validity, defined as the correlation between SET ratings and teacher self-evaluations or peer evaluations of teaching (Doyle and Chrichton, 1978). Correlations range from .20 (Centra, 1973; Blackburn and Clark, 1975) to the mid

.60's (Braskamp, Caulley, and Costin, 1979; Marsh, 1982b) when comparing SET ratings and instructor self-evaluations. When comparing SET ratings and peer evaluations, correlations are a bit higher, often ranging from .60 to the mid .80's (Maslow and Zimmerman, 1956; Blackburn and Clark, 1975).

Thus, the validity of SET appears to be reasonably well established, within certain limits. For example, well-designed validity studies have typically drawn data from multisection courses in order to control nuisance variables and assure grading consistency. The validity of SET has therefore not been as carefully examined for upper-level courses that typically do not require multiple sections. Further, individual items appearing on the typical evaluation form, because they vary so much across research studies, have limited utility in meta-analyses or literature reviews focusing on SET validity. The result is that much of the integrative validity research has focused on the typical global evaluation item (e.g., "Rate your instructor's overall teaching effectiveness"), rather than other items or groups of items included on evaluation forms.

Reliability Studies

The reliability of SET, in the broadest sense, is a component of the "construct validity" of the rating instrument; i.e., does the questionnaire measure what it should? Two aspects of reliability of SET have been identified in the education literature—internal consistency and stability. Internal consistency of the SET instrument addresses the issue of consistency of item responses to a rating instrument administered to students or classes taught by the same instructor. Two common approaches are used to explore SET instrument internal consistency. One approach involves the rating of individual teachers where the unit of analysis is within a single class of students (Elliott, 1950; Feldman, 1977). Another requires rating of individual teachers across sections or classes (McKeachie, 1979). With both approaches, reliability indices are calculated from correlations between items on common evaluation forms. Results of these types of studies are consistent in providing moderately strong evidence for the internal consistency of evaluation forms, with reliabilities usually ranging from the mid-.80's to the .90's (Feldman, 1977) within classes, and from the .40's to .60's across classes (Morsch, Burgess, and Smith, 1956; Hogan, 1973).

A related concern focuses on the psychometric issue of interpretation of student responses to evaluation questionnaire items that are intended to measure a common theoretical construct. Numerous studies have used factor analysis to identify and interpret the underlying meaning of student responses to commonly-used instructor evaluation forms. Kulik and McKeachie (1975), summarizing results of factor analysis studies of university instruction and evaluation, found that four to six factors were commonly extracted. Although various authors often create their own verbal labels for these factors, many researchers (e.g., Linn, Centra, and Tucker, 1975; Marsh, 1982b; Marsh and Ware, 1982) have often favored those used by Isaacson, et al. (1964) and in Kulik and McKeachie's integrative work. The four most commonly found factors are skill, rapport, structure, and overload.

The skill factor is a general instructional ability construct. Rapport provides a measure of the empathy or friendliness that the instructor displays. Structure represents the degree of organization and control that the instructor exhibits in the classroom. Overload measures the academic workload faced by the student. Although these factors, or factors with similar meaning, commonly appear in most of the studies, the skill factor is almost always the most important, usually containing over half the student evaluation items that address overall teaching effectiveness (e.g., Abbott and Perkins, 1982). Although the studies using a factor analysis approach are usually not presented as reliability studies, they do provide an evaluation of internal consistency of SET instruments. Like the internal consistency research, the factor analysis approach focuses on determining the extent of agreement of student ratings of conceptually similar questionnaire items.

The second aspect of SET reliability that has been explored is the stability of SET ratings of an instructor across time. Stability coefficients are usually calculated by correlating student ratings of an instructor taken two or more times during an academic term (Kohlan, 1973) or during the term and after completing the class (Overall and Marsh, 1978; McKeachie, Lin, and Mendelson, 1978). Reliability coefficients have generally fallen in a range from the .50's to the .90's, even with a test-retest time span of as long as ten years (e.g., Drucker and Remmers, 1950). Thus, strong empirical support exists for the reliability of SET, in terms of internal consistency and test-retest stability.

Effects of SET Feedback on Instructor Performance

Of the four primary purposes for which SET is said to be useful (improving teaching, evaluating performance, helping students select instructors, and inducing students to think critically about their educational experience), the improvement of instruction through SET feedback is the most-often studied (Cohen, 1980). The typical research design involves comparing SET ratings taken at two or more times within an academic term and, occasionally, across terms. The nature of SET feedback given to instructors varies across studies from simple written presentation of summarized ratings to formal consultation with SET experts. Consistently, instructors who receive feedback from SET are rated higher on the second SET administration than are control group instructors who receive no feedback. Instructors receiving feedback with some form of consultation also receive higher end-of-term student ratings than those receiving only summarized rating results. Moreover, rating improvements with feedback are found regardless of whether the second SET administration is within the same academic term as the first (feedback) administration or in the subsequent term. A few studies (summarized in Levinson-Rose and Menges, 1981) have examined the effect of SET feedback on student learning, with mixed results.

Nuisance Variables and SET

Perhaps the most common objection that instructors raise about SET is that student ratings are unduly influenced by factors other than teaching effectiveness. Most widely-available evaluation instruments include items designed to measure some of these factors (e.g., "What grade do you expect to receive in this course?"). The appearance of these items on SET instruments may encourage the belief that they do have significant explanatory power with respect to SET ratings. With few exceptions, however, these nuisance variables have little effect on student ratings of teaching effectiveness (Marsh, 1980 a,b; Marsh, 1984). Although numerous researchers have identified many potential nuisance variables, nine are most often cited and studied. These variables, and summarized empirical findings for each, are listed below.

1. Student and instructor personality traits. Instructor personality traits, as perceived by students, are consistently found to affect SET ratings (see, e.g., Baird, 1973; Costin and Grush, 1973; Elmore and Pohlman, 1978). The direction of the effect depends on the personality traits under consideration. Many researchers do not view perceived instructor personality traits as nuisance variables, arguing that they simply represent dimensions of an instructor's instructional performance. With respect to student personality traits, the literature is equivocal for most variables

studied (Abrami, Perry, and Leventhal, 1982). Literature reviews of the topic generally conclude that student personality traits do not have a biasing effect on instructor evaluations (see, e.g., McKeachie, 1979; Marsh, 1984).
2. Academic rank and within-course experience of instructor. Although the empirical evidence concerning the effect of instructor academic rank on ratings is ambivalent, results suggest that experience may have a positive effect on instructor ratings by students. An instructor teaching two sections of a course in one academic term tends to receive higher ratings in the later section (Marsh, 1980a,b). Also, when an instructor teaches a course during a second academic term, ratings are higher than during the first term (Marsh, 1982a).
3. Sex of instructor. The empirical evidence favors the conclusion that no systematic gender bias exists in overall instructor ratings (Ferber and Huber, 1975; Harris, 1976; Hesselbart, 1977; Kaschak, 1978). However, women do tend to be rated higher on evaluation items that measure interpersonal skills related to teaching (Bennett, 1982).
4. Grades expected by students. The bulk of empirical evidence reveals a positive relationship between expected grades and instructor ratings. Many studies exploring this relationship have used methodologies from which causal inferences can be tentatively drawn. Researchers using path analysis and cross-lagged panel correlation conclude that this widely-reported positive relationship probably reflects the two variables' common positive correlation with effective teaching (Howard and Maxwell, 1982; Marsh, 1984).
5. Student prior interest in subject matter. Several studies have demonstrated that student prior interest (often identified by comparing students taking a course as an elective with those required to take the course) is positively (but weakly) associated with instructor ratings (Menges, 1973; Feldman, 1976, 1977, 1978; Kulik and McKeachie, 1975; McKeachie, 1979; Howard and Maxwell, 1980).
6. Course subject matter. Empirical research has consistently demonstrated that students evaluate instructors teaching courses in certain disciplines (e.g., the humanities) higher than those in other disciplines (Feldman, 1978; Kulik and Kulik, 1974; McKeachie, 1979; Marsh and Overall, 1981).
7. Class size. A negative relationship between class size and instructor ratings has been the most common finding (Bausell and Bausell, 1979; Frey, 1978; Marsh, Overall, and Kesler, 1979).
8. Course difficulty. Instructors teaching courses that students perceive as more difficult tend to receive higher ratings than those teaching courses perceived as less difficult (Marsh, 1980a; Marsh, 1982a). Although this finding may seem counterintuitive, course difficulty is one of the more compelling predictive variables in terms of its relative explanatory power.
9. Stated purpose of evaluation. Most studies have shown that instructor ratings obtained for research purposes are quite similar to ratings to be used for evaluation purposes (Borresen, 1967; Driscoll and Goodwin, 1979; Centra, 1976; Meier and Feldhusen, 1979).

Several other potential biases to SET have been examined, including instructor reputation, academic level of the evaluated course, timing of evaluation administration, and perceived confidentiality of evaluations.

Even though statistical significance is obtained in research examining many of these nuisance variables, recent study has also focused on the relative explanatory power of these variables as a means of evaluating their practical impact on instructor ratings. Literature reviews by leading researchers typically conclude that reported significant results are of such small relative magnitude that they do not seriously threaten the validity of SET (Marsh, 1980a,b; Marsh and Overall, 1981; Marsh, 1982a; Cashin and Perrin, 1983). Marsh (1984), concluding a comprehensive review and critique of the literature, provides an excellent summation:

> Research described in this article clearly demonstrates that student ratings are clearly multidimensional, quite reliable, reasonably valid, relatively uncontaminated by many variables often seen as sources of potential bias, and are seen to be useful by students, faculty, and administrators. . . . Despite the generally supportive research findings, student ratings should be used cautiously, and there should be other forms of systematic input about teaching effectiveness, particularly when they are used for tenure/promotion decisions.

ACCOUNTING EDUCATION RESEARCH

Although student evaluation responses often serve as dependent variables in the accounting education literature (see, e.g., Tennant and Lawrence, 1975), only two recent research efforts have been reported that address the validity/reliability issues summarized above. In addition to these, Wright, Whittington, and Whittenburg (1984) provide brief summaries of findings drawn from selected studies reported in the general education literature. Both the empirical studies report findings that are consistent with similar studies in education. Porcano (1984) used factor analysis to identify salient dimensions of student ratings of instructors in principles, cost, and tax accounting courses. Having concluded that the derived factor structures were similar to those typically reported in the education literature, he used regression analysis to assess the ability of these factors to explain final grades in each of these courses. Results indicated that the factors exhibited significantly different explanatory power across the three different courses. Hooper and Page (1986) reported split-half reliabilities and limited within-questionnaire item associations for an internally developed SET questionnaire administered at the University of Virginia. As in the general education literature, reliabilities were high, and the questionnaire items most highly correlated with the global evaluation items were those typically reported.

RESEARCH OPPORTUNITIES IN ACCOUNTING EDUCATION

Future accounting education research in this area might continue to explore the extent to which reported reliability and validity results in the education literature carry over into accounting. Porcano's (1984) study demonstrated that the evaluative dimensions reported in earlier factor analysis studies are quite similar to those generated in accounting courses, providing some evidence that the consistent reliability findings in education are probably applicable to accounting. The validity issue, as addressed in the education literature, also deserves attention by accounting researchers. Research into the fundamental problem of defining and measuring effective teaching and its outcomes is the most significant component of the validity issue. Researchers might address the validity of SET in accounting by examining the relationship between student academic performance and instructor ratings. In accounting, a number of outcomes of effective teaching, other than high student academic performance, seem to be desirable. Socially significant criteria other than grades should be explored as measures of student achievement and as bases for SET. Student performance on the CPA exam and on-the-job performance evaluations after graduation may provide more socially significant measures of achievement of educational goals than exam and course grades. The standardized CPA exam, the formal performance evaluation programs used by many CPA firms, and the rather visible hiring and career advancement policies in many large firms provide accounting researchers with the opportunity to make an important contribution to the education literature.

The nature of the accounting profession itself may increase the importance of affective educational goals (e.g., the extent of professionalization of students) and of a more precise delineation of learning outcomes that might serve as criteria for validating SET. These outcomes might include the nurturing of specific accounting student attributes such as learning motivation, values awareness, knowledge acquisition, technical competency, communication and interaction skills, problem-structuring strategies, etc.

An apparently overlooked aspect of SET validity is concerned with institutional outcomes of effective teaching, rather than student achievement of educational goals. For example, effective teaching may yield more loyalty among alumni, increase employers' demand for graduates, generate more donations from external constituents, and attract more highly-qualified students. The validity of specific SET questionnaire items and dimensions needs to be addressed, as it has been in other disciplines (e.g., Cohen, 1982), in terms of institutional and professional goals as well as in terms of student achievement.

The education literature focuses primarily on two uses of SET: performance evaluation of instructors and improvement of teaching. Research surveying the ways that SET is currently used in accounting programs could provide useful information from which improvements could be made. In particular, multi-institutional field studies might examine SET practices in different types of programs (e.g., research vs. teaching institutions, graduate vs. undergraduate programs), for different faculty groups (e.g., tenured vs. untenured), and for different students/courses (majors vs. nonmajors, introductory tax vs. systems). Researchers might assess the extent of reliance on SET in performance evaluation of instructors, how (and if) student ratings of instruction are adjusted for perceived nuisance variables, and how SET fits into the overall performance evaluation framework. Researchers should also attempt to determine how SET can improve accounting instruction, perhaps by focusing on the form of the feedback about student ratings, given that form of SET feedback has been shown to be an important determinant of teaching improvement. Related issues that need to be addressed include the determination of appropriate comparison (norm group) ratings and the discovery of specific teacher behaviors that may yield higher, more valid ratings of teaching effectiveness (e.g., Murray, 1983).

FACULTY PERFORMANCE EVALUATION

EDUCATION RESEARCH FROM OTHER DISCIPLINES

For many reasons, the evaluation of faculty performance has become a rather significant issue in higher education in recent years. Declining student enrollments, an oversupply of Ph.D.s in many disciplines, and rather restrictive education budgets provide a drastically different economic environment for higher education now than in earlier years. The legal and political context for higher education has also shifted toward increased accountability for the achievement of certain societal goals. As in all segments of our society, the demonstration of compliance with federal and state statutes governing racial and sexual equality is a necessary component of performance evaluation. State legislatures, as well as students and faculty acting as litigants, continue to raise the issue of educational quality assessment through formal performance evaluation programs. Thus, the bulk of research devoted to faculty performance evaluation is quite recent, reflecting its increasing importance in higher education (see Seldin, 1984 for a more complete discussion of the recent history and current status of faculty performance evaluation).

Faculty performance evaluation (FPE) has two primary goals. First, it provides a basis for decisions concerning salary, promotion, and tenure for faculty. Second, FPE assists faculty in identifying and correcting deficiencies in their performances. FPE, used as an evaluative instrument to aid in administrative decisions, is called "summative" evaluation. FPE that is intended to provide a basis for self-assessment and improvement is called "formative" evaluation. Most of the empirical work devoted to FPE is descriptive research examining the criteria used for summative evaluation.

The Relative Importance of FPE Criteria

The typical study examining FPE uses a mailed questionnaire to gather information from various educational institutions. Comparisons of the relative importance of criteria used in FPE across types of institutions (e.g., research universities, doctoral granting universities, etc. as identified by the Carnegie Commission on Higher Education [1973]) are made. Whether the decision at hand is promotion, salary increase, or tenure, the two most important evaluation criteria are research and teaching, with service a distant third. Although researchers use a variety of survey instruments to gather information about evaluation criteria, several dimensions of research and teaching are commonly identified. Research is often evaluated in terms of quality of publications, number of publications, and research activity not yielding publications. Teaching is evaluated by students, peers, administrators, and the teacher himself, along a large number of dimensions. Service is apparently rather difficult to define, both in terms of its objective (the academic discipline, the academic department, the university, the community, the profession, society-at-large?), and its measurement. Thus, research findings about service as a performance evaluation criterion are rarely comparable. Even so, most studies report that service, however defined, is at best a minor factor in FPE (Centra, 1977). Other FPE criteria sometimes identified include personal qualifications and experience, personality factors, and marketability. As one would expect, the weights attached to various performance evaluation criteria differ across types of educational institutions.

Survey results generally support the notion that quality research is the most important FPE criterion at major universities, with teaching a close second. For smaller institutions, effective teaching is the most important criterion, with research and personal qualifications and experience only slightly less important (Centra, 1980). Smaller institutions also attach relatively more weight to public and institutional service than do major universities (Nitzsche, 1978; Centra, 1977).

Faculty Performance Measurement

Survey results also reveal that teaching is evaluated based on systematic student evaluations, formal chairman evaluations, colleagues' opinions', videotaped teaching, alumni ratings, and classroom visits (Centra, 1977). Of these modes of measuring teaching effectiveness, student and colleague evaluations of teaching are the most widely-used among administrators. Student evaluation of teaching, perhaps because of its formal, measurable output, is the most researched topic in the higher education literature and is therefore discussed elsewhere in this chapter. In comparison, the empirical research literature devoted to other modes of evaluating teaching effectiveness is rather small.

Most studies testing the validity of colleague teaching evaluations compare colleague ratings with whatever other measures of teaching effectiveness are available for a particular teacher, typically student ratings or administrator's ratings (Blackburn and Clark, 1975). Correlations usually range from the .60's to .80's, indicating substantial agreement between the groups of raters (Centra, 1980). Even so, faculty may be unwilling to accept colleague ratings of teaching effectiveness (Fenker, 1974) because academic colleagues are rarely direct observers of classroom behavior. When classroom teaching is observed by colleagues who are asked to base their evaluations solely on limited classroom observations, colleague ratings are unreliable and do not correlate well with student ratings of the same instructor. The conclusion tentatively drawn is that colleagues may actually evaluate teaching effectiveness based largely on input they have from students, so that the typical high correlations between colleague and student evaluations are misleading (Centra, 1975).

Researchers have examined several other methods of evaluating teaching. Self-evaluations of teaching effectiveness, although valuable as tools for self-improvement, have not been shown to be useful for summative evaluation. Self-ratings are found to correlate positively with student ratings, but they exhibit significant upward bias (Blackburn and Clark, 1975; Centra, 1973). Self-evaluation through videotape playback appears to be increasingly popular among faculty; its utility as a formative evaluation device has some support in the literature (Centra, 1980). Alumni ratings are highly correlated with student ratings of teaching effectiveness, although they are rarely used in formal FPE programs. For summative evaluation purposes, the most valid, reliable method for assessing teaching effectiveness is through student ratings, in conjunction with other evaluative input.

Centra (1977), surveying department heads at 134 institutions, found that the three most important means of evaluating research are the number of articles in quality journals, the number of books published, and the quality of research as judged by peers. Obviously, research quality is rather difficult to assess. Peer evaluation (typically by faculty colleagues, occasionally by peers at other institutions, Seldin, 1984) is increasingly used to assess research quality (Centra, 1977), but its validity has not yet been established. Citation counts are seldom used in FPE, but they appear to be a reasonably objective indicator of research quality (Centra, 1980). Apparently, research quality as assessed by faculty peers is the most important criterion in FPE, even though the validity of peer evaluations has not been empirically examined.

Faculty performance evaluation is clearly a developing field of endeavor, both in practice and as a research topic. Most of the descriptive research in the area suggests that the primary criteria used in FPE are research productivity and teaching effectiveness. Research is typically evaluated by faculty colleagues, while teaching evaluation by students is the most valid and popular means of assessing teaching effectiveness. Several other evaluation techniques may make important contributions to faculty improvement in teaching and research.

ACCOUNTING EDUCATION RESEARCH

Campbell, Gaertner, and Vecchio (1983) surveyed U.S. accounting faculty in order to examine the relative importance attached to various measures of teaching, research, service and other aspects of performance in promotion and tenure decisions. Their results were consistent with those found in the general education literature, indicating that the relative importance of various measures of faculty performance differs across types of educational institutions, faculty rank, and faculty tenure status. They also confirmed the typical finding that research and teaching are significantly more important than service in faculty performance evaluation. Edwards, Ingram, and Sanders (1981), while examining the need for teaching skills development in Ph.D. programs, noted that accounting administrators and directors in doctorate-granting programs deemed research most important in promotion/tenure deliberations. Teaching effectiveness was considered the most important evaluative factor by administrators in programs not offering the doctorate (cf. Centra, 1977; Seldin, 1984).

Several studies reported in the last few years, though perhaps not specifically designed to do so, may address one of the more difficult FPE issues. The many studies that describe and/or compare accounting publication rates, often by type of school, faculty rank, and journal orientation, may provide some general bases for performance evaluation of accounting faculty research productivity. These studies include Benjamin and Brenner (1974); Bazley and Nikolai (1975); Andrews and McKenzie (1978); Weber and Stevenson (1981); Windal (1981); Coe and Weinstock (1983); Bublitz and Kee (1984); and Jacobs, Hartgraves, and Beard (1986). Rouse and Shockley (1984), suggesting a reassessment of publication expectations, reported descriptive statistics of various attributes of faculty publishing in two leading accounting journals over a five-year period. Statistics presented included publicaltion rates by faculty rank and coauthorship status, and elapsed time from the author's terminal degree attainment to publication date.

RESEARCH OPPORTUNITIES IN ACCOUNTING EDUCATION

Faculty performance evaluation should probably be a more important research topic in accounting than in most other areas of higher education. In addition to the increased societal concern with FPE in education in general, continuing pressures in the accounting academic marketplace create a rather challenging context for FPE of accounting faculty. The combination of the high demand for accounting education and the short supply of accounting educators may have a significant impact on FPE in the field. If accounting programs attempt to meet the demand rather than restrict it, a strong incentive to lower FPE criteria in order to avoid faculty attrition may exist. This obvious threat to the quality of accounting education might be abrogated by the exploration of reasonable performance expectations for accounting faculty. Researchers should examine formative evaluation techniques as a means of enhancing the likelihood of positive summative outcomes and thus reducing faculty attrition.

Faculty performance evaluation in accounting needs to be addressed in terms of the activities and outcomes of faculty work. The widely-recognized components of faculty work—research, teaching, and service—are in need of clearer definition for evaluation (and research) purposes in higher education. The specification of "service" activities for FPE purposes has been particularly problematic in higher education, possibly because most prior research has not considered the differences that exist across disciplines. In accounting, as in other disciplines, the fundamental FPE issues seem to be straightforward—What "counts?" How much? How might it be assessed? The answers to these questions vary across types of institutions and among disciplines. The importance of the relationship between the accounting profession and accounting education may have an impact on the faculty activities that "count," and on the relative weights that might be attached to them. Accounting faculty work is intended to contribute to the attainment of the goals of the discipline, the academic community, *and* the profession. Each academic program in accounting provides its own unique context for faculty work. Researchers exploring FPE in accounting must be sensitive to the multiple dimensions of accounting faculty work in terms of its contribution to a diverse set of goals that vary across institutions and individuals.

RESEARCH

EDUCATION RESEARCH FROM OTHER DISCIPLINES

"Publish or perish" is an often-quoted maxim in academia, perhaps reflecting the widely-held belief among professors that research productivity is the sine qua non of an academic career. While that is a frequently challenged assertion, the education literature generally supports the underlying philosophy that the generation of knowledge is the single most important dimension of faculty work. Educators, as well as sociologists and psychologists, frequently advise academics about how research might best be done. Most of the empirical work reported in the literature addresses the relationship between research and teaching. Other issues commonly addressed include reasons for the failure of many academics as researchers, the salubrious outcomes of research activities, and the characteristics of successful researchers. The rather surprising finding in the literature is that most academics do not publish or publish very little (Ladd and Lipset, 1978; Cole, 1981).

Perceptions of the Causes of Poor Research Productivity

Several studies have explored the reasons that academics are not more involved in research activities, typically relying on a simple survey of faculty in various disciplines (Boice and Jones, 1984). The most common reason proffered is lack of time due to teaching, administrative, and service commitments (Glidden, 1975; Dorsel, 1981). Another often-cited reason for not publishing is the writing block, which may help explain what makes writing difficult for many professors. Reasons for writing blocks, or writing apprehension, are numerous. Early experiences with intimidating teachers and aggressive reviewers may induce anxiety about writing itself, or, more commonly, anxiety may result from evaluation apprehension (Daly and Miller, 1975). Personality factors that contribute to writing blocks have also been identified by several researchers. For example, Type A individuals, often characterized as hypersensitive and overly conscientious, may stifle their creative potential by consistently trying to overachieve (Crisp and Moldofsky, 1965). Fortunately, researchers have determined that several remedies for writing block may be quite effective (Rainer, 1978), while noting that some of the reasons given for not publishing (e.g., lack of time) do not really explain the tendency for faculty to fail to publish (Gould, 1980). The bulk of empirical research suggests that successful writing is achieved by focusing on the establishment and maintenance of momentum, rather than by waiting for "the right mood" or creative insight. Apparently, creativity in writing is more a function of consistent work habits and organization than of some notion of spontaneous inspiration (Boice and Jones, 1984).

Rewards and Correlates of Research Productivity

At major universities, and increasingly at smaller liberal arts colleges, three recognized organizational missions are the advancement of knowledge through research, the education of successive student generations, and the provision of service benefitting society. Although the relative importance of these goals is often debated, current faculty reward structures strongly suggest that research is the most valued of the three possible faculty activities. The pecuniary rewards and many nonpecuniary rewards accruing to faculty successfully involved in research are far greater than those available for either excellent teaching or meritorious service. Even so, all three organizational goals require time and energy of faculty. According to a recent survey, only 14 percent of responding faculty members viewed themselves as contributing significantly in all three areas (Baker and Zey-Ferrell, 1984). The allocation of limited faculty resources among research, teaching, and to some extent, service, has been the subject of several research efforts.

The typical empirical studies in this area deal with the relationship between research and teaching and often attempt to explore the hypothesis that faculty involvement in research enhances the quality of their teaching (Michalak and Friedrich, 1981). Research is quantified in a variety of ways, including faculty estimates of time spent on research (Harry and Goldner, 1972), government research grants received, number of articles published (Bresler, 1968), number of citations in the literature (Dent and Lewis, 1976; Linsky and Straus, 1975), and point assignments for different kinds of scholarly output (Voeks, 1962; Aleamoni and Yimer, 1973). Teaching effectiveness is usually measured by ratings on student evaluations of instructors (Bresler, 1968; Hicks, 1974; Voeks, 1962). Data analysis techniques range from simple correlational analyses to analysis of covariance. The results of these studies are mixed, typically indicating no relationship or a weak positive relationship between research and teaching effectiveness. Many of these studies are overly simplistic in design and execution. They rely only on cross-sectional analyses to examine an hypothesized relationship that necessarily develops over time. Most have virtually no theoretical basis from which to identify appropriate causal variables. At best, the conclusion that can be drawn is that research appears to have very little *measurable* beneficial effect on teaching effectiveness.

Although several authors have defended the need for faculty involvement in research by arguing that research enhances teaching, society at large and educational institutions place a very high value on research. The significant benefits accruing to faculty actively engaged in research indicate that research is a valuable societal commodity (Haim, 1981). A number of studies have demonstrated that several institutionally dispensed rewards are directly related to research productivity. Many researchers have attempted to build regression models that explain variation in faculty salaries in terms of independent variables that theoretically represent various components of faculty productivity, including research. Results consistently indicate a significant positive relationship between publications and absolute salary level (Fulton and Trow, 1974; Siegfried and White, 1978; Tuckman and Tuckman, 1984), salary increments (Hoyt, 1974), and merit pay (Kasten, 1984). Moreover, various nonpecuniary rewards are often granted to research-oriented faculty by their institutions, including early promotion (Salthouse, McKeachie, and Lin, 1978), teaching assignments in higher-level courses (Hayes, 1971), and tenure (Kasten, 1984). The empirical evidence has also shown that large extra-institutional rewards are frequently granted in return for research, and that teaching and service command much lower such returns (Kasten, 1984).

Several studies have explored faculty research in order to discover the factors that enhance productivity. Most have focused on the logical antecedents to the development of research skills and whether such skills yield higher research productivity. Researchers typically use the number of publications or the number of citations to one's work in the literature as measures of research productivity and perform simple correlation or regression analysis. Four variables have been shown to be reasonably predictive of research productivity among academics. Undergraduate selectivity scores, which measure the scholarly achievements of undergraduate programs by evaluating the quality of their students (e.g., ACT, SAT, or I.Q. scores), have been shown to be positively associated with research productivity of scientists (Long, 1978) and academics (Hargens and Hagstrom, 1982) matriculating at "selective" institutions. Prestige of the department from which the doctorate is received and of the department of first academic appointment are positively correlated with both faculty research productivity and eventual high-visibility position attainment (Reskin, 1977; Long, 1978; Hargens and Hagstrom, 1982). Elapsed time between Bachelor's and Doctorate degrees exhibits a negative relationship with research productivity (Clemente, 1973; Crowley and Chubin, 1976; Hargens and Hagstrom, 1982). Clearly, the most likely factors that influence research productivity are individual difference variables such as motivation, ability, personality, etc. These variables have not yet been extensively explored in the education literature.

ACCOUNTING EDUCATION RESEARCH

Two studies have appeared recently in the accounting education literature that address research specifically as a faculty activity. Cargile and Bublitz (1986) surveyed a sample of accounting faculty in order to assess their perceptions of factors contributing to research productivity. Associations between various respondent attributes and self-reported research productivity measures were reported. They reported that the most important perceived factors contributing to research productivity were computer access, reduced teaching loads/service commitments, and high quality colleagues and graduate students, although they found some evidence that the relative importance of these (and other) factors varies across types of institutions. They also found that faculties at different types of institutions face different teaching workloads, and perceive different relative weights attached to research, teaching, and service activities (cf. Edwards, Ingram, and Sanders, 1981).

Seiler and Pearson (1986) compared accounting faculty at doctoral-granting programs with faculty at programs not offering the doctorate in terms of their perceived satisfaction with several work-related variables. Questionnaire responses indicated that faculty in doctoral-granting programs are more satisfied than their colleagues in other programs. The authors discuss the findings as indicative of a positive relationship between research involvement and satisfaction.

RESEARCH OPPORTUNITIES IN ACCOUNTING EDUCATION

Studies that explore the reasons that more accounting faculty do not engage in research might lead to corrective actions by research-oriented universities. The correlates of faculty research productivity identified in higher education and other determinants of research and publishing should be explored, taking into account accounting's academic and professional constituencies. Exploration of the conflicts and synergies among research, teaching, and service activities of accounting educators could help better structure faculty evaluation programs and compensation schemes. The identification of the characteristics of successful research and researchers and the causes of unsuccessful research outcomes could provide useful information to those involved in educating Ph.D.s and maintaining faculty vitality. Other researchable issues include the examination of the economic marketplaces for research, teaching, and service activities; the evaluation of research criteria; and the relationships among faculty research activities and the accounting profession.

TEACHING

EDUCATION RESEARCH FROM OTHER DISCIPLINES

Almost all public statements by universities and colleges acknowledge the paramount importance of teaching. Although research and service are often mentioned in the public forum, teaching is unequivocally presented as the fundamental mission of the institution. Surveys of various faculty groups reveal that they do not quite agree with these institutional public sentiments. Virtually every faculty group surveyed by numerous researchers consider research to be equally important, and often more important, than teaching (Centra, 1977; 1980). Several researchers have attempted to assess the rewards associated with effective teaching. The largest literature dealing with teaching as a faculty activity examines relationships among faculty attitudes or personality characteristics and a variety of teaching behaviors. Some research is devoted to identifying the characteristics and behaviors of effective teachers. The literature exploring the relationship between teaching and research is discussed in the "Research" section.

Rewards and Determinants of Effective Teaching

Although many survey results indicate that teaching and research are about equally important, many authors assert that effective teaching is at best a necessary but insufficient component of an academic career in higher education. Several studies (e.g., Salthouse, McKeachie, and Lin, 1978; Kasten, 1984) exploring the factors that influence salary, promotion, and tenure reveal that the rewards for effective teaching are quite small relative to those garnered by scholarly research. Most research in this area relies on surveys of various groups of faculty and administrators at various institutions, or on controlled studies within a single university or college. Several of the more innovative studies present contrived groups of candidates for salary, promotion, or tenure decisions to various groups of faculty and administrators (Kasten, 1984). Others analyze extensive publicly-available data bases to explore the relationship between salaries and various measures of achievement (Tuckman and Hagemann, 1976). In both the simple surveys and more elaborate experiments, the question addressed is the relative importance of effective teaching in salary, promotion, and tenure decisions. Regression analysis is often used to assess the relative weights attached to research, teaching, and service activities, as well as to the importance of various personal characteristics and training. Researchers have measured teaching activity and effectiveness in a variety of ways, including measurement through student evaluations, class enrollments, credit hours generated, student achievement, and receipt of an outstanding teaching award. Although several studies report a significant positive effect of effective teaching on faculty rewards (Rossman, 1976; Siegfried and White, 1978), the weights attached to teaching are rather low. Research on the institutional rewards for teaching is largely inconclusive, due to serious measurement problems and largely inconsistent results. However, the consistent finding is that effective teaching yields much lower rewards than scholarly research (Kasten, 1984).

Several researchers have attempted to determine which instructor characteristics are important enough to be assessed by student evaluation of instructor instruments. Many surveys of students, faculty, administrators, and alumni have identified several instructor behaviors and characteristics that affect teaching effectiveness. Specific instructor behaviors rated high by all groups include preparing well for class, exhibiting genuine interest in the subject matter, and communicating well (Hildebrand, Wilson, and Dienst, 1971). Desirable instructor characteristics include (Centra 1980):

1. Communication skills
2. Favorable attitudes toward students
3. Knowledge of subject
4. Good organization of subject matter and course
5. Enthusiasm about subject
6. Fairness in examinations and grading

7. Flexibility
8. Encouragement of students to think for themselves
9. Good speaking ability

Results of factor analyses of survey results typically identify three to four factors representing student-teacher interaction, manner of instruction, stimulating students to learn, and personal traits of the instructor (Miron, 1983). Similar factors are identified from factor analyses of student ratings of their instructors (Kulik and McKeachie, 1975). Certain observable classroom instructor behaviors (e.g., vocal modulation, gesturing, and eye contact) have been shown to be strongly associated with both instructor ratings and student learning (Smith, 1977; Ware and Williams, 1980; Murray, 1983). Even though the research findings are converging, most researchers agree that effective teaching is, at best, a very poorly understood construct.

Research into attitudes of teachers has yielded additional evidence about the characteristics of an effective teacher. Gathering data through surveys, researchers often find that effective teachers (however defined) display some common general characteristics. Effective teachers are oriented toward the student, value the learning process, need to influence individual behavior, and believe that they have the power to effect desirable change in the student (Baker, Boggs, and Putnam, 1983).

Numerous studies have evaluated a wide variety of faculty attitudes and how they affect the educational process. Various models of instructor's cognitive processes as decision makers have been put forth and tested. Research paradigms and theories based in cognitive psychology are widely used, and research methods employed range from case studies to policy capturing, lens models, and process-tracing. Various instructor attitudes and characteristics have been shown to influence their teaching behavior (Shavelson and Stern, 1981). For example, an instructor's level of cognitive complexity has been shown to influence the choice of alternative teaching styles (Gordon, 1977). Instructor locus of control has been found to be an important determinant of the type of motivational techniques used in the classroom (Trice and Wood-Shuman, 1984). Instructors' expectations of and behavior toward different types of students have been found to vary systematically with several personality traits (Mitman, 1985). Many of these studies are descriptive attempts to identify interrelationships among variables rather than searches for solutions to practical educational problems. The diversity of variables studied reflects the complexities of the teacher's role in the educational process.

RESEARCH OPPORTUNITIES IN ACCOUNTING EDUCATION

Obviously, the identification and assessment of effective teaching in an accounting context is the issue of greatest potential interest. Unlike many disciplines, a typical accounting curriculum is quite diverse in terms of the nature of the courses required of accounting majors. Effective teaching in auditing or systems may be quite different from effective teaching in intermediate accounting or tax. Accounting researchers can make an important contribution to the education literature by exploring the relationship between effective teaching behaviors across different types of courses, students, and contexts, and in terms of unique accounting student outcomes (e.g., CPA examination performance). Other possible accounting education research topics include the assessments of alternative means of evaluating and rewarding effective teaching, the development of teaching skills in Ph.D.s, and the ways to attract highly-qualified individuals into doctoral programs in accounting.

FACULTY DEVELOPMENT

EDUCATION RESEARCH FROM OTHER DISCIPLINES

"Faculty development," a topic often discussed in education, encompasses two distinct bodies of literature. The first is normative, focusing on prescribed means for institutional goal achievement via various programs for encouraging faculty productivity. Little empirical evidence is available to support most of these prescriptions, and authors tend to rely on various developmental psychology theories to support their assertions about what should be done to enhance the continued growth and productivity of academics. The second body of literature is less ambitious and probably should logically precede the larger prescriptive literature. Largely empirical, this research investigates faculty career patterns, typically tracing changes in productivity and attitudes. The research to date is exploratory, marked by searches for causal relationships and tests of competing pretheoretical paradigms.

Faculty Maturation and Developmental Models

The typical empirical study examining faculty development is a cross-sectional analysis of faculty attitudes and performance. Faculty at differing academic ranks, ages, or experience levels are interviewed or asked to respond to a questionnaire concerning their performance and attitudes (e.g., Bayer and Dutton, 1977). Some studies use more objective performance measures such as articles and books published and number of scholarly works cited in the literature. Whatever the dependent variables, groups of faculty are typically compared at a single point in time and conclusions are drawn about existing differences. Most researchers discuss their results in terms of systematic faculty changes that occur over time. However, their cross-sectional research rarely allows such an inference to be unambiguously drawn.

Empirical findings tend to reveal an inverse relationship between publication rate and chronological age (Blackburn, Behymer, and Hall, 1978; Long, 1978; Bayer and Dutton, 1977), although some have indicated a saddle-shaped curve, with peaks at ages in the thirties and fifties (Pelz and Andrews, 1976). The research evidence also supports the idea that fundamental work-oriented values and self-perceptions of faculty change predictably as they move through their careers. Younger faculty members tend to view themselves primarily as researchers within a given discipline, while older professors view themselves as teachers and as members of a particular educational institution (Baldwin and Blackburn, 1981). Finally, opinion surveys suggest that academicians believe that the relative emphasis in graduate programs has shifted in recent years toward scholarly productivity and away from teaching, so that assistant professors are expected to be strong scholars, and at least adequate teachers. These findings provide the accepted knowledge base from which researchers have attempted to develop three general theoretical frameworks (Lawrence and Blackburn, 1985).

Developmental models (e.g., Hodgkinson, 1974) assert that changes in professors' productivity and values over time are the result of natural psychosocial aging processes. Some of these changes, notably the decline in research productivity, are assumed to result from the self-appraisal that accompanies transition periods. For example, proponents of these models attribute older professors' decline in scholarly activity as an outcome of the final resolution of developmental tasks that predominate during the age 40 transition. At about this age, according to these models, professors may pause to re-evaluate their careers and take steps to assure that their professional lives have integrity and wholeness. They move away from research and toward an emphasis on teaching and service. Many who have not achieved their scholarly ideals begin to build support structures around new identities involving less research (Baldwin and Blackburn, 1981). Others may reorient toward teaching and service in order to achieve a more balanced set of roles, reflecting the desire to make a meaningful contribution to their institutions, perhaps because such a goal might be more readily attainable than a comparable research goal.

Cohort models emphasize the impact of socialization to the profession, discipline, and/or institution on apparently changing roles that professors adopt (Trow, 1977). Assuming that people are more responsive to socialization experiences early in their careers, differences in productivity and values are accounted for by cohort flows rather than aging effects. A group of professors completing graduate work and achieving tenure at roughly the same time comprise a demographic cohort with a common general set of values. The next academic generation will likewise share a common value orientation, so that observed differences in teaching, research, and service activities between cohorts may reflect underlying differences in socially-induced values rather than simple aging effects (Pfeffer, 1983). These models would explain reported differences between age groups in terms of the general shift toward scholarly endeavor in recent years, resulting in different values among successive academic generations of cohorts.

Historical models are less developed and explain proportionately less of the phenomena than do the other two models. Historical models attribute changes in faculty performance and values to general changes within society, often after some precipitating event (Lawrence and Blackburn, 1985). Thus, historical effects (e.g., the social movements of the 1960s) manifest themselves across all age groups or cohorts. Their effect is assumed to be the same across all groups, but may be differentially modified by intervening age or cohort group factors (Cutler and Bengston, 1974). Thus, these models would explain the recent increase in research exploring the status of women in higher education in terms of the general societal concern over equality for women. Demographic differences in the researchers who tend to address the question would be attributed to the differential effect of this societal concern on different cohorts of researchers.

Faculty Demography and Developmental Models

The current interest in faculty vitality (discussed in chapter 6) is largely driven by the concern that the continuing trends in faculty demographics might have adverse effects on the balanced development and growth of the academic disciplines. Several factors have contributed to what is called the "graying" of the professorate. Some of the more frequently cited are an oversupply of Ph.D.s, a declining or stable demand for higher education (Hansen, 1985), the recent increase in the mandatory retirement age in the United States, and tenure policies (AAUP, 1982). For whatever reasons, the average age of faculty is expected to continue increasing. In 1980, about 40 percent of tenured faculty in four-year institutions were between the ages of 36 and 45. The Carnegie Council on Policy Studies in Higher Education (1980) projects that, as this cohort of faculty ages, it will comprise about 45 percent of the faculty population by 1990, with little change well into the next decade.

The policy implication frequently drawn is that the aging faculty must be "developed," "vitalized," or at least refurbished periodically. Many of these developmental programs encourage faculty to continue to bear responsibility for those tasks that, according to the developmental models discussed earlier, would normally be passed on to younger colleagues if they were available. In general terms, educators are concerned that certain dimensions of faculty work (e.g., research productivity) will suffer because the faculty is not at the developmental stage that best matches the needed work (Reskin, 1985).

The potential effects of an aging faculty may not be as widespread or as well understood as the developmental models seem to suggest. The widely-reported empirical work on the relationships between faculty age and research productivity, for example, is overgeneralized and often seriously flawed (cf. Reskin, 1985). Much of this research aggregates data for very different disciplines and types of institutions. The declining or saddle-shaped career productivity pattern is a coarse aggregate of very diverse career productivity patterns that vary widely across disciplines (Bayer and Dutton, 1977), institutions, and individuals (Blackburn, Beyhmer, and Hall, 1978; Reskin, 1977; 1978). Most of the studies are cross-sectional comparisons of the recent productivity of different age groups at a single point in time. They do not assess the potentially confounding effects attributable to other differences in age cohorts that arise as they move through changing academic cultures.

ACCOUNTING EDUCATION RESEARCH

One recent study by Beard, Jacobs, and Hartgraves (1985) assessed the career publication productivity pattern of accounting faculty in the U.S. Using number of articles published as the measure of productivity, they examined the relationship between productivity and the time between the publication year of articles in a selected group of journals and the year in which the doctorate was received by the author. Their findings, though not cast in terms of the faculty development literature, provide some evidence that the declining career research productivity often reported in the education literature generalizes to accounting.

Several other studies have addressed various faculty development concerns. For example, Kyle and Williams (1972) used a mailed questionnaire to examine accounting department chairpersons' perceptions of the utility of CPA certification of faculty. In a similar vein, Raabe and Stevens (1985) examined the proportions of professionally certified faculty at various ranks and in different types of accounting programs.

These and other research efforts have been devoted to aspects of faculty development that, although certainly not unique to accounting, are not common to most academic disciplines. Recent changes in accreditation criteria for accounting programs required CPE for many professional accountants, and the extent of reliance of accounting programs on private support have prompted concern over the relationship between accounting educators and practitioners (Russell and Glezen, 1984). Accounting education researchers have responded to the changing environment on several fronts. Sedki and Petrello (1984) and Schwartz and Fogg (1985) surveyed faculty to assess the extent to which formal practitioner/faculty advisory boards are used by accounting programs, and to explore the benefits of such programs. Rouse, Davis, and Friedlob (1986) surveyed selected accounting departments concerning the AACSB's "relevant experience" accreditation requirement, while Gray, Cooper, and Cornick (1984) surveyed Fortune 500 executives' interest in accounting faculty residencies. Finally, Carver and King (1986) assessed practitioner's attitudes toward various dimensions of accounting education and educators.

RESEARCH OPPORTUNITIES IN ACCOUNTING EDUCATION

Given that the most fundamental faculty development issues have only begun to be addressed in the accounting education literature, several researchable topics are readily apparent. The faculty development strategies that are so numerous in the "professional" education journals should be empirically tested. Very little is known about the effectiveness of intervention strategies (e.g., sabbaticals, internships) intended to enhance faculty development. Indeed, most of the empirical work devoted to faculty development attempts to simply identify the more easily measured potential causes of changes in faculty productivity during their careers. Promotion, tenure attainment, and faculty relocation seem to be visible career events that might be associated with changes in productivity and developmental activity. Other questions that might prove to be useful researchable topics include evaluation of the policy implications arising from identified accounting faculty career patterns, and the factors that influence research productivity and other faculty activities throughout a faculty career.

THE STATUS OF WOMEN AND MINORITY FACULTY

EDUCATION RESEARCH FROM OTHER DISCIPLINES

Women

The changing social, economic, and political status of women has been a dominant force in this country for almost two decades, affecting virtually every aspect of our society. Much has been written in the popular press, government reports, and academic journals about women's progress toward equality, including many analyses of the current condition of women as faculty in higher education. These studies must be approached with caution, however. Perhaps more than any other recent change in our society, the movement toward equality for women has progressed dramatically. Any study of the "current" status of women, whether in higher education or any other profession, may very well be out of date before it is published. Fortunately, many studies of women in higher education have appropriately focused on assessing the extent of progress toward equality rather than simply describing the current situation.

At least in terms of the number seeking and holding academic positions, women have made significant gains in recent years. Hyer (1985) developed an index to measure change in faculty composition and other variables thought to be important in evaluating affirmative action compliance and applied it to doctorate-granting institutions for the period from 1971 through 1980. Although she found substantial variation across institutions, she reported a 52 percent increase in the number of women faculty, and a 26 percent increase in the ratio of female-to-male faculty during the ten-year period examined. Hyer also found a 110 percent increase in the number of female full professors and a 53 percent increase in the number of tenured women. Over roughly the same period, the number and proportion of women seeking Ph.D.s also increased dramatically (Roemer, 1983). Further, women have begun to move more rapidly into major administrative positions in academia. An analysis of early career paths of ACE Fellows (Green, 1984) revealed that women appointed from 1978 to 1983 have moved into administrative positions (Dean or above) as rapidly as men, and much more quickly than in previous years. Even so, few authors are willing to assert that women have achieved equality in academia. The evidence seems to indicate a strong trend toward continuing improvement, but the problems of discrimination against women are certainly not solved and perhaps not yet completely understood.

Although significant gains have been made in many academic disciplines' hiring practices (Cole, 1979), the picture still appears to be rather bleak with respect to other aspects of the careers of women academics. Several empirical studies have unequivocally demonstrated that women faculty do not fare as well as men in terms of salary, promotion, and tenure policies in higher education. Many authors refer to the "revolving door" phenomenon that women face in academia. Many more women than men Ph.D.s either leave academia or move from one institution to another, possibly in response to failure to achieve adequate salary levels, promotion, or tenure (Stapp, 1979).

In academic year 1977–78, the modal academic rank of men was full professor; for women, the model rank was assistant professor (Sandler, 1979). Even in relatively nontechnical disciplines where women have been represented for many years, they tend to be concentrated at lower ranks. Of those who earned Ph.D.s in history between 1975 and 1978, 27 percent of the men had achieved the rank of associate professor, while only nine percent of the women had been promoted by 1980 (Winkler, 1981). Similarly, a 1980–81 survey of graduate psychology departments revealed that women were proportionately more highly represented in lower academic ranks than men (Russo, Olmedo, Stapp, and Fulcher, 1981). Women Ph.D.s also appear to be over-represented in the ranks of the unemployed. Tuckman and Tuckman (1984), analyzing Ph.D. unemployment rates for selected years between 1973 and 1981, reported that about one-third of female Ph.D.s are unemployed at graduation, while 25 percent of comparable male Ph.D.s are unemployed.

Tenure and salary policies in higher education seem to affect women more adversely than men. In academic year 1980–81, 74 percent of higher education faculty were men, and 70 percent of them were tenured. In the same year, only 50 percent of women faculty were tenured (Menges and Exum, 1983). With respect to salary equity, the conclusion drawn in virtually every study is that men and women faculty with comparable qualifications do not earn comparable salaries. Women are paid less, whether the institution under study is a particular university, discipline, an entire state, or all of higher education. Although the relative difference between men's and women's salaries may be gradually declining, men were recently reported as earning, on average, six to 13 percent more than women in higher education (Koch, 1982).

Recently, researchers have begun to explore the disparities between men and women faculty in terms of the underlying possible causes of apparent discrimination. The distribution of women faculty across disciplines and types of educational institutions is different from that of men. Women tend to be more likely than men to be employed by institutions without graduate programs, where they face heavier teaching loads and less publication pressure. Women also are more highly concentrated in academic disciplines with an oversupply of Ph.D.s, earn their doctorates at a later age than men (Koch, 1982; Menges and Exum, 1983; Tuckman and Tuckman, 1984), and are more likely to serve as part-time faculty (Emmons, 1982). Very little is known about the reasons for these differences, yet these factors are obviously very important possible determinants of the observed disparities between men and women in studies that focus on salary, promotion, and tenure experiences.

A few recent studies probably indicate the future direction of research into the status of women in higher education and represent significant methodological advances in research in this area. These studies move beyond the presentation of descriptive statistics typical of most studies to the controlled search for causal factors (Koch, 1982). For example, Emmons (1982), performed a seven-year longitudinal study of the careers of a cohort of assistant professors in psychology. She pair-matched a sample of men with women accepting their first tenure-track academic appointments in 1971, controlling for the proportion holding Ph.D.s and recency of highest degree attainment. She found no differences in employment status, location, or academic rank seven years later. She also reported that women faculty were no more likely to be caught by the academic revolving door than men. Further, Emmons used regression analyses to predict unemployment, mobility, quality of the 1978 employing institution, and academic rank attained for her sample. Independent variables were sex, five educational characteristics, four 1971 employment characteristics, number of citations in the literature through 1975, and interaction terms created by cross-products of sex and the other predictor variables. The only significant interaction effect was sex by quality of the 1978 institution where the faculty were employed, indicating that women were associated with higher quality institutions than men. Emmons' model used a roughly temporal ordering of independent variables, so that interactions entered late in the equation (e.g., citations, for which there was a significant univariate difference between men and women) were less likely to reveal possible existing effects as significant. Even so, the author concluded that well-controlled research endeavors paint a more optimistic picture of the status of women than previous, methodologically weaker studies. Indeed, several authors have noted that the assessment of sexual equity issues should be addressed in terms of the complex set of factors that presumably influence salary, promotion, and tenure decisions (Koch, 1982; Over, 1985).

Minorities

Like the progress toward equal opportunity for women, the movement toward equality for minorities has profound moral and societal implications. Many aspects of the historical struggle for minority equality are similar to those of women, yet minorities face an additional constraint that is reflected both in their relative progress toward equality and the available literature documenting their changing status in higher education. Unlike women, minorities comprise, by definition, a much smaller segment of the general U.S. population. Due to the nature of long-lived social and economic barriers, many minorities have been drastically under-represented in academia at all levels. One result of minority under-representation among higher education faculties is an academic literature exploring minority faculty issues that is much smaller than that devoted to women faculty concerns. Moreover, the education literature is not comprehensive in its coverage of the diverse groups labelled "minorities." Although the nonempirical professional education literature is replete with analyses and admonitions concerning minority issues, the empirical literature focuses almost entirely on exploring the status of blacks in higher education.

Surveys conducted by academicians and various governmental agencies reveal that blacks and other minorities have made few significant gains in the academic marketplace in recent years. In 1958, about 200 blacks were teaching on a full-time basis in predominantly white institutions in this country. By 1976, black faculty still accounted for only 4.4 percent of all faculty at institutions of higher learning, even though blacks constituted about ten percent of the college student population. At the same time, other prominent minority groups (notably Hispanics and Asian-Americans) comprised three to four percent of faculty at U.S. colleges and universities (Menges and Exum, 1983). Thus, minority faculty gains in recent years have been less dramatic than many believe. Indeed, many educators assert that black progress toward adequate representation among faculties in higher education reached a plateau in the late 1970s (Billingsley, 1982).

Black faculty members also apparently face different salary, promotion, and tenure experiences than their white colleagues in higher education. Survey research conducted by academics and government agencies provides strong evidence that blacks are earning lower salaries than other faculty groups at the same academic rank and are less likely to achieve promotion to associate or full professor (Traynham and Green, 1977; DHEW,

1978; Menges and Exum, 1983). Even at predominantly black colleges and universities, blacks are proportionately under-represented at all ranks except instructor, with the degree of under-representation increasing with professorial rank (Billingsley, 1982). In 1976, 36 percent of black faculty were tenured, compared to 54 percent of white faculty in higher education (Menges and Exum, 1983).

The prospects of a resurgence of the past trend toward increasing black faculty employment are not encouraging. Black enrollments in graduate and professional programs of education have remained relatively static or declined slightly over the years since the mid-1970s. From 1976 to 1978, when blacks accounted for about 11.5 percent of the population, less than six percent of graduate students in the U.S. were black. Moreover, historically black colleges, few of which offer doctoral degrees, produce about 20 percent of the Master's degrees awarded to blacks (Lehner, 1980). Many educators argue that these students are less likely to pursue the doctorate and that they are also more likely to choose an academic career, often without further graduate work (Billingsley, 1982). Since 1977, only three to four percent of the Ph.D.s awarded each year have been earned by blacks.

Many authors and researchers have attempted to identify potential causes of the continuing stagnation of the movement toward black equality in higher education. Although hiring practices in academia have generally been shown to be equitable, problems arising from the unique situation of black academics are often cited as major concerns. The first, already mentioned, is the failure of doctoral programs to attract an appropriate number of qualified black candidates. Thus, the availability pool of black Ph.D.s is too small relative to the need. After the initial academic appointment, institutional and professional service requirements are often disproportionately heavy among black faculty members in predominantly white contexts. A black faculty presence on various internal committees (notably student and faculty recruiting and student advising) is viewed as a means of assuring that appropriate representation is achieved. Black visibility in an academic unit's interactions with external parties is also often encouraged by university administrations in order to demonstrate the desire for continued racial equalization. Further, many black educators assert that they have a moral obligation to the development of the black academic community, requiring a significant proportion of their resources and time. The result is often failure to achieve promotion and tenure due to low academic productivity (Scott, 1981; Billingsley, 1982).

Many authors note that the presentation of simple comparisons of black faculty with other faculty groups ignores several probable causes of existing differences in salary, promotion, and tenure experiences. Black Ph.D.s tend to be concentrated in the social sciences and education rather than in high-demand areas such as computer science, the physical sciences, and engineering. On average, blacks earn their doctorates at a later age than white Ph.D.s, so that their productive careers are shorter. The traditionally black colleges and universities typically offer lower faculty salaries, a heavier teaching load, and fewer available resources to their predominantly black faculties. Perhaps most importantly, too few blacks in academia hold the Ph.D. In 1977, only about one-third of black faculty held the doctorate, compared with 56 percent of white faculty, at predominantly black institutions (Billingsley, 1982).

RESEARCH OPPORTUNITIES IN ACCOUNTING EDUCATION

The status of women and minorities in accounting education has not been addressed in the accounting education literature. Given the recent strong influx of women and minorities into the accounting profession, accounting researchers should focus on determining the causes and cures of problems of equality for women and minority faculty. Studies of women and minority faculty in accounting education should examine the equity issues in light of the rapidity of recent changes and taking into account the important institutional and other background variables that may affect comparisons.

CONCLUSION

In this chapter, we view faculty as inputs into the educational process. Many education research issues that are important faculty concerns are discussed in chapter 6. Those addressed in this chapter include the following:

1. Faculty performance evaluation
2. Student evaluation of teaching
3. Research
4. Teaching
5. Faculty development
6. The status of women and minorities

For each of these concerns, several broad research topics were suggested. Clearly, these topics are related to each other in varying degrees, and much of the research in these different topical areas has a common thread. All of them, or at least major portions of each of them, are concerned with or dependent on some assessment of the achievement of valued outcomes of various faculty activities. Much research is devoted to assessing the utility of research productivity, the correlates/causes of effective teaching, and the definition of service activities. A limited amount of research into the effectiveness of various faculty development strategies has been reported, including several preliminary studies in accounting education. The literature devoted to the status of women and minorities is largely an assessment of the progress toward achievement of societal goals.

From an accounting education research perspective, numerous opportunities for research certainly exist, many of which are relatively unique to academic disciplines that support well-defined professions. In accounting, should teaching effectiveness be judged differently (e.g., is student professionalization a desired educational outcome?) than in other disciplines? How should research productivity be enhanced and evaluated in accounting programs, given various institutional goals and an orientation toward serving a well-defined profession? Is faculty service to the profession a more important component of faculty workload in accounting than in other academic disciplines? What is achieved by the various faculty development strategies employed in accounting, some of which induce faculty involvement in the practice of accounting? To what extent is accounting academia contributing to the achievement of racial and sexual equality, given the relatively high visibility of the accounting profession in the business community? These and many other questions offer research opportunities that may provide contributions to both accounting education and the broader general education literature, as well as to the accounting profession.

CHAPTER 4 BIBLIOGRAPHY

Abbott, R. D., and D. Perkins, "Reliability and Validity Evidence for Scales Measuring Dimensions of Student Ratings of Instruction," *Educational and Psychological Measurement* (Summer 1982), pp. 563–569.

Abrami, P. C., R. P. Perry, and L. Leventhal, "The Relationship Between Student Personality Characteristics, Teacher Ratings, and Student Achievement," *Journal of Educational Psychology* (1982), pp. 111–125.

Aleamoni, L. M., and M. Yimer, "An Investigation of the Relationship Between Colleague Rating, Student Rating, Research Productivity, and Academic Rank in Rating Instructional Effectiveness," *Journal of Educational Psychology* (June 1973), pp. 274–277.

American Association of University Professors, "Uncapping the Mandatory Retirement Age," *Academe: Bulletin of the AAUP* (Sep./Oct. 1982), pp. 14–18.

Andrews, W. T., and P. B. McKenzie, "Leading Accounting Departments Revisited," *The Accounting Review* (January 1978), pp. 135–138.

Baird, L. L., "Teaching Styles: An Exploratory Study of Dimensions and Effects," *Journal of Educational Psychology* (1973), pp. 15–21.

Baker, G. A., G. R. Boggs, and S. Putnam, "Ideal Environment Nurtures Excellence," *Community and Junior College Journal* (October 1983), pp. 27–29.

Baker, P. J., and M. Zey-Ferrell, "Local and Cosmopolitan Orientations of Faculty," *Teaching Sociology* (October 1984), pp. 82–106.

Baldwin, R., and R. Blackburn, "The Academic Career as a Developmental Process: Implications for Higher Education," *Journal of Higher Education* (1981), pp. 598–614.

Bausell, R. B., and C. R. Bausell, "Student Ratings and Various Instructional Variables From a Within-Instructor Perspective," *Research in Higher Education* (1979), pp. 167–187.

Bayer, A. E., and J. E. Dutton, "Career Age and Research/Professional Activities of Academic Scientists: Tests of Alternative Nonlinear Models and Some Implications for Higher Education Faculty Policies," *Journal of Higher Education* (1977), pp. 259–282.

Bazley, J. D., and L. A. Nikolai, "A Comparison of Published Accounting Research and Qualities of Accounting Faculty and Doctoral Programs," *The Accounting Review* (July 1975), pp. 605–610.

Beard, L. H., F. A. Jacobs, and A. L. Hartgraves, "Publications: A Valid Measure of Faculty Contribution?" *Journal of Accounting Education* (Fall 1985), pp. 155–161.

Benjamin, J. J., and V. C. Brenner, "Perceptions of Journal Quality," *The Accounting Review* (July 1974), pp. 360–362.

Bennett, S. K., "Student Perceptions Of and Expectations For Male and Female Instructors: Evidence Relating to the Question of Gender Bias in Teaching Evaluation," *Journal of Educational Psychology* (1982), pp. 170–179.

Billingsley, A., "Building Strong Faculties in Black Colleges." *The Journal of Negro Education* (Winter 1982), pp. 4–15.

Blackburn, R. T., and M. J. Clark, "An Assessment of Faculty Performance: Some Correlates Between Administrators, Colleagues, Students, and Self-Ratings," *Sociology of Education* (Spring 1975), pp. 242–256.

———, C. Behymer, and D. Hall, "Research Note: Correlates of Faculty Publications," *Sociology of Education* (April 1978), pp. 132–141.

Boice, R., and F. Jones, "Why Academicians Don't Write," *Journal of Higher Education* (September/October 1984), pp. 567–582.

Bolton, B., D. Bonge, and J. Marr, "Ratings of Instruction, Examination Performance, and Subsequent Enrollment in Psychology Courses," *Teaching of Psychology* (April 1979), pp. 82–85.

Borresen, H., "The Effects of Instructions and Item Content on Three Types of Ratings," *Educational and Psychological Measurement* (1967), pp. 855–862.

Braskamp, L. A., D. Caulley, and F. Costin, "Student Ratings and Instructor Self-Ratings and Their Relationship to Student Achievement," *American Educational Research Journal* (Summer 1979), pp. 295–306.

Bresler, J. B., "Teaching Effectiveness and Government Awards," *Science* (April 1968), pp. 164–167.
Bublitz, B., and R. Kee, "Measures of Research Productivity," *Issues in Accounting Education* (1984), pp. 39–60.
Campbell, D. K., J. Gaertner, and R. P. Vecchio, "Perceptions of Promotion and Tenure Criteria: A Survey of Accounting Educators," *Journal of Accounting Education* (Spring 1983), pp. 83–92.
Campbell, D. T., and J. C. Stanley, *Experimental and Quasi-Experimental Designs for Research* (Chicago: Rand McNally, 1963).
Cargile, B. R., and B. Bublitz, "Factors Contributing to Published Research by Accounting Faculties," *The Accounting Review* (January 1986), pp. 158–178.
Carnegie Commission on Higher Education, *A Classification of Institutions of Higher Education* (Berkeley, Calif.: Carnegie Commission on Higher Education, 1973).
Carnegie Council on Policy Studies in Higher Education, *Three Thousand Futures* (San Francisco: Jossey-Bass, 1980).
Carver, M. R., and T. E. King, "Attitudes of Accounting Practitioners Towards Accounting Faculty and Accounting Education," *Journal of Accounting Education* (Spring 1986), pp. 31–43.
Cashin, W. E., and B. M. Perrin, "Do College Teachers Who Voluntarily Have Courses Evaluated Receive Higher Student Ratings?" *Journal of Educational Psychology* (August 1983), pp. 595–602.
Centra, J. A., "Self-Ratings of College Teachers: A Comparison with Student Ratings," *Journal of Educational Measurement* (Winter 1973), pp. 287–295.
———, "Colleagues as Raters of Classroom Instruction," *Journal of Higher Education* (1975), pp. 327–337.
———, "The Influence of Different Directions on Student Ratings of Instruction," *Journal of Educational Measurement* (Winter 1976), pp. 277–282.
———, "How Universities Evaluate Faculty Performance: A Survey of Department Heads," GREG Research Report No. 75-5bR (Princeton, N.J.: Educational Testing Service, 1977).
———, "Determining Faculty Effectiveness" (San Francisco: Jossey-Bass, 1980).
Clemente, F., "Early Career Determinants of Research Productivity," *American Journal of Sociology* (September 1973), pp. 409–419.
Coe, R. K., and I. Weinstock, "Evaluating the Accounting Professor's Journal Publications," *Journal of Accounting Education* (Spring 1983), pp. 127–129.
Cohen, P. A., "Effectiveness of Student-Rating Feedback for Improving College Instruction: A Meta-Analysis of Findings," *Research in Higher Education* (1980), pp. 321–341.
———, "Validity of Student Ratings in Psychology Courses: A Research Synthesis," *Teaching of Psychology* (April 1982), pp. 78–82.
———, "Comment on a Selective Review of the Validity of Student Ratings of Teaching," *Journal of Higher Education* (July/August 1983), pp. 448–458.
Cole, J. R., *Fair Sciences: Women in the Scientific Community* (New York: Free Press, 1979).
———, "Women in Science," *American Scientist* (July/August 1981), pp. 385–91.
Cook, T. D., and D. T. Campbell, *Quasi-Experimentation: Design and Analysis Issues for Field Settings,* (Boston: Houghton Mifflin, 1979).
Costin, F., and E. Grush, "Personality Correlates of Teacher-Student Behavior in the College Classroom," *Journal of Educational Psychology* (1973), pp. 35–44.
Crisp, A. H., and H. Moldofsky, "A Psychosomatic Study of Writer's Cramp," *British Journal of Psychiatry* (December 1965), pp. 841–858.
Crowley, C. J., and D. E. Chubin, "The Occupational Structure of Science: A Log-Linear

Analysis of the Inter-Sectoral Mobility of American Sociologists," *Sociological Quarterly* (Spring 1976), pp. 197–217.

Cutler, N., and V. Bengston, "Age and Political Alienation: Maturation, Generation, and Period Effects," *The Annals of the American Academy of Political and Social Science* (1974), pp. 160–175.

Daly, J. A., and M. D. Miller, "The Empirical Development of an Instrument to Measure Writing Apprehension," *Research in the Teaching of English* (1975), pp. 242–249.

Dent, P. L., and D. J. Lewis, "The Relationship Between Teaching Effectiveness and Measures of Research Quality," *Educational Research Quarterly* (Fall 1976), pp. 3–16.

Department of Health, Education, and Welfare (DHEW), Office of Education, National Advisory Committee on Black Higher Education and Black Colleges and Universities, *Higher Education Equity: The Crisis of Appearance versus Reality* (Washington, D.C.: DHEW 1978).

Dorsel, T. N., "Conflicting Goals: A Dilemma for the Teacher-Researcher," *Teaching of Psychology* (February 1981), pp. 52–53.

Dowell, D. A., and J. A. Neal, "A Selective Review of the Validity of Student Ratings of Teaching," *Journal of Higher Education* (Jan./Feb. 1982), pp. 51–62.

Doyle, K. O., and L. I. Chrichton, "Student, Peer, and Self-Evaluations of College Instructors," *Journal of Educational Psychology* (1978), pp. 815–826.

Driscoll, L. A., and W. L. Goodwin, "The Effects of Varying Information About the Use and Disposition of Results on University Students' Evaluations of Faculty and Courses," *American Educational Research Journal* (1979), pp. 25–37.

Drucker, A. J., and H. H. Remmers, "Do Alumni and Students Differ in their Attitudes toward Instructors?" *Purdue University Studies in Higher Education* (1950), pp. 62–74.

Edwards, J. B., R. W. Ingram, and H. P. Sanders, "Developing Teaching Skills in Doctoral Programs: The Current Status and Perceived Needs," *The Accounting Review* (January 1981), pp. 144–157.

Elliott, D. N., "Characteristics and Relationships of Various Criteria of College and University Training," *Purdue University Studies in Higher Education* (1950), pp. 5–61.

Elmore, P. B., and J. T. Pohlman, "Effect of Teacher, Student, and Class Characteristics on the Evaluation of College Instructors," *Journal of Educational Psychology* (1978), pp. 187–192.

Emmons, C., "A Longitudinal Study of the Careers of a Cohort of Assistant Professors in Psychology," *American Psychologist* (November 1982), pp. 1228–1238.

Feldman, K. A., "Grades and College Students' Evaluations of Their Courses and Teachers," *Research in Higher Education* (1976), pp. 69–111.

———, "Consistency and Variability Among College Students in Rating Their Teachers and Courses: A Review and Analysis," *Research in Higher Education* (1977), 223–274.

———, "Course Characteristics and College Students' Ratings of Their Teachers: What We Know and What We Don't," *Research in Higher Education* (1978), pp. 199–242.

Fenker, R. M., "Teacher Evaluation at TCU: An Analysis of the Perceived Roles of Faculty by Students, Administrators, and Faculty," *The Evaluation of College Teaching*, R. I. Miller (New York: Jossey-Bass, 1974).

Ferber, M., and J. Huber, "Sex of Student and Instructor: A Study of Student Bias," *American Journal of Sociology* (1975), pp. 949–963.

Frey, P. W., "A Two-Dimensional Analysis of Student Ratings of Instruction," *Research in Higher Education* (1978), pp. 69–91.

Fulton, O. and M. Trow, "Research Activity in Higher Education," *Sociology of Education* (Winter 1974), pp. 29–73.

Glidden, L. M., "Confessions of an Experimental Psychologist: How I Tried to do Research in the Teaching of Psychology and Failed, and Did Not Try Again," *Teaching of Psychology* (October 1975), pp. 130–131.

Gordon, M., "Mathematics Presentation as a Function of Cognitive/Personality Variables," *Journal of Research in Mathematics Education* (May 1977), pp. 205–210.

Gould, J. D., "Experiments in Composing Letters: Some Facts, Some Myths, and Some Observations," *Cognitive Processes in Writing*, edited by L. W. Gress and E. R. Steinberg (Hillsdale, N.J.: Erlbaum, 1980).

Gray, O. R., W. D. Cooper, and M. F. Cornick, "A Survey of Fortune 500 Companies' Interests in Accounting Faculty Residencies," *Journal of Accounting Education* (Fall 1984), pp. 177–180.

Green, M. F., "Women and Minority ACE Fellows in the Ascent Toward Administrative Posts," *Education Record* (Summer 1984), pp. 46–49.

Haim, G., "Academic Ideologies and Styles of Research Among Academic Researchers," *Research in Higher Education* (1981), pp. 291–304.

Hanson, W. L., "Changing Demography of Faculty in Higher Education," *Faculty Vitality and Institutional Productivity*, eds. S. M. Clark and D. R. Lewis (New York: Teachers College Press, 1985), pp. 27–54.

Hargens, L. L. and W. O. Hagstrom, "Scientific Consensus and Academic Status Attainment Patterns," *Sociology of Education* (October 1982), pp. 183–196.

Harris, M. B., "The Effects of Sex, Sex-Stereotyped Descriptions, and Institutions on Evaluations of Teachers," *Sex Roles* (1976), pp. 15–21.

Harry, J., and N. S. Goldner, "The 'Null' Relationship Between Teaching and Research." *Sociology of Education*, 45 (Winter 1972), pp. 47–60.

Hasselback, J. R., *Accounting Faculty Directory*, (Prentice-Hall, 1976 through 1988).

Hayes, J. R., "Research, Teaching, and Faculty Fate," *Science* (1971), pp. 227–230.

Hesselbart, S., "Sex Role and Occupational Stereotypes: Three Studies of Impression Formation," *Sex Roles* (1977), pp. 409–422.

Hicks, R. A., "The Relationship Between Publishing and Teaching Effectiveness," *California Journal of Educational Research* (May 1974), pp. 140–146.

Hildebrand, M., R. C. Wilson, and E. R. Dienst, *Evaluating University Teaching* (Berkeley: Center for Research and Development in Higher Education, University of California, 1971).

Hodgkinson, H. L., "Adult Development: Implications for Faculty and Administrators," *Educational Record* (Fall 1974), pp. 263–274.

Hogan, T. P., "Similarity of Student Ratings Across Instructors, Courses, and Time," *Research in Higher Education* (1973), pp. 149–154.

Hooper, P. and J. Page, "Measuring Teaching Effectiveness by Student Evaluation," *Issues in Accounting Education* (Spring 1986), pp. 56–64.

Howard, G. S., and S. E. Maxwell, "Correlation Between Student Satisfaction and Grades: A Case of Mistaken Causation?" *Journal of Educational Psychology* (1980), pp. 810–820.

———, and ———, "Do Grades Contaminate Student Evaluations of Instruction?" *Research in Higher Education* (1982), pp. 175–189.

Hoyt, D. P., "Interrelationships Among Instructional Effectiveness, Publication Record, and Monetary Reward," *Research in Higher Education* (1974), pp. 81–88.

Hyer, P. B., "Assessing Progress in the Status of Women Faculty," *Research in Higher Education* (1985), pp. 169–184.

Isaacson, R. L., W. J. McKeachie, J. E. Milholland, Y. G. Lin, M. Hofeller, J. W. Baerwaldt, and K. Zinn, "Dimensions of Student Evaluations of Teaching," *Journal of Educational Psychology* (1964), pp. 344–351.

Jacobs, F. A., A. L. Hartgraves, and L. H. Beard, "Publication Productivity of Doctoral Alumni: A Time-Adjusted Model," *The Accounting Review* (January 1986), pp. 179–187.

Kaschak, E., "Sex Bias in Student Evaluations of College Professors," *Psychology of Women Quarterly* (Spring 1978), pp. 235–243.

Kasten, K. L., "Tenure and Merit Pay as Rewards for Research, Teaching, and Service at a Research University," *Journal of Higher Education* (July/August 1984), pp. 500–514.

Koch, J. V., "Salary Equity Issues in Higher Education: Where Do We Stand?" *AAHE Bulletin* (October 1982), pp. 7–14.

Kohlan, R. G., "A Comparison of Faculty Evaluations Early and Late in the Course," *Journal of Higher Education* (November 1973), pp. 587–595.

Kulik, J. A., and C. C. Kulik, "Student Ratings of Instruction," *Teaching of Psychology* (1974), pp. 51–57.

———, and W. J. McKeachie, "The Evaluation of Teachers in Higher Education," in F. N. Kerlinger (ed.), *Review of Research in Education* (Itasca, Illinois: F. E. Peacock, 1975).

Kyle, D. L., and J. R. Williams, "The Significance of the CPA Certificate for Accounting Professors," *Journal of Accountancy* (May 1972), pp. 85–87.

Ladd, E. C., and S. M. Lipset, *Final Report: Survey of the Social, Political, and Educational Perspectives of American College and University Faculty* (Storrs: University of Connecticut Press, 1978).

Lawrence, J. H., and R. T. Blackburn, "Faculty Careers: Maturation, Demographic, and Historical Effects," *Research in Higher Education* (1985), pp. 135–154.

Lehner, J. C., "A Losing Battle: The Decline in Black Participation in Graduate and Professional Education," National Advisory Committee on Black Higher Education and Black Colleges and Universities (Washington, D.C., 1980).

Levinson-Rose, J., and R. J. Menges, "Improving College Teaching: A Critical Review of Research," *Review of Educational Research* (Fall 1981), pp. 403–434.

Linn, R. L., J. A. Centra, and L. Tucker, "Between, Within, and Total Group Factor Analyses of Student Ratings of Instruction," *Multivariate Behavorial Research* (July 1975), pp. 277–288.

Linsky, A. S., and M. A. Straus, "Student Evaluations, Research Productivity, and Eminence of College Faculty," *Journal of Higher Education* (January/February 1975), pp. 89–102.

Long, J. S., "Productivity and Academic Position in the Scientific Career," *American Sociological Review* (1978), pp. 889–908.

Marsh, H. W., "The Influence of Student, Course, and Instructor Characteristics on Evaluations of University Teaching," *American Educational Research Journal* (Summer 1980a), pp. 219–237.

———, "Research on Students' Evaluations of Teaching Effectiveness," *Instructional Evaluation* (1980b), pp. 5–13.

———, "Factors Affecting Students' Evaluations of the Same Course Taught by the Same Instructor on Different Occasions," *American Educational Research Journal* (Winter 1982a), pp. 485–497.

———, "Validity of Students' Evaluations of College Teaching: A Multitrait-Multimethod Analysis," *Journal of Educational Psychology* (1982b), pp. 264–279.

———, "Students' Evaluations of University Teaching: Dimensionality, Reliability, Validity, Potential Biases, and Utility," *Journal of Educational Psychology* (1984), pp. 707–754.

———, and J. U. Overall, "The Relative Influence of Course Level, Course Type, and

Instructor on Students' Evaluations of College Teaching," *American Educational Research Journal* (Spring 1981), pp. 103–112.

———, ———, and S. P. Kesler, "Class Size, Students' Evaluations, and Instructional Effectiveness," *American Educational Research Journal* (1979), pp. 57–70.

———, ———, and ———, "Validity of Student Evaluations of Instructional Effectiveness: A Comparison of Faculty Self-Evaluations and Evaluations by Their Students," *Journal of Educational Psychology* (1979), pp. 140–160.

———, and J. E. Ware, Jr., "Effects of Expressiveness, Content Coverage, and Incentive on Multidimensional Student Rating Scales: New Interpretations of the Dr. Fox Effect," *Journal of Educational Psychology* (1982), pp. 126–134.

Maslow, A. H., and W. Zimmerman, "College Teaching Ability, Scholarly Activity, and Personality," *Journal of Educational Psychology* (1956), pp. 185–192.

Mathis, B. C., "Faculty Development," *Encyclopedia of Educational Research*, 5th edition, ed. by H. E. Mitzel (New York: The Free Press, 1982), pp. 646–655.

McKeachie, W. J., and D. Solomon, "Student Ratings of Instructors: A Validity Study," *Journal of Educational Research* (January 1958), pp. 379–382.

———, Y-G Lin, and C. N. Mendelson, "A Small Study Assessing Teacher Effectiveness: Does Learning Last?" *Contemporary Educational Psychology* (October 1978), pp. 352–357.

———, "Student Ratings of Faculty: A Reprise," *Academe* (October 1979), pp. 384–397.

Meier, R. A., and J. F. Feldhusen, "Another Look at Dr. Fox: Effect of Stated Purpose of Evaluation, Lecturer Expressiveness, and Density of Lecture Content on Student Ratings," *Journal of Educational Psychology* (1979), pp. 339–345.

Menges, R. J., "The New Reporters: Students Rate Instruction," in C. R. Pace (ed.), *Evaluating Learning and Teaching: New Directions for Higher Education, No. 4* (San Francisco: Jossey-Bass, 1973).

———, and W. H. Exum, "Barriers to the Progress of Women and Minority Faculty," *Journal of Higher Education* (March/April 1983), pp. 123–144.

Michalak, S. J., and R. J. Friedrich, "Research Productivity and Teaching Effectiveness at a Small Liberal Arts College," *Journal of Higher Education* (Nov./Dec. 1981), pp. 578–597.

Miron, M., "What Makes a Good Teacher," *Higher Education in Europe* (April/June 1983), pp. 45–53.

Mitman, A. L., "Teachers' Differential Behavior Toward Higher and Lower Achieving Students and Its Relation to Selected Teacher Characteristics," *Journal of Educational Psychology* (April 1985), pp. 149–161.

Morsch, J. E., G. G. Burgess, and P. N. Smith, "Student Achievement as a Measure of Instructor Effectiveness," *Journal of Educational Psychology* (1956), pp. 79–88.

Murray, H. G., "Low-inference Classroom Teaching Behaviors and Student Ratings of College Teaching Effectiveness," *Journal of Educational Psychology* (February 1983), pp. 138–149.

Nitzsche, J. C., "How to Save Your Career," *Change* (February 1978), pp. 40–43.

Over, A., "Early Career Patterns of Men and Women in British Universities," *Higher Education* (June 1985), pp. 321–331.

Overall, J. U., and H. W. Marsh, "Long-Term Stability of Students' Evaluations of Instruction: A Longitudinal Study," paper presented at 1978 Annual Meeting of the Association for Institutional Research (Houston: May 1978).

Pelz, D. C., and F. M. Andrews, *Scientists in Organization* (New York: Wiley, 1976).

Perry, R. P., P. C. Abrami, L. Leventhal, and J. Check, "Instructor Reputation: An Expectancy Relationship Involving Student Ratings and Achievement," *Journal of Educational Psychology* (1979), pp. 776–787.

Pfeffer, J., "Organizational Demography," in L. Cummings and B. Staw (eds.), *Research in Organizational Behavior* (Greenwich, CT: JAI Press, 1983).

Porcano, T. M., "An Empirical Analysis of Some Factors Affecting Student Performance," *Journal of Accounting Education* (Fall 1984), pp. 111–126.

Raabe, W. A., and W. P. Stevens, "Who is Educating Today's Accountants? Some Observations," *Journal of Accounting Education* (Fall 1985), pp. 147–154.

Rainer, T., *The New Diary* (Los Angeles: J. P. Tarcher, 1978).

Reskin, B. F., "Scientific Productivity and the Reward Structure of Science," *American Sociological Review* (June 1977), pp. 491–504.

———, "Scientific Productivity, Sex, and Location in the Institution of Science," *American Journal of Sociology* (March 1978), pp. 1235–1243.

———, "Aging and Productivity: Careers and Results," in *Faculty Vitality and Institutional Productivity*, eds. S. M. Clark and D. R. Lewis (New York: Teachers College Press, 1985), pp. 86–97.

Roemer, R., "Changing Patterns of Degree Selection Among Women: 1970–78," *Research in Higher Education* (1983), pp. 435–454.

Rossman, J. E., "Teaching, Publication, and Rewards at a Liberal Arts College," *Improving College and University Teaching* (Autumn 1976), pp. 238–240.

Rouse, R. W., and R. A. Shockley, "Setting Realistic Expectations for Publishing in Leading Accounting Research Journals," *Journal of Accounting Education* (Fall 1984), pp. 43–52.

———, J. R. Davis, and G. T. Friedlob, "The Relevant Experience Criterion for Accounting Accreditation by the AACSB—A Current Assessment," *Journal of Accounting Education* (Spring 1986), pp. 147–160.

Russell, K. A., and G. W. Glezen, "An Investigation of Certain Interactions Between Large CPA Firms and Accounting Educators," *Journal of Accounting Education* (Spring 1984), pp. 55–69.

Russo, N. F., E. L. Olmedo, J. Stapp, and R. Fulcher, "Women and Minorities in Psychology," *American Psychologist* (November 1981), pp. 1315–1363.

Salthouse, T. A., W. J. McKeachie, and Y. Lin, "An Experimental Investigation of Factors Affecting University Promotion Decisions," *Journal of Higher Education* (March/April 1978), pp. 177–183.

Sandler, B. R., "You've Come a Long Way, Maybe—Or Why It Still Hurts To Be a Woman in Labor," *Current Issues in Higher Education* (1979), pp. 11–14.

Schwartz, B. N., and S. L. Fogg, "Department of Accounting Advisory Board: A Method of Communicating with the Business and Professional Community," *Journal of Accounting Education* (Spring 1985), pp. 179–184.

Scott, R. R., "Black Faculty Productivity and Interpersonal Contacts," *Journal of Negro Education* (Summer 1981), pp. 224–236.

Sedki, S. S., and G. J. Petrello, "The Accounting Practitioners/Accounting Educators Dialogue," *Journal of Accounting Education* (Spring 1984), pp. 163–166.

Seiler, R. E., and D. A. Pearson, "Work Satisfaction Through Research—An Empirical Test," *Issues in Accounting Education* (Spring 1986), pp. 65–75.

Seldin, P., *Changing Practices in Faculty Evaluation* (San Francisco: Jossey-Bass, 1984).

Shavelson, R. J., and P. Stern, "Research on Teachers' Pedagogical Thoughts, Judgments, Decisions, and Behavior," *Review of Educational Research* (Winter 1981), pp. 455–498.

Siegfried, J. J., and K. J. White, "Teaching and Publishing as Determinants of Academic Salaries," *Journal of Economic Education* (March/April 1978), pp. 177–183.

Smith, D. G., "College Classroom Interactions and Critical Thinking," *Journal of Educational Psychology* (1977), pp. 180–190.

Stapp, J., "Minorities and Women: Caught in an Academic Revolving Door," *APA Monitor* (November 1979), p. 14.

Sullivan, A. M., and G. R. Skanes, "Validity of Student Evaluation of Teaching and the Characteristics of Successful Instructors," *Journal of Educational Psychology* (1974), pp. 584–590.

Tennant, K., and C. Lawrence, "Teaching Strategies: Effects on Student Evaluations of Teachers," *The Accounting Review* (October 1975), pp. 899–904.

Traynham, E. C., and G. Green, "Affirmative Action Programs and Salary Discrimination: A Case Study," *Negro Educational Review* (January 1977), pp. 36–41.

Trice, A. D., and S. Wood-Shuman, "Teacher Locus of Control and Choice Between Intrinsic or Extrinsic Motivational Techniques," *Educational Research Quarterly* (1984), pp. 11–13.

Trow, M., "Departments as Contexts for Teaching and Learning," in D. McHenry, et al. (eds.), *Academic Departments* (San Francisco: Jossey-Bass, 1977), pp. 12–13.

Tuckman, B. H., and H. P. Tuckman, "Unemployment Among Graduating Ph.D.s: Do Economic Conditions Matter?" *Research in Higher Education* (1984), pp. 385–398.

Tuckman, H. P., and R. P. Hagemann, "An Analysis of the Reward Structure in Two Disciplines," *Journal of Higher Education* (1976), pp. 447–464.

Voeks, V. W., "Publications and Teaching Effectiveness," *Journal of Higher Education* (April 1962), pp. 212–218.

Ware, J. E., and R. G. Williams, "A Reanalysis of the Dr. Fox Experiments," *Instructional Evaluation* (1980), pp. 15–18.

Weber, R. P., and W. C. Stevenson, "Evaluations of Accounting Journal and Departmental Quality," *The Accounting Review* (July 1981), pp. 596–612.

Windal, F. W., "Publishing for a Varied Public: An Empirical Study," *The Accounting Review* (July 1981), pp. 653–658.

Winkler, K. J., "Women Historians Have Greater Access to Some Jobs but Remain Concentrated in 'Underpaid Ranks,'" *Chronicle of Higher Education* (January 12, 1981), p. 8.

Wright, P., R. Whittington, and G. E. Whittenburg, "Student Ratings of Teaching Effectiveness: What the Research Reveals," *Journal of Accounting Education* (Fall 1984), pp. 5–30.

CHAPTER 5

Research Related to the Educational Process

The literature on the elements of the educational process occupies a central place in the body of educational research. Here scholars deal with the subjects of knowledge communication, learning, and evaluation. We have chosen to categorize this literature into four areas: testing and grading; teaching methods; learning; and contextual variables. Given the great volume of non-accounting research on these subjects, we necessarily have chosen to reference only literature which describes the important theoretical and empirical findings related to the educational process. Admittedly we have exercised much selectivity in choosing these references. As a result many important papers have necessarily been omitted, but we do believe that we have provided the reader with coverage of the major research issues. An overview of the topics covered in this chapter is shown in Figure 4.

TESTING AND GRADING

EDUCATION RESEARCH IN OTHER DISCIPLINES

The education literature on the subject of testing and grading spans more than 50 years and involves exploration of hundreds of topics. There are, however, a few very broad measurement issues that give the interested reader an entry into the literature on testing and grading. These issues are of enough significance to be of interest to any student of the educational process, but are not subjects with which most accounting researchers would likely be familiar. Accounting education journals contain a great many studies that are concerned with the effectiveness of various teaching methods. Much of this research describes the use of classroom examination scores as a dependent variable. The validity of such research hinges on the validity of the examinations used in the experiments, yet few, if any, authors give the subject of examination validity any experimental concern. Readers interested in an additional general reference on educational measurement may wish to refer to Thorndike (1971). A more recent and most readable treatment of the subject of testing and grading is Milton, Pollio, and Eison (1986).

The specific topics discussed here deal with two basic issues: test validity and test anxiety. The first issue can perhaps best be examined by asking the following questions: How can we assess the validity of an examination? Do the examinations we give assess the qualities we intend? The second issue, involving the psychological aspects of testing, is concerned with the extent to which anxiety either impedes or enhances examination performance.

Test Validity

Perhaps the broadest question that can be asked about a test is, what does it measure? The process of assessing the accuracy of a given examination's inferences or predictions is known as validation (Cronbach, 1971). The subject of validity can also be somewhat more broadly said to include other descriptive and explanatory interpretations of testing such as the psychological qualities of the examinee.

In order to give the concept of test validity greater operational meaning, the American Psychological Association (1966) distinguished between three types of validity. Cri-

FIGURE 4
THE EDUCATIONAL PROCESS

Testing and Grading
  Test validity
    Criterion validity
    Content validity
    Construct validity
  Test anxiety
  Timing of exams
  Question sequencing
  Exam strategy
  Grades and grading

Teaching Methods
  Computer-assisted instruction
  Personalized systems of instruction
  Effects of homework on learning
  Lecture method
  Other issues

Learning

Contextual Issues

---

terion or predictive validation compares test scores with direct observation or measurement of a quality or behavior predicted by the test score. Content validation is concerned with determining whether a test is a representative sample of the subject matter about which conclusions are to be drawn. Content validity may also be defined in terms of responses: do the subject's responses constitute a representative sample of the responses that the subject would make in an actual situation involving the area of interest to the examiner (Lennon, 1956)? Finally, construct validation is the process of determining what is meant by a given response. More explicitly, are the traits which a test purports to measure actually measured by the test?

Most educators would agree that exhaustive validation studies of day-to-day quizzes and periodic examinations are not practical activities. Other examinations, such as the ACT, GMAT, and CPA exams certainly ought to be subjected to a broad range of validation studies. In the interest of effective testing, however, the preparer of an examination should be aware of the underlying issues with which validation is concerned, even if formal validation of the examination is not anticipated.

Criterion validity. The question of interest in criterion validity is whether a test accurately measures achievement or mastery of a subject. Such an examination, almost by design, might yield restricted score distributions. The typical examination administered in principles of accounting would presumably contain an objective of measuring achievement in a criterion reference sense. But such a test would normally also have an objective of discriminating between students in terms of levels of achievement in a norm-referenced sense. This duality of objectives creates a problem in that high discrimination power on a test emphasizes aptitude and de-emphasizes achievement (Messick, 1975). Examinations can be designed to address the issues of criterion achievement and level of achievement simultaneously, although careful attention to the objectives of each type of assessment is required to design such tests properly. It is clear that both types of assessment are necessary in academic subjects.

A norm-referenced examination score indicates where (on a scale of 1 to 100) a particular subject scores in comparison to others who have taken a given examination. The test score by itself does not indicate what kind of concepts or abilities have been demonstrated by the examinee. Examples of such examinations are those used to measure aptitude for graduate study: the GRE and GMAT are essentially norm-referenced tests. Norm-referenced examinations also have a place in the classroom, perhaps, but norm-referenced assessment by itself omits evaluation of the learning process.

The concept of criterion-referenced testing was developed in the 1960s but has its roots in earlier work dealing with absolute versus relative standards of measurement. A recent and thorough treatment of this subject together with a complete literature review of the subject, is found in Berk (1984). Specifically, a criterion-referenced test is one that yields measurements which are interpretable in terms of specific performance standards. The domain of tasks or behaviors assessed by the test may be either ordered (ranked) or unordered. An example of a test which yields an assessment of an ordered domain is one in which the level of proficiency is specified, such as an "expert," "intermediate," or "novice" level. Criterion-referenced tests with unordered domains might predict the presence or absence of a given behavior or trait (Nitko, 1984).

Content validity. Although it is difficult to generalize about the nature of the examinations which accounting professors give in the classroom, it does seem reasonable to suggest that the principal validation issues underlying these exams are of a criterion validity nature. Hence a question of importance deals with content validity: do the questions on these examinations accurately sample the population of issues that the teacher chooses to sample? While the content validity of a given examination is largely a question of fact, the adequacy of content validity can be addressed more formally by comparing scores on test forms which have been independently constructed. Even where such a practice is not practical, the apparent utility of such a procedure suggests that instructors should test frequently in order to minimize the effect on overall grades which could result from an exam which lacked content validity. A question related to content validity is whether an examination measures achievement of an important educational objective. This question might be addressed by comparing the tasks on the examination with the educational objectives as stated by persons other than the preparers of the test.

Construct validity. The concept of construct validity is more closely associated with tests of a psychological nature which are designed to describe individuals rather than to evaluate their achievement or performance (Cronbach, 1971). However, Messick (1975) has argued that the validity of examinations cannot be judged on the basis of content or criterion considerations alone, but that the meaning of the examination scores must be evaluated in order to make decisions based on the score. For example, simply asking how much accounting a student knows is an almost ridiculous question, devoid of meaning. Yet such a result is precisely what a norm-referenced examination attempts to achieve. Complete assessment of a student's ability requires that the professor also evaluate the nature of the knowledge that a student has, and this evaluation requires that attention be focused on the learning process and not just on the outcome (test score) alone.

An examination with high construct validity is one in which the measure of the material learned is an accurate description of the nature of the subject's actual knowledge. Teachers of technical subjects are concerned with whether a student can accomplish prescribed tasks. A low score on a given examination tells the teacher that the student *did not* perform certain tasks. If the examination possesses adequate construct validity, we can also infer that the student *could not* perform those tasks. It must be emphasized that the processes of inferring presence or absence of underlying ability involve assessment of learning processes and are thus construct oriented conclusions involving a description of the student. In addition, it is just as important that a test score not measure an unintended construct. A question worded in a particular way or one which includes unfamiliar words may end up being more a test of vocabulary than of the underlying process (construct) which the professor sought to examine. Similar problems also arise for timed examinations. A timed examination may be affected greatly by the reading speed of the student, particularly when the time allowed is marginally adequate or inadequate. The resulting score might not then be a valid measure of the underlying processes which the test was designed to assess.

Test Anxiety

Test anxiety is a "form of self-preoccupation—characterized by self-awareness, self-doubt, and self-depreciation—that influences overt behavior. . . ." (Sarason and Stoops, 1978). Some research suggests that its severity is accentuated by the existence of student skill deficiencies (Russo, 1984; Culler and Holahan, 1980). A basic question of interest to educators is whether test anxiety will affect test performance. Extensive research has been conducted on this question. Early work in this area indicated that individual performance is either improved or worsened by test anxiety and that the direction of change depends on the particular anxiety response of the subject (Sarason, Mandler, and Craighill, 1952). Specifically, it was argued that individuals with anxiety responses which were defined as incompatible or debilitating would be adversely affected by the onset of anxiety. Students without such negative responses would enjoy improved performance.

Measures of anxiety are obtained using anxiety scales, of which a number have been developed. Sarason, Mandler, and Craighill's conclusions were based on research which used the Mandler-Sarason TAS anxiety scale (Mandler and Sarason, 1952), a unidimensional scale in which all responses are either debilitating or not debilitating. A typical question on such a scale asks respondents whether they worry before and during exams. Other questions deal with such responses as reaction to time pressure, level of preparation, or effects of previous grades. Scale measurements require respondents to indicate a range of responses typically based on a five-point scale.

Later research has refined the unidimensional measurement scale into a measurement of two aspects of achievement anxiety. One set of questions measures facilitating anxiety and another set of questions measures debilitating responses (Alpert and Haber, 1960). Should respondents score low on both measures, they could be considered to be unaffected by anxiety in either direction. Alpert and Haber constructed this scale in a way which minimizes the correlation between the facilitating and debilitating scales. Employing both scales, the authors were able to significantly improve the prediction of GPA over predictions using either scale alone. Subsequent research by Munz, Costello, and Korabik (1975) confirms these findings.

We would observe that these anxiety scales merely measure tendencies and could not necessarily be used to make precise predictions about the behavior of individual students. Even with the use of both facilitating and debilitating anxiety scales, the multiple correlation coefficients published by Alpert and Haber ranged from .32 to .54 for three different groups of male students.

More recent research confirms the influence of test anxiety in performance prediction but indicates that study habits, study organization, and test-taking skills are more strongly associated with academic performance than test anxiety (Brown and Nelson, 1983; Kirkland and Hollandsworth, 1979; Galassi, Frierson, and Sharer, 1981). It is important, however, that professors be aware of the existence of test anxiety in order to counsel students who may be affected by it.

A number of studies are concerned with treatment or counseling to reduce text anxiety or to conduct examinations in a manner which reduces it. Barger (1983) conducted a study in which students were given information about the types of questions to be asked. Performance of the experimental group was not observed to be superior to that of a control group, although anxiety was reduced. Reductions in anxiety have also been observed in research into the effectiveness of open-book exams (Francis, 1982). Work by Fulkerson and Martin (1981) indicates that more frequent testing may reduce anxiety while improving performance and student evaluations of instructors. Weinstein, et al. (1982) found that test anxiety had a profound impact on students using deep-level processing strategies but found no such impact where superficial level processing was employed.

Timing of Examinations

In a study of the effect of timing of final examinations on performance, McClain (1983a) found that students did better on exams that fall early in the final examination week as compared with later. Students of comparable ability in an introductory psychology class were assigned to four different examination times over a one-week period. Those receiving grades of A, B, and C all performed better when the final was taken during the first period as compared with the other times. All subjects took the same exam but were not told the exam would be identical. McClain suggests that fatigue and increased anticipation of vacation contribute to the poorer performance of the later groups. An additional potential explanation for these findings is misallocation of preparation time by students who delay studying for their later examinations.

Question Sequencing

Substantial research has been done attempting to determine whether arrangement of test items according to item difficulty affects test performance. Barcikowski and Olsen (1975) note that most previous research generally concludes that arrangement of test items according to difficulty does not affect performance. The purpose of this study was to test Helson's adaptation level theory, which suggests that subjects will perceive that items arranged in Hard-Medium-Easy (H-M-E) order are easier than items arranged in a Easy-Medium-Hard (E-M-H) order. The subjects were 85 students in three sections of Teaching Reading and Language Arts at Ohio University. Students were given the same tests, with 42 students given tests when the items were arranged E-M-H, and 43 students given tests with the items arranged H-M-E. The authors ran multivariate ANOVA on both the test scores and the perceptions of item difficulty. The findings were that subjects did perceive the test items to be easier when arranged H-M-E as compared with E-M-H. The scores of the two groups were not significantly different for five of six subtests, a finding which is consistent with the preponderance of the research on item ordering (Barcikowski and Olsen, 1975, p. 87).

Examination Strategy

McClain (1983b) employed a method akin to protocol analysis to study the strategies employed by introductory psychology students on multiple-choice tests. The subjects were required to verbalize their thoughts while taking a test, and these verbalizations were recorded for later use by the researcher. The subjects were selected from a group of volunteers on the basis of their grades on previous tests; thus, three groups of 20 students A, C, and F averages were selected. McClain found that A students used different strategies than did C or F students, whose strategies were very similar. The performance on this examination by the three groups was consistent with previous performance. The strategies employed by the A students were characterized by a more thorough consideration of the alternative answers to each question. For example, A students generally read all answer choices, whereas C and F students tended to frequently stop reading when they came to the answer which they believed was correct. Among the three groups, only A students anticipated answers frequently. In their verbalizations, A students critiqued incorrect alternatives far more frequently than did the other groups. McClain's study is subject to the limitations imposed by all protocol analysis studies. The method is somewhat subjective, because the subjects cannot verbalize all thought processes and may not put forth maximum effort to do so. At best, protocol analysis provides only a partial tracing of decision processes. In addition, the subjects in this study were volunteers, rendering generalization of the findings to other groups a fragile, if not altogether inappropriate, procedure.

Grades and Grading

Extensive research by Milton (Milton, Pollio, and Eison, 1986; Milton and Associates, 1978; Milton, 1972; Milton and Shoben, 1968) raises serious questions about the quality of classroom tests, about the predictive ability of grades, and about the role that the educational system assigns to grades in the educational process. For example, we have reviewed substantial literature on the prediction of achievement which indicates that high school and college grades are among the best predictors of undergraduate and graduate achievement. Warren (Milton, Pollio, and Eison, 1986, p. 14) observes that the median value of the correlation coefficients reported in studies predicting graduate grades from undergraduate GPA is approximately .3. Even more disconcerting is the existence of other research which finds very little relationship between college grades and post-college achievement in a variety of fields (Milton, Pollio, and Eison, 1986, p. 14). Since these studies employed grade-point averages as predictor variables, we should not really find the conclusions surprising. GPA is the result of averaging evaluations given by individual professors whose grading criteria are not related to the criteria of other instructors in any precise way. Furthermore, much research predicts very low long-run retention of material which is learned in a course and not subsequently reviewed or used. Finally, we can hardly expect to find highly similar grading criteria across institutions.

Some defense must be made of standardized tests, however. While the correlation between GRE or GMAT and graduate GPA may be low, this result may well be because the relationship between the two scores is nonlinear. As a result, standardized tests may serve very well as discriminators or reference points in deciding who will be admitted to a course of study. Indeed, that is their real purpose, and their utility for such decisions cannot be rejected on the basis of low correlation with subsequent GPA.

Added to these imperfections in the grading system is the problem of testing. As we note in the section of this chapter on learning, factors which affect student motivation have a profound affect on the way subjects are learned. Tests are clearly among the most important factors affecting motivation. For example, Milton, Pollio, and Eison (1986, p. 20) note that perhaps the two most frequently asked questions in any course are, "Will that be on the final?" and "Will the test be objective or essay?" They note that should the answer to the first question be no, learning often ceases, and if the answer to the second question is objective, students abandon the use of higher-order learning techniques in favor of rote memory efforts. An unfortunate truth is that many classroom tests are poorly prepared because they are not only ambiguous, but also because they overemphasize the use of simple recall and exclude testing of students' complex cognitive skills. While some simple recall questions are appropriate to test basic knowledge in a discipline, examinations should also assess the students' ability to use basic skills and knowledge in problem analysis.

A movement toward redressing these significant problems would include serious re-evaluation of the content and purpose of tests on the part of every professor and a reappraisal of the basic structure of the grading system to eliminate the artificial precision that it implies. Among the suggestions worthy of serious consideration are those of Milton, Pollio, and Eison (1986), who suggest that tests be placed in the service of the learning process, and that grading systems attempt only to identify the extraordinarily distinguished or unsatisfactory students. Regarding the concept of a GPA, they recommend that it simply be abolished. Such a step would preclude the use of this statistic in a variety of inappropriate ways, particularly that of screening applicants from opportunities in graduate programs and professional positions.

Many of the steps which might be taken to improve examinations are merely common sense. These steps include such procedures as peer review of examinations with the objective of eliminating ambiguous language and assuring that the examinations test higher-order learning processes. In addition, much more emphasis should be placed on providing quality feedback to students. This feedback should include subsequent discussion of test results as well as written comments by the instructor on individual papers.

ACCOUNTING EDUCATION RESEARCH

Recent accounting literature on the subject of testing and grading has concentrated on the subject of test construction. Articles have appeared which deal with the subject of test validity and reliability, and there are even more specific studies of various questions related to test construction.

Test Validity

The increasing use of multiple-choice questions on college accounting examinations as well as on the CPA examination indicates a need to measure the validity and reliability of these types of examinations as compared with ones which are primarily of a problem nature. Collier and Mehrens (1985) relate the concepts of reliability and validity to multiple-choice (MC) examinations for accounting students and provide the reader with guidance in the construction of MC examinations. The authors believe that proper use of MC examinations increases reliability and validity of all types of accounting examinations, including the CPA exam.

An empirical study by Frakes and Lathen (1985) lends credibility to the validity of MC examinations and also points out some potential limitations of both MC and problem (PR) examinations. This study was conducted on two sections of introductory accounting taught at Washington State University. Every section was given three examinations, each designed to test the same material in both MC and PR format. The authors had intended also to test for effects of question ordering but abandoned that attempt when the second examination had to be deleted from the study because students did not have time to finish it. The second test was the only one of three in which MC questions were sequenced last on the exam. Tests on the data from the remaining two examinations show no significant differences in the mean test scores of the MC items as compared with the PR items. In addition, the rankings of the students' scores on the MC examinations were strongly associated with the rankings from the PR examinations. The data do indicate, however, a greater variability in the problem grades, and if grades had been based on either set of data alone, some rank shifts would have occurred as compared with the other data set. This study provides some support for the use of carefully written MC items, but it must be emphasized that these papers do not establish the validity of MC examinations for assessing all important learning outcomes. The almost universal use of problem exams and essay questions in accounting classes is evidence of the support these approaches have among accounting educators. The research we have reviewed in the section of this chapter on learning strongly suggests that the CPA examination MC questions have a dismal record of assessing higher order cognitive skills.

Test Anxiety

Given the intensity of the examination environment in quantitative courses such as accounting, it is surprising that the subject of test anxiety has not been more thoroughly studied. A recent paper by Wright (1986) investigates the impact of an available prior examinations policy (APEP) on test anxiety, student evaluations (SET), and performance. Wright's study indicates that an APEP positively affects SET scores, lowers test anxiety, and increases perceived learning by the students, but the actual performance of the APEP group was not significantly different from the non-APEP group.

Question Sequencing

Paretta and Chadwick (1975) conducted an experiment on elementary accounting students consisting of a fully-crossed 3×3 ANOVA of question sequence and student ability. Questions were sequenced difficult at end, random, and difficult at beginning. Subjects were partitioned into above-average, average, and below-average by academic record. The results were based on a single final exam given to 306 students. All questions were multiple choice. The authors found that question sequencing affects only average students. They believe that below-average students are unaffected by sequencing because they lack the sensitivity to distinguish between difficult and easy questions, and above-average students find all questions relatively easy. Students with average ability did substantially poorer on examinations with difficult questions at the beginning than where sequencing was random or where difficult questions were placed at the end of the examination.

A more recent paper by Howe and Baldwin (1983) reports the results of a test of the effects of item sequencing on 499 students in introductory accounting over three interim examinations and a final examination. The exams were composed of a combination of conceptual and problem-type examinations. In addition, an attitudinal questionnaire which elicited responses about accounting, the instructor, and the course was administered at the end of the course. There were ten class sections and five instructors involved in the study. Sequencing of questions on the examinations was arranged three ways—hard to easy, easy to hard, and random. The data were analyzed using ANCOVA, with a diagnostic skills test administered during the first week of class as the covariate. No significant association between examination scores and question sequencing was found, nor did there appear to be an association between question sequencing and withdrawal behavior. A less positive attitude toward the class was associated with the random sequencing group, however.

The study implies that question sequencing is not a factor which affects performance, a finding which is consistent, in the authors' views, with most educational measurement research. This conclusion differs from the findings of Paretta and Chadwick (1975). A possible explanation posed by Howe and Baldwin is that Paretta and Chadwick based their findings on a single examination and are thus limited in scope. It might also be possible that the covariate used by Howe and Baldwin was not effective in controlling for the effects of student ability on the variable of interest. Their results might have been different had they been able to obtain GPA data and conducted their analysis using a nested ANOVA, as was done in a later paper (Baldwin and Howard, 1983).

This final paper (Baldwin and Howard, 1983) shows that topical sequencing, the arrangement of the order in which topics are covered, can have an effect on grades attained. Baldwin and Howard conducted an experiment on an introductory accounting class and a tax class. Subjects in the classes were tested using either an ordered sequence of questions (questions ordered by chapter and within the chapter) or a scrambled sequence (no systematic ordering either within chapters or between chapters). Grade-point average of subjects was nested in each class, giving the experiment a 6×2 design. ANOVA was conducted on "time to complete the exam" and "exam scores." Baldwin and Howard found no significant effects for time to complete, perhaps because most students used the full time anyway. The main effect of sequencing, however, was significant for examination scores. In addition, the student quality/sequencing interaction was also significant.

The data indicate that for both classes, high GPA students perform relatively poorer on the randomly-sequenced examination as compared with ordered exams than do either the medium or low GPA group. The low GPA group actually did better on the random-sequenced exams. A plausible explanation for this finding is that good students are well prepared and learn the material in a sequenced manner, whereas more poorly prepared students who skim material are unaffected by question ordering. This research implies that scrambling questions to preclude cheating may penalize good students. The authors suggest that, for multiple-choice items, a compromise which avoids this potential penalty while still controlling cheating is to scramble the answers, but not the questions themselves.

Computerized Testing

Burton, McKeown, and Shlosberg (1978) describe a system of administering examinations using an interactive computer system (ICS). The system described has the capacity to generate multiple-choice, journal entry, and computational type questions. The authors tested the system on 375 students over an entire term, some on line and others on paper. The study concludes that the ICS obtains results consistent with those which might be obtained through conventional means and that the ICS is efficient in terms of examination security and instructor time.

Grades and Grading

The extensive literature on grades and grading reviewed previously points to the conclusion that traditional measures of achievement cannot necessarily be used to make precise predictions of future salary, promotion, or career achievement. Recent accounting work confirms this inference for students entering the CPA profession. Ferris (1982) finds that these traditional measures have little or no ability to predict subsequent achievement. In a survey of staff accountants at a single large accounting firm, Ferris found that possession of an advanced degree had a temporary impact on salary but that later performance was not related to level of achievement, quality of instruction, or level of attainment.

RESEARCH OPPORTUNITIES IN ACCOUNTING EDUCATION

The subjects of testing and grading have been barely scratched in accounting literature. Two major areas of testing offer potential for needed research—classroom testing and professional examinations. Experiments are needed which deal with the cognitive processes inherent in solving accounting problems. The subject of test anxiety on accounting examinations has apparently not been researched at all. Given the potential impact of test anxiety on individual performance, such research would be of immediate interest. Regarding professional examinations, studies which improve our understanding of the validity of these examinations are very much needed in spite of the fact that the sponsoring organizations may be actively engaged in studies of their own on this subject. Given the potential availability of performance data on the CPA examination from associations of State Boards of Accountancy, researchers should find it possible to design studies concerned with various aspects of the CPA examination.

TEACHING METHODS

EDUCATION RESEARCH IN OTHER DISCIPLINES

A traditional question asked about the subject of teaching methods addresses the issue of which teaching method is best. More recently, educational psychologists have begun to ask "Which method of instruction is best for whom?" (Snow and Peterson, 1980). The answer to this question must be formulated in terms of student aptitude. In addition to broad aptitude measures such as that implied by the ACT score, there are many finer measures of aptitude relevant to study of the learning process. The association between aptitude and teaching method is a phenomenon called aptitude-treatment interaction, or ATI. Substantial research demonstrates its existence (Cronbach and Snow, 1977; Snow, 1977 and 1978).

Snow and Peterson (1980) have outlined the principal research issues which refine our understanding of aptitude and teaching methods. Generally, high ability students tend to be more effective in unstructured environments, whereas low ability students improve their performance in more highly structured environments. As an example, high ability students seem to increase their achievement in a discussion environment, whereas the low ability student performs better in a lecture class. Similar findings resulted from research on the effectiveness of self-paced instruction, a method which is characterized by a high level of instructional control. Research shows that low ability students benefit from the self-paced environment. High ability students seem to fare equally well in self-paced classes as compared with traditional classes.

Other research into aspects of ATI is concerned with specific cognitive skills or psychological traits. Students with strong abstract reasoning ability (field independence) have been found to require less guidance in problem solving courses than field-dependent students. Students with good short-term memory are more effective notetakers than students without such talent and thus are better adapted to lecture environments. Students scoring high on the achievement via independence (Ai) scale of the California Psychological Inventory and low on the Achievement via Conformance (Ac) scale, performed best in a low-structure/high-participation environment. Conversely, students scoring high on Ac and low on Ai performed best in a high-structure/low-participation environment (Snow and Peterson, 1980). The existence of ATI implies that generalization about the effects of teaching strategies and methods are always tentative, because all students do not react in the same way to environmental changes. Evaluation of the discussion of teaching methods which follows must be tempered by an appreciation of the fact that ATI can confound research results.

A number of studies have been published on the effects of alternative methods of instruction on student achievement. Four teaching method issues seem particularly important in education research. These issues are personalized systems of instruction (PSI), computer-assisted instruction (CAI), homework, and the lecture method. The reason for inclusion of a review of the first two topics is that both have been extensively researched in a number of different disciplines, including accounting. The third issue, homework, seems particularly important because the practice of assigning it is so pervasive, particularly in undergraduate courses. The final issue, the lecture method, is included because of its often maligned status and its continuing preeminence, in spite of such criticism. Much of the research on PSI and CAI involves a research design whereby the performance of an experimental group of students is compared with a control group taught in a traditional lecture/discussion format. Most of the studies cited employ subjects from only a single institution and are confined to a single course. The measure of achievement selected as the dependent variable is almost exclusively the grade received in the course included in the experiment.

At the outset, it must be strongly emphasized that there is strong support for the idea that alternative teaching methods should not be tested from an achievement perspective—that without knowledge of the relationship between teaching and learning it is not possible to properly study the impact of teaching on achievement. After reviewing over 100 comparative studies of teaching methods, Dubin and Traveggia (1968, p. 45) concluded, "We have found no shred of evidence to indicate any basis for preferring one teaching method over another as measured by performance of students on course examinations." This reaction is echoed by Clark (1983) who concludes that "most current summaries and meta-analyses of media comparison studies clearly suggest that media do not influence learning under any conditions" (p. 443). Adherents to this point of view maintain that it is the content of a course, and not the media used to convey it, that affects learning. Other researchers are not convinced that innovative teaching methods are not superior to conventional methods. Dunkin's (1986) extensive literature review leads to the conclusion that alternative methods such as computer-based teaching, audio-tutorials, and programmed instruction are marginally superior to conventional instruction. Dunkin also argues that Keller plans, where students proceed at their own pace and are tested when they so request, are considerably superior to conventional instruction. Keller plans do not seem to reduce the achievement gap between lower- and higher-ability students, however, and tend to encourage a high drop-out rate (Snow and Peterson, 1980, p. 2).

To some extent, the superiority some researchers find in innovative teaching methods is a result of their newness, a factor which diminishes as time passes. Researchers must also control for curriculum effects which potentially affect the learning process. On balance, we are inclined to conclude that, as a minimum, innovative teaching methods are as good as conventional instruction in many circumstances. Teachers should be encouraged to use them to develop courses with the objective of increasing student interest and instructional efficiency. Finally, the test instruments used by the researcher must be constructed so that they are not biased toward a particular learning approach.

Computer-Assisted Instruction (CAI)

Perhaps the strongest case that can be made for CAI is its potential for improving the cost-effectiveness of instruction. Little research has appeared on this subject; however, a framework for the pursuit of such research is given by Dalgaard, Lewis, and Boyer (1984). They review other research which supports the use of CAI because it improves student attitudes and achievement. As with other innovative teaching methods, CAI has differing effectiveness across ability groups and personality types. Swartz, Davison, and Bonello (1980) argue that failure to disaggregate the subjects into distinguishable groups by ability may result in conclusions which erroneously report that the teaching innovation is ineffective. As a test of their hypothesis, they measured the effect of CAI on a population of 219 students disaggregated into quartiles. Independent variables in their regression analysis were a pretest on the Test of Understanding of College Economics (TUCE), combined SAT, grade-point average and high school grades, and computer time using CAI. The analysis indicated that CAI had markedly different ability to explain variation in the achievement level across ability groups.

Ellinger and Frankland (1976) conducted an experiment comparing test performance of two groups of introductory geography students. One group studied a module of material on the subject of spatial competition under a traditional lecture-discussion format, and the other group studied the same material using a computer game (case). Subjects were given pretests and post-tests simultaneously, and the amount of time devoted to the learning unit was the same for each group. T-tests for the differences in mean, mode, and median between pretest and post-test scores do not reject the hypothesis of no difference for any of the three measures for the experimental group as compared with the control group. There were significant increases in the total test scores for post-test, as compared with pretest indicating that learning did occur for both groups. The strength of this study is its use of pretests to control for differing student ability. However, the failure of the authors to stratify students into ability groups may have contributed to the finding no difference in learning between the experimental and control groups.

Wooley (1978) conducted an experiment designed to determine whether the type of feedback given in CAI affected the amount learned. Subjects were introductory astronomy students at Eastern Michigan University. Three CAI groups were established. Group I completed a CAI module designed to improve a student's knowledge of mathematical concepts used in introductory astronomy. These subjects received three items of feedback: (A) knowledge of results ("wrong if incorrect"), (B) knowledge of correct response, and (C) response contingent feedback (an explanation). Group II completed the same module but received only category (A) feedback. Group III completed a series of CAI questions presented by the modules. This group served as a control group for investigating improvement in math ability. Wooley employed ANCOVA with pretest as a covariate for Groups I and II and concluded that the type of feedback had no effect on the amount learned. Both Groups I and II had significantly higher post-test scores than did Group III, indicating that the CAI module was effective in imparting knowledge of the math concepts. His findings regarding feedback are inconsistent with some earlier research he cites. It should be noted that the subjects in this study and in the Ellinger and Frankland study above used computer equipment which is extraordinarily primitive when compared with modern personal computers. The extent to which their results would have been affected by employing the latest technology is, of course, unknown.

In conclusion, CAI offers the potential for cost-saving in certain kinds of instruction. The research on CAI to date indicates that it is at least as effective as traditional instruction in the areas where it has been tried, and student attitudes toward it have been positive. Finally, the use of CAI does aid in the development of computer literacy, and that in itself is a positive accomplishment.

Personalized Systems of Instruction

Research on the subject of personalized systems of instruction (PSI) generally favors the technique over the lecture/discussion approach when group means are used to measure achievement. It should be reiterated, however, that PSI and other nontraditional teaching methods may be of greater benefit to some ability groups than to others. PSI instruction also invites a problem of student procrastination. One paper in the accounting literature (Crosby, 1984) finds a higher withdrawal rate for a PSI class than for a control group in a lecture discussion class. To some extent, PSI and CAI are related in that computers can be used to implement the PSI approach. Thus, research which demonstrates the effectiveness of PSI might also be said to support CAI when it is employed in a PSI format. A final cautionary note relates to the choice of experimental subjects. Virtually all PSI experiments reported in the literature are conducted in survey courses. Different findings potentially exist for upper division classes where students are more homogeneous regarding their majors and interests.

The potential for more cost-effectiveness of nontraditional teaching methods was tested by Fisher, Guenther, and MacWhinney (1977). The subjects in this study were 623 upper division genetics students at three different campuses of the University of California. All subjects were science majors. The authors attempted to control for a number of subject demographic, socioeconomic, and background variables. They conclude that the results provide strong evidence that the video-autotutorial approach is more effective for large group science instruction. This conclusion is based on the finding that the experimental group did significantly better than the control group on the post-test at every ability level. Other experiments involving survey courses in science at other universities reach virtually identical conclusions regarding the effectiveness of PSI (Hedges, 1978; Coombs, 1978).

A similar experiment in principles of economics courses at Western Illinois produced positive results for the achievement of the experimental group. The course used a variety of media, including video tapes, textbooks, programmed text materials, and small group discussions. The computer was used to make testing of the self-paced mode effective. Students were tested at the computer terminal from a bank of questions and given immediate feedback with explanations on missed questions and objectives. The researchers controlled for ACT scores and grade point average of the subjects. Statistical comparison of the two groups led the authors to conclude that the experimental group learned as much, retained more, made better grades, and enjoyed the course more than did the control group (Marlin and Niss, 1982).

Knight, Williams, and Jardon (1975) conducted an experiment on students in introductory psychology that was designed to determine whether programmed student achievement (PA) procedures would increase examination performance. PA procedure required students to retake weekly quizzes until all questions were answered correctly. Two PA groups were established. PA-F students were given three attempts at the weekly quizzes and would receive an F in the course if they did not receive a perfect score by the third try. PA-P students would lose one letter grade for failing to receive a perfect score by the third attempt. A third control group took the weekly quizzes but was not subject to PA procedures. All three groups were also given two major exams during the semester and those examinations were not subject to PA procedures. The quizzes counted 50 percent of the final grade, with only the first score counted for each group. The major examinations comprised the remaining 50 percent of the final grade. Employing one-way ANOVA, the authors found significant differences between the two PA groups and the control group for both weekly quizzes and major examination scores. The two PA group scores were not significantly different. The effects of the PA contingency did not generalize to the other courses the students in the experimental groups took.

Vredeveld (1982) notes that the use of programmed instruction (PI) was touted as the wave of the future in economic education in the late 1960s, but that the approach has not caught on and interest in the subject has declined considerably. He reviews a substantial amount of literature which concludes that PI is either as effective as or more effective than traditional teaching methods. He notes further that the limited number of studies available indicate that properly conducted PI courses take less instructor and student time than traditional methods.

Vredeveld believes that the failure of PI to become more widely used is a result of several factors. Faculty members have no incentive to reduce the time a student spends on a class and thus basically treat student time as a free good. In addition, faculty would rather use traditional methods and teach small classes rather than teach larger classes with PI methods because the former are more satisfying personally. Finally, the faculty reward system is not based on student performance, and there is no incentive to increase the amount learned and retained by using PI techniques.

The most visible limitation of PSI, self-paced courses is the problem of student procrastination. Students without the self-discipline required to proceed through a self-paced course often fail to complete the course or withdraw. Wesp and Ford (1982) conducted an experiment where pacing was varied. The subjects were 182 students in three introductory psychology classes. Approximately one-third of the students were required to complete one core unit per week. Another one-third were required to complete three core units every three weeks. The final one-third were only required to complete 12 units by the end of the twelfth week. The authors found that the middle, moderately-paced group performed at a higher level than did either of the other two groups. They conclude that some degree of pacing increases the performance of PSI classes, but that some flexibility must be allowed.

Effects of Homework on Learning

A topic of particular interest to many accounting teachers is the effect of homework assignment and collection practices on learning. Research on this topic seems to indicate that the important issue related to homework is not whether or not it is collected, but is, rather, the promptness and effectiveness of feedback. Students in mathematics classes who were allowed to ask questions on homework before it was collected made higher scores than did another class where questions were not permitted until homework was returned (Austin, 1980). The two groups were given common exams and were taught by the same instructor, who made an effort to control for problems assigned and discussed.

When feedback is not a variable, the collection of homework does not seem to improve performance. Milligan and Reid (1973) compared the performance of two sections of a mechanical engineering class at the University of Tennessee in which the students in one section were required to turn in homework and the students in the other section were not. After collecting the homework, the instructor worked the problems on the board. However, he did not work the problems in the section in which no problems were collected. A comparison of test scores on identical departmental examinations revealed that the students in the section in which no homework was collected performed substantially better than the other group. Similar findings for industrial engineering students are also reported by Stephens (1977). Neither Milligan and Reid nor Stephens made any effort to control for background variables—including GPA and the number of majors/non-majors in each section. Milligan and Reid also surveyed other students in the college on a number of homework related areas. Among their findings was that a requirement for students to put a solution on the board substantially increased the percentage of problems attempted before class.

Other research on the subject of homework reviewed by Wiebe (1982) indicates that achievement levels of college students are similar for homework and no-homework groups. In addition, no significant differences in performance have been observed between students tested frequently and those receiving infrequent tests. Wiebe constructed an experiment which examined the effects of homework and quizzes together. The subjects were students in six sections of a theory of arithmetic course at Arizona State University. Two treatments were assigned randomly—one to each of the six sections. Treatment 1 involved the collection of homework, unannounced weekly quizzes, and graded attendance, combined with periodic exams. Treatment 2 involved assigned homework which was reviewed but not collected, quizzes distributed as study guides, and grades based on periodic exams only. The subjects' math ability was controlled for through the use of a pretest. The findings were that there were no significant differences in the achievement levels of the treatment groups as measured by a post-test. In addition, an attitude questionnaire revealed no differences in attitude toward the course or toward mathematics in general. There were also no differences in the withdrawal rates between treatment groups. Significant differences were found in the attitude toward the treatments, however, with each group favoring the treatment to which they had been subjected.

The Lecture Method

The lecture method is sometimes popularly criticized as having been obsolete since the invention of the printing press. More recently the availability of computers and audio visual aids has provided critics of the lecture approach with new fuel. However, since the popularity of the lecture approach persists, this persistence must not be without reason.

McKeachie (1980) has evaluated the lecture method in light of the extensive research which has appeared on it as well as in terms of the cognitive processes that students employ while learning from lectures. It seems logical that lectures ought not to mimic the textbook. Books are superior to lectures because reading can proceed at the pace set by the student, and printed material is more accessible than a lecture. Ideally, the lecture should serve as a means of disseminating the most recent information about the subject, to summarize widely dispersed information, to adapt information to a particular audience, and to provide learning structures which help the students learn to read. Lectures may also act as important motivational stimuli to the students. Every student can probably recall a professor whose inspired lectures greatly affected his attitude toward and interest in a subject.

Research on the subject of note-taking indicates that the effect of note-taking on cognitive processes has implications for the organization of lectures. Students have a limited capacity to store information in active memory and need to be able to integrate the lecture into previously developed mental structures or frameworks in order to efficiently process it. It is therefore important that lectures be designed to allow time for mental processing by the use of redundancy and appropriate pauses where students can catch up on their notes (Hartly and Davis, 1978).

The appropriate organizational structure of a lecture is essentially a function of the nature of the subject matter. McKeachie lists several potential organizational structures including time sequence, cause to effect sequence, and problem to solution sequence. Some courses may require only one basic structure for all lectures, while others might best make use of several different structures. Equally important in determining the format and structure of a lecture is the background of the students and their expectations about the course.

Regardless of structure, all lectures should begin by challenging the students to learn specific topics about which they have a need to know. This procedure can be accomplished with a statement or list of objectives, or perhaps with prequestions. Such introductory material enables students to process the body of the lecture more efficiently. The essential feature of the main part of any good lecture is that it not be overly ambitious in terms of the amount of material to be covered, given the time allowed. If students are placed in an information overload situation, they are likely to gain little from the lecture. Another feature related to this very essential element is the need for a certain amount of redundancy. An analogy to reading shows how important redundancy is in a lecture. When students read, they are afforded the opportunity of reviewing and re-reading passages until they fully understand the material. Most students will certainly review and re-read to some degree when studying any rigorous academic topic. Since this important learning technique is not available to the student listening to a lecture, some redundancy and review should be built into the lecture itself. Finally, a lecture should conclude with a review and recapitulation of the major points covered. Perhaps the singlemost consistent failure of college professors is not taking the time to include a well stated conclusion in their lecture. Research on the effectiveness of lectures as compared with discussions, peer teaching, and team teaching does not indicate that one is strongly more appropriate than another for any particular topic. Extensive research reviews conducted over several decades have suggested a slight preference for discussion over lecture where the course seeks to require students to employ complex cognitive skills (Dunkin, 1986).

Closely related to the lecture is the subject of notetaking. Extensively studied, research on notetaking deals with its effect on learning, the nature of effective notes, and the role of notes in studying. In general, the processes of reviewing notes seem to have a greater effect on learning than the mere act of taking notes. Given that notes appear to be useful in studying, students who take them can be expected to improve their performances as a result. Evidence also indicates that notes taken by students are better learning facilitators than canned notes provided by the instructor. Other research has addressed the subject of when notes should be taken (during or after lectures), the relationship between test mode, test interval, test performance, and notetaking, and the influence of the organizational structure of subject matter on notetaking (Carrier and Titus, 1979).

Other Teaching Method Issues

Wetzel, et al. (1982) employed regression analysis to determine if teaching and learning style affected achievement as measured by the TUCE (Test of Understanding of College Economics). The subjects were principles of economics students at Virginia Commonwealth University. Both students and instructors in the classes tested were asked to complete a questionnaire which determined the learning/teaching style which they preferred/used. The authors categorized learning/teaching styles into three basic groups: (1) dependent—a highly structured format centered on the lecture, (2) independent/unstructured, and (3) collaborative—where group projects are emphasized. Multiple regression analysis was then employed, with achievement as the dependent variable and the teaching style, learning styles, age, gender, and other student factors as the independent variables. The authors concluded that inclusion of the teaching/learning style variables greatly increased the power of the models to explain changes in achievement.

Some courses are offered in large lecture sections, with one hour a week devoted to small group discussion with a graduate assistant. Aamodt (1983) surveyed 180 students in general psychology classes to determine their preferences for type of discussion material. The results of the responses were stratified by achievement level, and very little response variation was observed. The study concludes that the most popular small group activities were discussions of lecture material and demonstrations of lecture material. The findings quite logically conclude that students wish to discuss material that is perceived to be relevant to test questions.

In an earlier paper, Aamodt (1982) examined the effect of review session attendance on students enrolled in a large general psychology course. Students were given the opportunity of attending an optional study session. Test scores were analyzed in a 3×2 ANOVA design stratifying the students by Wonderlic Personality Inventory (high, medium, low) score and attendance/nonattendance at the study session. The Wonderlic inventory measures abilities in math, vocabulary, and logic. Aamodt found that attendance at the study session improved the performance of the high- and middle-ability groups and that the high group students benefited more from attendance than did the middle group. Attendance at the study session did not appear to benefit the low-ability students. The paper does not provide concrete theoretical explanation for the results, although several potential explanations are proposed.

ACCOUNTING EDUCATION RESEARCH

While such topics as programmed instruction have received attention in accounting literature, the topic receiving the greatest current attention is computer-assisted instruction. Virtually all of this work has been descriptive, consisting of papers which explain how computers can be used in teaching accounting. Little published work exists which tests the effectiveness of the new computer-assisted techniques. Even if it is assumed that computer-assisted instruction is appropriate in accounting, research is still needed to determine how to proceed with further developments and whether currently used practices are effective.

Effectiveness of CAI

A study of the effectiveness of CAI in elementary accounting was conducted by McKeown (1976). The subjects were enrolled in four sections of elementary accounting at the University of Illinois. Two instructors were involved, with each teaching one experimental group and one control group section. The experimental sections were taught using the PLATO tutorial system. The control group was taught in a conventional manner. Each group was given three interim examinations and a comprehensive final. McKeown employed ANOVA to measure statistical differences in the examination scores of the two groups. While there were no differences in the interim examination scores, the experimental group did significantly better on the final than did the control group. McKeown also observed that the experimental group spent less time on the course and completed more of the assignments than did the control group. A similar study by Groomer (1981) found that students using PLATO for out-of-class assistance performed better than a control group using graduate student tutors. In a study of Intermediate II students, Freidman (1981) found that students who used the computer as a problem solving tool outside of class performed better on the AICPA Level II examination than did a control group.

In an earlier paper Streuling and Holstrum (1972) tested the effectiveness of audio-visual equipment in teaching introductory material on capital gains. While this study did not use computers, the experiment could have been conducted using microcomputers, had they been available. The authors compared the performance of students in the experimental group with a control group taught by the same instructors. Three full time professors at the University of Texas participated in the study. Performance on two post-tests were analyzed, using analysis of covariance with GPA as the covariate. The results were mixed. The control group did better on the first post-test, and the experimental group did better on the second. The authors offer several potential explanations for their findings, including the possibility that the use of the audio-visual approach causes the students to retain knowledge gained for a longer period of time. None of these studies stratified the participants by ability level; thus the extent of aptitude ability interaction is unknown. Also, given the relatively short time periods covered by the experiments, the effects of the newness of the teaching methods is also unknown.

Research which does address the subject of ability group differences has noted that the performance of weaker students tends to improve more than that of the average student. Fetters, McKenzie, and Callaghan (1986) tested the effects on performance of intermediate accounting students who were assigned computer cases on the topics of price-level accounting and leasing. The performance of these students was compared with a control group who were assigned CPA exam questions on the same subjects and did not use the computer. The authors found some enhancement of performance in the experimental group, particularly among weaker students, and no detrimental effects in terms of lack of understanding of concepts.

Dickens and Harper (1986) conducted an experiment in which four sections of intermediate accounting students solved problems with the aid of menu-driven BASIC computer programs. One-half of the students did an assignment on earnings per share, and one-half did an assignment on income tax allocation. Students were allowed to use the microcomputer only on one set of problems. Assignments to the two groups were random. No significant differences were observed in the achievement of the experimental groups as compared to the control group. Student ability was controlled for with a pre-test. There were also no significant differences attributed to differences in instructors. Attitude toward use of the computer by students was generally favorable. Another study comparing performance of students using manual vs. computerized practice sets found no differences in either performance or attitude between the two groups. The computer group did spend less time on the practice set (Alkafaji and Schroeder, 1986).

Descriptive Studies of CAI in Accounting Classes

A number of papers have been published in accounting journals which describe applications of computers in the classroom. These papers generally make no effort to empirically measure the differences between the approach described and conventional teaching methods, but are simply written to describe how the computer was used in a particular course. While such research may provide guidance in course design and organization, it does not address the important questions of cost effectiveness and student achievement.

Most descriptive research in computer use typically explains how a particular algorithm may be solved using the computer. These studies may also indicate some empirical evidence on student reaction to the computer exercise. Anderson (1976) describes a computer application in which students use the computer to perform a number of managerial accounting analyses including CPV analysis and profit forecasts. Based on student reaction, Anderson concludes that the exercise is a valuable experience for the students.

A similar study on the subject of computerized financial statement analysis was done by Throckmorton and Talbott (1978). A paper by Blocher and Robertson (1976) describes a computer-assisted approach to the teaching of Bayesian sampling in auditing classes.

More recent papers have dealt with more sophisticated exercises in the auditing and systems areas, as well as with microcomputers. Scheiner and Kiger (1983) developed a method of exposing students to generalized audit software in an auditing course. Specifically, students are required to complete a project using the Deloitte, Haskins, and Sells auditape. The authors conclude that the experience is useful for the students and is efficient in terms of computer time required and class hours consumed. A similar paper describing the use of the TREAT package was done by Vasarhelyi and Lin (1985). Chandler (1984) describes a course in accounting information systems which required students to participate in a group project involving the design and implementation of a computer-based accounting application for actual businesses. Chandler uses student evaluations in support of his conclusion that the projects constituted a valuable experience for the students. Thomas (1983) describes the use of microcomputer spreadsheets in the preparation and grading of complex financial accounting problems such as earnings per share and consolidations. He concludes that such an approach has substantial value and suggests applications in areas other than the specific cases which he used.

Additional studies address the general subject of the role of the microcomputer and the current trends in hardware and software acquisition by accounting programs. Romney (1983) provides an overall look at the role of the microcomputer in accounting education, together with a description of how microcomputers can be used in courses in systems, tax, auditing, and administration. Thomas (1984) has recently surveyed college and university accounting departments and reported on the ways that accounting programs are currently using microcomputers. This survey describes the programming languages required at the schools surveyed together with the types of software and CAI packages currently in use.

Izard and Reeve (1986) point out how a recent innovation, spreadsheet software, offers opportunity for expanded computer application in problem solving. These spreadsheets "have the advantage of relative ease and efficiency over other algorithmic approaches. . . ." (Izard and Reeve, p. 162). Other papers explaining potential spreadsheet applications include Thomas (1983), and Kalbers (1984). Research is needed to test the achievement effects of using these techniques in a variety of classroom settings.

Computer Integration

The increasing availability of microcomputers to accounting faculty and students has focused attention on integration of these machines into course work where computers have not traditionally been used. The research on CAI tends to indicate that integration of computers into such classes is likely to be well received from an attitude perspective, but is not likely to strongly impact achievement. Such a finding does not suggest that integration should not take place, however. At the very least, use of the microcomputer in classes will (1) give students needed hands on experience, (2) provide a base for faculty to study ways in which the computer might ultimately affect achievement, and (3) shift some of the laborious calculation work on accounting homework from the student to the computer and from the classroom to the computer lab. Two recent papers thoroughly discuss the issues of computer integration. A comprehensive framework for integration of the computer throughout the accounting curriculum was recently published by Armitage and Boritz (1986). This paper offers many useful suggestions on the process of computer integration. Another study by Helmi (1986) discusses computer integration in terms of the various ways the computer can be used in courses as well as listing pitfalls to avoid in the process.

A further potential change is the use of the computer as a teaching aid in place of the traditional chalkboard and overhead projector. Our review indicates that little, if any, published research has appeared on this subject; however, two recent papers are indicative of the kinds of research opportunities that exist.

Borthick and Clark (1987) conducted an experiment in which information systems students used word processing equipment to prepare written assignments on personal computers. The experimental group also used language analysis programs to test the quality of their syntax and writing structure. The control group did not use these programs. The authors controlled for a number of potentially confounding factors, including the number of hours worked on the assignments, grade-point averages, and student gender. The findings were that the experimental group exhibited improved performance as a result of using the language analysis system.

The microcomputer is more effective as a learning tool when it is used to solve integrative problems than when it is used to solve small problems which can easily be solved by other means. It should be emphasized, however, that teachers should not expect dramatic evidence of improved learning and performance from any single computer exercise. The beneficial effects of computer integration may be significant only after computer use is fully integrated into the accounting curriculum (Borthick and Clark, 1986).

Personalized Systems of Instruction

PSI courses in accounting appear to have become less fashionable in recent years. Some evidence indicates that these courses tend to experience high withdrawal rates and have no particularly consistent record of increasing student achievement. A paper by Crosby (1984) describes a method of using PSI at a community college to teach principles of accounting and presents data which compare the grades of PSI students with those of lecture section students. The PSI group experienced a substantially higher withdrawal rate than the lecture group in one of the two terms of the experiment. Moreover, a large number of PSI students received incompletes in both terms (39 percent and 32 percent, respectively) as compared with almost no incompletes (zero percent and three percent) for the lecture groups. It is also possible that personality may interact with performance in PSI instruction. In an experiment comparing self-study students with traditional lecture students in elementary accounting McNeill and Collins (1975) found that students scoring high on a personality scale for autonomy tended to perform very well in a self-study mode.

Two accounting studies are strongly positive on the PSI approach. Bailes (1979) conducted an experiment employing PSI in introductory managerial accounting. The experiment involved two instructors and four sections of elementary managerial accounting. Each instructor taught one section using PSI and another section using the traditional lecture method. Employing ANOVA and testing for a difference in final examination scores, Bailes found that the main effect of teaching method was significant. Bailes also asked students to state whether they would recommend the course to others. This question was asked at the beginning of the term and again at the end of the term. A chi square test was employed, and the responses of the PSI group were not significantly different for the two groups at the beginning of the term. However, at the end of the term, the PSI group had a significantly more favorable recommendation rate than did the lecture group. The responses to the second query are potentially affected by differential withdrawal rates.

Liao (1978) constructed an experiment designed to evaluate the effectiveness of PSI in intermediate accounting classes. Students in two sections of intermediate accounting were enrolled in a self-paced section in which they were required to demonstrate competency in a module before they were allowed to continue to the next module. Liao used two intermediate sections taught in the previous year by the same instructor as a control group. Comparison of mean scores on AICPA achievement tests revealed that the PSI group had a significantly higher mean score as measured by a t-test. When the scores were stratified by GPA, students of average ability tended to perform better under the PSI approach, while the top students fared equally well under either mode. Poorer students tended to perform better and withdraw less frequently in the traditional lecture sections. A similar paper by Laughlin, Gentry, and May (1976) finds no measurable impact of the PSI approach but concludes that students' past performance, as measured by GPA, better predicted performance in the PSI setting than in the traditional setting.

Other research is less supportive of the PSI approach. Battista (1978) compared the performance of introductory students in self-paced instructional groups with conventional classes. There were four classes and two instructors involved in the experiment. Each instructor taught one experimental and one control-group class. The groups were compared using a combination of achievement questions testing both intellectual ability and knowledge. The results indicate that the students in the conventional class outperformed the self-paced group, and a test comparing performance based on locus of control (whether subjects were internally or externally oriented) indicated no significant differences attributable to that factor.

A few programmed textbooks in introductory accounting were published in years past, but the idea did not catch on. Markell and Pemberton (1972) conducted a two-semester experiment comparing introductory accounting classes using standard textbooks with classes using a programmed textbook. A comparison of grades in the two groups indicates that the programmed classes did as well as or better than the classes using the standard textbook. The comparisons made did not control for GPA, however. A second test correlating accounting grades with a predicted grade-point index weakly supports the conclusion that the programmed group performed at a higher level.

The Lecture Method

A question of interest is whether there are ways of improving upon the traditional lecture/discussion method other than completely abandoning it in favor of alternative formats such as PSI. Baldwin (1980) suggests that the positioning of daily quizzes has a potential effect on student achievement as measured by interim and final examinations. Baldwin employed ANCOVA to compare the performance of two sections of introductory students where each section was given 12 daily quizzes and four examinations. In one section the quizzes were "pre-quizzes" given before the lecture/discussion, and in the other section the quizzes were "post-quizzes." The covariate was GPA. The results indicate that the pre-quiz group performed significantly better than the post-quiz group. Students were also surveyed regarding the attitude toward the two formats, and no significant differences were observed.

Other Research on Teaching Methods

There have been a number of other research papers which discuss the use of cases, television instruction, internships, and other nontraditional approaches to teaching. Most of this work focuses on whether student attitudes were positive or negative toward the experience and whether student achievement as measured by examination scores was significantly different for the experimental group as compared with the control group. Virtually all of these studies are case studies using students in a particular course for one term at a single institution. A well designed study typically involves the use of several sections of a particular course, with each instructor involved teaching an equal number of experimental group and control group sections. Analysis of variance and analysis of covariance are commonly employed to identify significant differences in the attitudes and achievement of the two groups.

Existing research in these areas is published almost exclusively in the education section of *The Accounting Review*, with a few recent papers appearing in the *Journal of Accounting Education* and *Issues in Accounting Education*. Notable examples of these studies include (1) the use of business games/cases (DeCoster and Prater, 1973; Pointer and Ljungdahl, 1973); (2) the effectiveness of televised instruction (Snowball and Collins, 1980); (3) examination content (Edmonds, 1984; Pawliczek, 1977); (4) course format (Howell and Johnson, 1982; Benis, Brody, and Johnson, 1976; Stout and Bonfield, 1986); (5) internships (Goodman, 1983; Koehler, 1974); (6) textbook selection (Adelberg and Razek, 1984); (7) systems understanding aids (Arens and Ward, 1984); and (8) the effect of high school accounting courses on performance (Baldwin and Howe, 1982; Bergin, 1983; Schroeder, 1986).

RESEARCH OPPORTUNITIES IN ACCOUNTING EDUCATION

Opportunities for additional research on teaching methods appear to be ample, particularly in the area of microcomputer use. Many accounting programs have only recently had such equipment available for their students. Work which studies the impact on student achievement would be particularly timely, since previously published research has been largely devoted to describing how the microcomputer can be used in accounting courses. Of particular importance in the design of these experiments is the need for carefully selected experimental and control groups and for control of the effect of nuisance or background variables in the experiments. Another desirable attribute of the research is that achievement levels be stratified by ability groups, because outstanding students may be affected differently by the treatments tested than average or below-average students.

We wish to repeat the warning made at the beginning of this section on teaching methods that much evidence indicates that studies of teaching impact may not be discernible when course examination scores are used as the dependent variable of interest. An alternative research approach is that researchers investigate the links between teaching and learning and that we search for the commonalities between different teaching methods rather than for differences (Dubin and Traveggia, 1968). Finally, should the researcher choose the traditional approach of employing test scores as measures of achievement, much attention must be given to assure that the examinations used are capable of making the distinctions which are demanded of them. Virtually every paper on the subject of teaching impact reviewed here and elsewhere ignores this important consideration (Anderson, 1972, pp. 165–168). Another problem to which little attention has been paid relates to the teaching materials used in tests of alternative teaching methods. In many of the studies cited, particularly those related to CAI and PSI, the control and experimental groups used different text and reading materials. Given the significance of the textbook and related materials to the overall learning process, it is possible that virtually all of the measurable effects of alternative teaching methods are attributable to the differences in the reading materials, rather than to the mode of instruction. In many courses the textbook used has more to do with what the student learns than all other factors combined (Milton, 1972, p. 24).

LEARNING

EDUCATION RESEARCH IN OTHER DISCIPLINES

Early literature on the subject of learning appeared almost exclusively in articles written by experimental psychologists. These articles were frequently characterized by experiments in which subjects were required to perform some mundane learning activity which the experimenter then measured. The problem might have involved the memorization of nonsense syllables followed by attempts by the experimenter to measure memory decay—the rate at which subjects forgot what they had learned. The essential feature of this type of research is that it centered on the observation of an outcome, and not on the learning process itself. While such research was important, it did not involve study of processes associated with the classroom experience.

More recently, researchers have become interested in the learning process directly. This work is concerned with the motivational issues, learning styles or approaches, and learning processes. Since there are literally thousands of research studies related to questions about learning, this monograph must necessarily attempt to give the reader only an entry into the literature. Bransford (1979) provides a taxonomy of learning research and reviews a substantial number of papers related to all aspects of his taxonomy. Bransford divides questions about learning into four categories:

1. Characteristics of the learner (skills, knowledge, attitudes, etc.)
2. Criterial tasks (recognition, recall, transfer, problem solving, etc.)
3. Nature of the materials (modality, physical structure, psychological structure, conceptual difficulty, sequencing of materials, etc.)
4. Learning activities (attention, rehearsal, elaboration, etc.)

Bransford's book is essentially a systematic treatment of research on the above four types of questions and how they relate to each other.

There is at least one very basic issue which we believe should be discussed. This subject deals with student motivation and has a profound effect on the way in which college level subjects are learned. Marton (1976) asserts that the way in which instructional tasks are interpreted results in a conscious choice to learn in a particular way. The method of learning thus has an effect on the level of understanding achieved. Marton specifies two different types of motivational/process combinations as deep-level processing and surface processing. Even where (deep-level) understanding is clearly the desirable goal, subjects have been found to seek to attain the goal in different ways. Pask (1976) has specified two different learning styles emanating within deep-level processing. Some subjects attempted to develop, from the beginning, a broad view of the learning task which explains how the subject related to other topics. Pask calls this the *holist* strategy. The *serialist* strategy, conversely, involves an attempt to develop understanding from component details in a linear sequence. Pask believes that some students are predisposd to choose one or the other strategies, even where one of them may be clearly more appropriate than the other. Other subjects are able to discern which strategy will best serve their objectives and choose accordingly. Ultimately, deep-level comprehension is achieved only when both strategies are employed, because both an overview of a subject as well as its component processes must be understood. Pask notes that some students will fall short of this ideal using only one or the other strategy. Such an approach results in incomplete learning. Entwistle, Hanley, and Hounsell (1979) develop an inventory of the learning process which specifies the relationships between the principal motivational aspects, approaches, and processes of learning. The methodological approach is one of factor-analyzing the subjects' responses to queries about their study habits and intellectual orientation. They identify three motivational classes—understanding, reproducing, and achieving high grades, each of which may incorporate one or more of the various learning approaches and processes and result in either deep-level, incomplete, or surface-level understanding. Related research has also been done by Ramsden (1983), Biggs (1976, 1979), and O'Neil and Child (1984).

The other principal approach used involves a qualitative analysis of a subject's learning process. This technique centers around a variety of interview techniques including some experimental settings. Carefully done, these techniques offer the potential of giving extraordinarily precise descriptions of the learning process. Recent examples of this approach include Laurillard (1979) and Ramsden (1979).

ACCOUNTING EDUCATION RESEARCH

Some scholars have suggested that the work environment of professional accountants demands individuals with a high level of cognitive complexity, because that environment is very complex. Existing research indicates that individuals with a low level of cognitive complexity (low CL) do not perform well in unstructured environments. Individuals with high levels of cognitive complexity (high CL) perform equally well in structured and unstructured environments. An important question is, therefore, whether these theories related to cognitive complexity are relevant to accounting courses.

Amernic and Beechy (1984) conducted an experiment which employed the paragraph completion (PCT) test to introductory accounting students dichotomized into high CL and low CL groups. ANCOVA was then employed to assess their performances on three examinations, each of which contained one highly structured and one highly unstructured question. The covariate was GPA, which was marginally different for the high CL and low groups. The findings were that the high and low groups did equally well on the structured questions but the high group did substantially better on the unstructured questions. The authors conclude that the course content of introductory accounting should include unstructured material so as to be more attractive to high CL students, because those are the kinds of individuals who have the greatest potential for success in professional accounting.

Baldwin and Reckers (1984) administered the Kolb (Kolb, 1976) Learning Style Inventory (LSI) to introductory accounting students to test for differences in learning style by accounting students as compared to other business majors. The findings indicate that accounting and finance majors have more abstract learning styles than other business majors. Administration of the instrument to accounting majors and accounting faculty revealed that faculty are markedly more abstract learners than students. Baldwin and Reckers believe that the use of instruments such as the Kolb LSI may potentially be used as a counseling device, with the objective of improving accounting education. A later paper by Baker, Simon, and Bazeli (1986) confirms the finding related to students.

A paper by Baker and Simon (1985) offers damning evidence that the CPA exam does not test the ability of the candidate to use abstract reasoning and higher-level cognitive skills. Their research shows that on two recent CPA exams, more than 90 percent of the multiple-choice questions were at the concrete-operational level as opposed to the formal operational level, which calls upon abstract reasoning ability. On problem and essay questions the percentage of concrete-operational questions were approximately 80 percent.

Much psychological evidence indicates that persons under stress will resort to primitive or first-learned responses (Weick, 1983). In an experiment involving the learning of direct costing and absorption, Belkaoui (1975) confirmed the expected effects. In a later paper Belkaoui (1977) determined whether subjects were disposed to prefer one particular technique over another (ego involvement). He then required the subjects to solve an exercise using one of two techniques just learned. The paper concludes that the subjects will, under stress, tend to employ the technique which is "more dear or basic to them" (Belkaoui, 1977, p. 255).

RESEARCH OPPORTUNITIES IN ACCOUNTING EDUCATION

Accounting research is needed which deals with the way in which accounting subjects are learned and which explains the kinds of teaching/study methods that foster student knowledge retention. Educational research literature clearly shows that many factors affect learning and that simplistic explanations for achievement or failure are usually inadequate explanations for a particular case. In terms of Bransford's taxonomy, issues of particular interest to accountants include identification of cognitive skills which are associated with accounting aptitude and specification of the types of study habits which are consistent with success in accounting courses.

CONTEXTUAL ISSUES

EDUCATIONAL RESEARCH IN OTHER DISCIPLINES

Contextual variables are concerned with such issues as class size, physical environment, and time of day. Much of the research on this subject has been concerned with determining whether these variables have an impact on student evaluations, a subject which is covered elsewhere in this monograph. There has also been a substantial amount of research on these issues which is specifically concerned with elementary and secondary school environments and is of limited relevance to the objectives of this effort. The most visible issue from the standpoint of the college teacher is the subject of class size and how it impacts the attitudes and performance of students. McKeachie (1978) notes that most of the research on class size indicates that large classes are not as effective as small classes for retention of knowledge, critical thinking, and attitudinal change, but that achievement does not seem to be affected. Another study found that students tend to prefer small classes rather than large classes, but that achievement was not necessarily impaired by the large class environment (Seigfried and Fels, 1979). The issue of the effect of class size on achievement is not, however, fully resolved. Other research, particularly on precollege students, indicates that class size may have a dramatic effect on achievement, particularly when very small classes are offered (Klein, 1985).

A comprehensive study on the impact of class size on student attitudes was done by McConnell and Sosin (1984). They surveyed eight different large classes in accounting, economics, management, and marketing at the University of Nebraska. Multiple regression analysis was employed to model attitude survey scores on a number of background and attitudinal variables including student evaluation, grade, sex, major, college, GPA, year in school, and class size. Generally they found that students were not in favor of large classes. Given the need for some large classes, however, this paper provides guidance toward mitigating their unfavorable aspects. The research suggests that departments should employ their best instructors in large classes and that it is particularly important that a student's first large class be effectively taught, since the first impression will have a significant impact on subsequent attitude. The paper also recommends that majors in a subject be assigned to smaller sections where both large and small sections of a course are offered. Other findings include the fact that better students seem to be less contented with a large-class environment than below-average students and that female students tend to be less satisfied with large class experiences than male students.

ACCOUNTING EDUCATION RESEARCH

Buehlmann and Techavichit (1984) have studied the class size issue in accounting principles classes. Employing regression analysis, they were able to model performance in a large section as a function of GPA and experience with large sections. Buehlmann and Techavichit were unable to model two smaller sections using the same procedures. The implication is that the smaller sections were more supportive of less able and less mature students. The successful students in the large section were the more experienced and more able students. The authors also noted a higher withdrawal rate in the large section (38 percent) as compared with the smaller sections (25 percent).

RESEARCH OPPORTUNITIES IN ACCOUNTING EDUCATION

Additional work needs to be done to determine whether and how accounting can be taught effectively in large classes and what kinds of students are best able to succeed in such classes. A related question is whether computer integration and other technological innovations have any bearing on the class size issue. This research should consider student attitude measures as well as cognitive measures related to class size and class format. Another area of research of much importance concerns the cost/benefit aspects of nontraditional class formats.

CHAPTER 5 BIBLIOGRAPHY

Aamodt, M. G., "Academic Ability and Student Preference for Discussion Group Activities," *Teaching of Psychology* (April 1983), pp. 117–119.

―――, "Effect of the Study Session on Test Performance." *Teaching of Psychology* (April 1982), pp. 118–120.

Adelberg, A. H., and J. R. Razek, "The Cloze Procedure: A Methodology for Determining the Understandability of Accounting Textbooks," *The Accounting Review* (January 1984), pp. 109–122.

Alkafaji, Y., and N. Schroeder, "Manual vs Ccomputerized Practice Sets: A Test for Differences," *Journal of Accounting Education* (Fall 1986), pp. 19–25.

Alpert, R., and R. N. Haber, "Anxiety in Academic Achievement Situations," *Journal of Abnormal and Social Psychology* (September 1960), pp. 207–215.

American Psychological Association, *Standards for Educational and Psychological Tests and Manuals* (Washington: American Psychological Association, 1966).

Amernic, J. H., and T. H. Beechy, "Accounting Students' Performance and Cognitive Complexity: Some Empirical Evidence," *The Accounting Review* (April 1984), pp. 300–313.

Anderson, J. J., "Computer-Supported Instruction in Managerial Accounting," *The Accounting Review* (July 1976), pp. 617–624.

Anderson, R. C., "How to Construct Achievement Tests to Assess Comprehension," *Review of Educational Research* (Spring 1972), pp. 145–170.

Arens, A. A., and W. D. Dewey, "The Use of a Systems Understanding Aid in the Accounting Curriculum," *The Accounting Review* (January 1984), pp. 98–108.

Armitage, H., and J. Boritz, "Integrating Computers Into the Accounting Curriculum," *Issues in Accounting Education* (Spring 1986), pp. 86–101.

Austin, J. D., "When to Allow Student Questions on Homework," *Journal for Research in Mathematics Education* (January 1980), pp. 71–75.

Bailes, J. C., "Lectures Versus Personalized Instruction: An Experimental Study in Elementary Managerial Accounting," *The Accounting Review* (January 1979), pp. 147–154.

Baker, R. E., and J. R. Simon, "An Assessment of the Cognitive Demands of the Uniform CPA Examination and Implications for CPA Review/Preparation Courses," *Journal of Accounting Education* (Fall 1985), pp. 15–29.

———, ———, and F. Bazeli, "An Assessment of Learning Style Preferences of Accounting Majors," *Issues in Accounting Education* (Spring 1986), pp. 1–12.

Baldwin, B. A., "On Positioning the Quiz: An Empirical Analysis," *The Accounting Review* (October 1980), pp. 664–671.

———, and K. R. Howe, "Secondary-Level Study of Accounting and Subsequent Performance in the First College Course," *The Accounting Review* (July 1982), pp. 619–626.

———, and T. P. Howard, "Intertopical Sequencing of Sequencing of Examination Questions: An Empirical Evaluation," *Journal of Accounting Education* (Fall 1983), pp. 89–96.

———, and P. M. J. Reckers, "Exploring the Role of Learning Style Research in Accounting Education Policy," *Journal of Accounting Education* (Fall 1984), pp. 63–76.

Barcikowski, R. S., and H. Olsen, "Test Item Arrangement and Adaptation Level," *Journal of Psychology* (May 1975), pp. 87–93.

Barger, G. W., "Classroom Testing Procedures and Student Anxiety," *Improving College and University Teaching* (Winter 1983), pp. 25–26.

Battista, M. S., "The Effect of Instructional Technology and Learner Characteristics on Cognitive Achievement in College Accounting," *The Accounting Review* (April 1978), pp. 477–485.

Belkaoui, A., "Learning Order and Acceptance of Accounting Techniques," *The Accounting Review* (October 1975), pp. 897–899.

———, "The Primacy-Recency Effect, Ego Involvement and The Acceptance of Accounting Techniques," *The Accounting Review* (January 1977), pp. 252–253.

Benis, M., C. Brody, and R. T. Johnson, "Utilization of the Small Group Approach to Teaching Intermediate Accounting," *The Accounting Review* (October 1976), pp. 894–898.

Bergin, J. L., "The Effect of Previous Accounting Study on Student Performance in the First College-Level Financial Accounting Course," *Issues in Accounting Education* (1983), pp. 19–28.

Berk, R. A., ed., *A Guide to Criterion-Referenced Test Construction* (Baltimore: The Johns Hopkins University Press, 1984).

Biggs, J. B., "Dimensions of Study Behaviour; Another Look at ATI," *British Journal of Education Psychology*, 46 (1976), pp. 61–80.

———, "Individual Differences in Study Processes and the Quality of Learning Outcomes," *Higher Education* (July 1979), pp. 381–394.

Blocher, E., and J. C. Robertson, "Bayesian Sampling Procedures for Auditors: Computer-Assisted Instruction," *The Accounting Review* (April 1976), pp. 359–363.

Borthick, A. F., and R. L. Clark, "The Role of Productive Thinking in Affecting Student Learning with Microcomputers in Accounting Education," *The Accounting Review* (January 1986), pp. 143–157.

———, "Improving Accounting Majors' Writing Quality: The Role of Language Analysis in Attention Directing," *Issues in Accounting Education* (Spring 1987), pp. 18–27.

Bransford, J. D., *Human Cognition* (Belmont, CA: Wadsworth Publishing Company, 1979).

Brown, S. D., and T. L. Nelson, "Beyond the Uniformity Myth: A Comparison of Academically Successful and Unsuccessful Test Anxious Students," *Journal of Counseling Psychology* (July 1983), pp. 367–374.

Buehlmann, D. M., and J. V. Techavichit, "Factors Influencing Final Examination Performance in Large Versus Small Sections of Accounting Principles," *Journal of Accounting Education* (Spring 1984), pp. 127–136.

Burton, E. J., J. C. McKeown, and J. Shlosberg, "The Generation and Administration of Examinations on Interactive Computer Systems," *The Accounting Review* (January 1978), pp. 170–178.

Carrier, C. A., and A. Titus, "The Effects of Notetaking: A Review of Studies," *Contemporary Educational Psychology* (October 1979), pp. 299–314.

Chandler, J. S., "A Course on the Management of the Systems Development Process with Hands-on Computing," *Journal of Accounting Education* (Spring 1984), pp. 99–110.

Clark, R. E., "Reconsidering Research on Learning from Media," *Review of Educational Research* (Winter 1983), pp. 445–459.

Collier, H. W., and W. A. Mehrens, "Using Multiple Choice Test Items to Improve Classroom Testing of Professional Accounting Students," *Journal of Accounting Education* (Fall 1985), pp. 41–51.

Coombs, R. E., "Individualization and Student Freedom to Choose," *American Biology Teacher* (September 1978), pp. 365–368.

Cronbach, L. J. "Test Validation," in R. L. Thorndike, *Educational Measurement*, second ed. (Washington: American Council on Education, 1971), pp. 443–507.

———, and R. E. Snow, *Aptitudes and Instructional Methods* (New York: Irvington, 1977).

Crosby, L. G., "Experiences With the Personalized System of Instruction (PSI) to Teach Elementary Accounting," *Journal of Accounting Education* (Spring 1984), pp. 139–144.

Culler, R. E., and C. J. Holahan, "Test Anxiety and Academic Performance: The Effects of Study Related Behavior," *Journal of Educational Psychology* (February 1980), pp. 16–20.

Dalgaard, B., D. R. Lewis and C. M. Boyer, "Cost and Effectiveness Considerations in the Use of Computer Assisted Instruction in Economics," *Journal of Economic Education* (Fall 1984), pp. 309–323.

DeCoster, D., and G. Prater, "An Experimental Study of the Use of a Business Game in Elementary Accounting," *The Accounting Review* (January 1973), pp. 137–142.

Dickens, T. L., and R. M. Harper, "The Use of Micro-Computers in Intermediate Accounting: Effects on Student Achievement and Attitudes," *Journal of Accounting Education* (Spring 1986), pp. 127–146.

Dubin, R., and T. C. Traveggia, *The Teaching Learning Paradox* (Eugene, OR: Center for the Advanced Study of Educational Administration, 1968).

Dunkin, M. J., "Research on Teaching in Higher Education," in Wittrock, M. C., ed., *Handbook of Research on Teaching*, 3rd. ed. (New York: MacMillan, 1986), pp. 754–777.

Edmonds, T. P., "On the Benefits of Cumulative Exams: An Experimental Study," *The Accounting Review* (October 1984), pp. 660–668.

Ellinger, R. S., and P. Frankland, "Computer Assisted and Lecture Instruction: A Comparative Experiment," *Journal of Geography* (February 1976), pp. 109–120.

Entwistle, N., M. Hanley, and D. Hounsell, "Identifying Distinctive Approaches to Studying," *Higher Education* (July 1979), pp. 365–379.

Ferris, K. R., "Educational Predictors of Professional Pay and Performance," *Accounting Organizations and Society* (1982), pp. 225–230.

Fetters, M., J. McKenzie and D. Callaghan, "Does the Computer Hinder Accounting Education?" *Issues in Accounting Education* (Spring 1986), pp. 76–85.

Fisher, K. M., H. Guenther, and B. MacWhinney, "Does Video-Autotutorial Instruction Improve College Student Achievement?" *Journal of Research in Science Teaching* (November 1977), pp. 481–498.

Frakes, A. H., and W. C. Lathen, "A Comparison of Multiple Choice and Problem Examinations in Introductory Financial Accounting," *Journal of Accounting Education* (Spring 1985), pp. 81–89.

Francis, J., "A Case for Open Book Examinations," *Education Review* (February 1982), pp. 13–26.

Freidman, M., "The Effect on Achievement of Using the Computer as a Problem-Solving Tool in the Intermediate Accounting Course," *The Accounting Review* (January 1981), pp. 137–143.

Fulkerson, F. E., and G. Martin, "Effects of Exam Frequency on Student Performance, Evaluations of Instructor, and Text Anxiety," *Teaching of Psychology* (April 1981), pp. 90–93.

Galassi, J. P., H. T. Frierson, and R. Sharer, "Behavior of High, Moderate, and Low Test Anxious Students During an Actual Test Situation," *Journal of Consulting and Clinical Psychology*, Vol. 49 (1981), pp. 51–62.

Goodman, L., "An Analysis of the Effectiveness of Public Accounting Internship Programs at Major New York City CPA Firms," *Journal of Accounting Education* (Fall 1983), pp. 159–162.

Groomer, S. M., "An Experiment in Computer-Assisted Instruction for Introductory Accounting," *The Accounting Review* (October 1981), pp. 934–941.

Hartley, J., and I. K. Davies, "Note Taking: A Critical Review," *Programmed Learning and Educational Technology* (London: Kogan Page, Ltd., 1978), pp. 207–224.

Hedges, L., "Personalized Introductory Courses: A Longitudinal Study," *American Journal of Physics* (1978), pp. 207–210.

Helmi, M., "Integrating the Micro-Computer Into Accounting Education—Approaches and Pitfalls," *Issues in Accounting Education* (Spring 1986), pp. 102–111.

Howe, K. R., and B. A. Baldwin, "The Effects of Evaluative Sequencing on Performance, Behavior, and Attitudes," *The Accounting Review* (January 1983), pp. 135–142.

Howell, W. C., and L. T. Johnson, "An Evaluation of the Compressed-Course Format for Instruction in Accounting." *The Accounting Review* (April 1982), pp. 402–413.

Izard, C. D., and J. M. Reeve, "Electronic Spreadsheet Technology in the Teaching of Accounting and Taxation—Uses, Limitations, and Examples," *Journal of Accounting Education* (Spring 1986), pp. 161–175.

Kalbers, L. P., "Electronic Spreadsheets: Powerful and Flexible Educational Tools," *Journal of Accounting Education* (Fall 1984), pp. 163–168.

Kirkland, K., and J. G. Hollandsworth, Jr., "Test Anxiety Study Skills, and Academic Performance," *Journal of College Student Personnel* (September 1979), pp. 431–455.

Klein, K., "The Research on Class Size," *Phi Delta Kappan* (April 1985), pp. 578–580.

Knight, J. M., J. D. Williams, and M. Jardon, "The Effects of Contingency Avoidance on

Programmed Student Achievement," *Research in Higher Education* (1975), pp. 11–17.

Koehler, R. W., "The Effect of Internship Programs on Subsequent College Performance," *The Accounting Review* (April 1974), pp. 382–384.

Kolb, D. A., "Management and the Learning Process," *California Management Review* (Spring 1976), pp. 21–31.

Laughlin, E. J., J. W. Gentry, and C. May, "Comparison of Alternative Forms of Teaching Fundamentals of Accounting," *The Accounting Review* (April 1976), pp. 347–351.

Laurillard, D., "The Processes of Student Learning," *Higher Education* (July 1979), pp. 395–410.

Lennon, R. T., "Assumptions Underlying the Use of Content Validity," *Educational and Psychological Measurement* Vol. 16 (1956), pp. 294–304.

Liao, S. S., "Learner Directed Instruction: Additional Evidences," *The Accounting Review* (January 1978), pp. 155–161.

Mandler, G., and S. B. Sarason, "A Study of Anxiety and Learning," *Journal of Abnormal and Social Psychology*, Vol. 47 (1952), pp. 810–817.

Markell, W., and W. A. Pemberton, "Programmed Instruction in Elementary Accounting—Is It Successful?" *The Accounting Review* (April 1972), pp. 381–384.

Marlin, J. W., and J. F. Niss, "The Advanced Learning System, A Computer Managed, Self Paced System of Instruction: An Application in Principles of Economics," *Journal of Economic Education* (Summer 1982), pp. 26–39.

Marton, F., "What Does It Take to Learn? Some Implications of an Alternative View To Learning," in N. J. Entwistle, ed., *Strategies for Research and Development in Higher Education* (Amsterdam: Swets and Zeitlinger, 1976).

McClain, L., "Behavior During Examinations: A Comparison of A, C, and F Students," *Teaching of Psychology* (April 1983a), pp. 69–71.

———, "Students Perform Better on Early Final Exam," *Teaching of Psychology* (December 1983b), pp. 226–227.

McConnell, C. R., and K. Sosin, "Some Determinants of Student Attitudes Toward Large Classes," *Journal of Economic Education* (Summer 1984), pp. 181–190.

McKeachie, W. J., "Improving Lectures by Understanding Students' Information Processing," in McKeachie, W. J., ed., *Learning, Cognition, and College Teaching* (San Francisco: Jossey-Bass, Inc., 1980), pp. 25–35.

———, *Teaching Tips: A Guidebook for the Beginning College Teacher*, seventh ed. (Lexington, MA: D. C. Heath, 1978).

McKeown, J. C., "Computer-Assisted Instruction for Elementary Accounting," *The Accounting Review* (January 1976), pp. 123–130.

McNeill, I. E., and F. Collins, "Personality Tendencies and Learning Modes in Elementary Accounting," *The Accounting Review* (October 1975), pp. 888–897.

Messick, S., "The Standard Problem: Meaning and Values in Measurement and Evaluation," *American Psychologist* (October 1975), pp. 955–966.

———, "Test Validity and the Ethics of Assessment," *American Psychologist* (November 1980), pp. 1012–1027.

Milligan, M. W., and R. L. Reid, "Homework: Its Relationship to Learning," *Engineering Education* (October 1973), pp. 32–38.

Milton, O., *Alternatives to the Traditional* (San Francisco: Jossey-Bass Publishers, 1972).

———, and Associates, *On College Teaching* (San Francisco: Jossey-Bass Publishers, 1978).

———, H. R. Pollio, and J. A. Eison, *Making Sense of College Grades* (San Francisco: Jossey-Bass Publishers, 1986).

———, and E. J. Shoben, Jr., eds., *Learning and the Professors* (Athens: Ohio University Press, 1968).

Munz, D. C., C. T. Costello, and K. Korabik, "A Further Test of the Inverted U Hypothesis Relating Achievement Anxiety and Academic Test Performance," *Journal of Psychology* (January 1975), pp. 39–47.

Nitko, A. J., "Defining 'Criterion Referenced Test'," in R. A. Berk, ed., *A Guide to Criterion Referenced Test Construction* (Baltimore: The Johns Hopkins University Press, 1984), pp. 8–28.

O'Neil, M. J., and D. Child, "Biggs' SPQ: A British Study of Its Educational Structure," *British Journal of Educational Psychology* (June 1984), pp. 228–234.

Paretta, R. L., and L. W. Chadwick, "The Sequencing of Examinations and Its Effects on Student Performance," *The Accounting Review* (July 1975), pp. 595–601.

Pask, G., "Styles and Strategies of Learning," *British Journal of Educational Psychology* Vol. 46 (1976), pp. 128–148.

Pawliczek, R. B., "The Effect of Different Scoring Plans on Student Performance in an Elementary Accounting Course," *The Accounting Review* (July 1977), pp. 721–726.

Pointer, L. G., and P. W. Ljungdahl, "The Merit of Using the Case Method in Teaching the Specialized Accounting Course," *The Accounting Review* (July 1973), pp. 614–618.

Ramsden, P., "Student Learning and Perceptions of the Academic Environment," *Higher Education* (July 1979), pp. 411–427.

———, "Institutional Variations in British Students' Approaches to Learning and Experiences of Teaching," *Higher Education* (December 1983), pp. 691–705.

Romney, M., "The Use of Microcomputers in Accounting Education," *Journal of Accounting Education* (Fall 1983), pp. 11–19.

Russo, T. J., "Multimodal Approaches to Student Test Anxiety," *Clearing House* (December 1984), pp. 62–66.

Sarason, S. B., G. Mandler, and P. G. Craighill, "The Effect of Differential Instructions on Anxiety and Learning," *Journal of Abnormal and Social Psychology*, Vol. 47 (1952), pp. 561–565.

Sarason, I. G., and R. Stoops, "Test Anxiety and the Passage of Time," *Journal of Consulting and Clinical Psychology*, 46 (1978), pp. 102–109.

Scheiner, J. H., and J. E. Kiger, "Generalized Audit Software: A Classroom Approach," *Issues in Accounting Education* (1983), pp. 123–131.

Schroeder, N., "Previous Accounting Education and College-Level Accounting Exam Performance," *Issues in Accounting Education* (Spring 1986), pp. 37–47.

Seigfried, J. J., and R. Fels, "Research on Teaching College Economics: A Survey," *Journal of Economic Literature* (September 1979), pp. 923–969.

Snow, R. E., "Research on Attitudes: A Progress Report," in L. S. Shulman, ed., *Review of Research in Education*, Vol. 4 (Itasca, IL: Peacock Publishers, 1977).

———, "Aptitude-Treatment Interactions in Educational Research," in L. A. Pervin and M. Lewis, eds., *Perspectives in Interactional Psychology* (New York: Plenum Press, 1978).

———, and P. L. Peterson, "Recognizing Differences in Student Attitudes," in W. J. McKeachie, *Learning, Cognition, and College Teaching* (San Francisco: Jossey-Bass, 1980).

Snowball, D., and W. A. Collins, "Televised Accounting Instruction, Attitudes and Performance: A Field Experiment," *The Accounting Review* (January 1980), pp. 123–133.

Stephens, L. J., "What Role Does the Grading of Homework Play in Upper Level Engineering Courses," *Educational Research and Methods* (1977), pp. 64–65, 72.

Stout, D. E., and E. H. Bonfield, "Experimental Evidence on the Relationship Between Class Meeting Time Compression and Accounting Student Performance, Evaluations and Drop Out Experience," *Journal of Accounting Education* (Fall 1986), pp. 51–62.

Streuling G. F., and G. L. Holstrum, "Teaching Machines Versus Lectures in Accounting Education: An Experiment," *The Accounting Review* (October 1972), pp. 806–810.

Swartz, T. R., W. I. Davison, and F. J. Bonello, "Why Have We Ignored the Distribution of Benefits From College Instruction?" *Journal of Economic Education* (Spring 1980), pp. 28–36.

Thomas, A. L., "Use of Microcomputer Spreadsheet Software in Preparing and Grading Complex Accounting Problems," *The Accounting Review* (October 1983), pp. 777–786.

―――, "North American College and University Uses of Microcomputers in Teaching Accounting—1983 Survey," *Journal of Accounting Education* (Fall 1984), pp. 31–41.

Thorndike, R. L., ed., *Educational Measurement* (Washington: American Council on Education, 1971).

Throckmorton, J. J., and J. Talbott, "Computer-Supported Instruction in Financial Statement Analysis," *The Accounting Review* (January 1978), pp. 186–191.

Vasarhelyi, M. A., and W. T. Lin, "EDP Auditing Instruction Using An Interactive Generalized Audit Software," *Journal of Accounting Education* (Fall 1985), pp. 79–89.

Vredeveld, G., "Economics and Programmed Instruction," *Journal of Economic Education* (Summer 1982), pp. 14–25.

Wesp, R., and J. E. Ford, "Flexible Instructor Pacing Assists Student Progress in a Personalized System of Instruction," *Teaching of Psychology* (October 1982), pp. 160–162.

Weick, K. E., "Stress in Accounting Systems," *The Accounting Review* (April 1983), pp. 350–369.

Wetzel, J. N., W. J. Potter, and D. M. O'Toole, "The Influence of Learning and Teaching Styles on Student Attitudes and Achievement in the Introductory Economics Course: A Case Study," *Journal of Economic Education* (Winter 1982), pp. 33–39.

Weinstein, C., W. E. Cubberly, and F. C. Richardson, "The Effects of Test Anxiety on Learning at Superficial and Deep Levels of Processing," *Contemporary Educational Psychology* (April 1982), pp. 107–112.

Wiebe, J. H., "Using Graded Quizzes, Homework, and Attendance for Motivating Study in a College Math Class," *Mathematics and Computer Education* (Winter 1982), pp. 24–28.

Wittrock, M. C., ed., *Handbook of Research on Teaching*, 3rd. ed. (New York: MacMillan, 1986).

Wooley, J. K., "Factors Affecting Students' Attitudes and Achievement in an Astronomy Computer-Assisted Instruction Program," *Journal of Research in Science Teaching* (March 1978), pp. 173–78.

Wright, A., "On the Use of An Available Prior Examinations Policy," *Issues in Accounting Education* (Spring 1986), pp. 24–36.

CHAPTER 6

Research Related to Administration and Constituents

In Chapters 3–5, we have discussed academic issues related to students, faculty and the educational process in terms of general research in other educational fields, educational research in accounting, and research opportunities in accounting which warrant current investigation. In this chapter we turn our attention to several administrative and professional issues, following the same general format of presentation of the previous three chapters.

Some of the topics included in this chapter have broad application to many academic fields; others are uniquely found in professional fields of study, such as accounting. An overview of the topics contained in this chapter is shown in Figure 5.

ADMINISTRATIVE STRUCTURE AND FIVE-YEAR PROGRAMS

ACADEMIC RESEARCH IN OTHER DISCIPLINES

The subject of academic program administration must be approached with humility. Much research has been devoted to the topic, yet many fundamental questions remain unanswered. More than 25 years ago, Eells and Hollis reported "that some twenty thousand books, pamphlets, and magazine articles had been published on university administration in a ten-year period" (Dressel and Pratt, 1971, p. 30). A subsequent bibliography by Dressel and Pratt lists dozens of important studies which provide a framework within which to study the subject (Dressel and Pratt, 1971).

Given the volume and significance of this research, it seems appropriate to address herein only subjects which seem to be of particular importance to accounting. Accordingly, this chapter provides a summary of the theoretical and empirical nature of academic departmental organizations as a preview to the central empirical question regarding academic accounting programs—whether such an organization should consist of a department, a separate school, or some other type of structure. In conjunction with this analysis, some attention must also be devoted to the role and duties of the administrator, since the administrative function is inexorably entwined with the nature of the organizational structure. Also, because the emergence of the five-year accounting program has occurred in conjunction with schools of accounting, accounting research on five-year programs is covered later in this section.

A comprehensive study by Dressel, Johnson, and Marcus (1970) explores virtually every aspect of the departmental organization. The typical departmental structure of modern universities evolved from less differentiated organizations as the distinctions between disciplines became more defined. It is notable, for example, that accounting subjects were first taught in universities as economics courses with the evolution of accounting departments coming much later. This process of departmental evolution, which began almost as soon as universities were founded in the United States, still continues to change,

FIGURE 5

ADMINISTRATION AND CONSTITUENTS

Administrative Structure and Five-Year Programs
  Administrative structure
  Schools of accountancy
  Five-year programs

Accreditation of Programs
  Role of accreditation
  Development of accreditation
  Focus of accreditation process
  Accreditation standards

Faculty Vitality

Financing of Programs

Academic Program Ratings

Continuing Professional Education

---

although the department as we know it was well established in some institutions by the last 20 years of the nineteenth century.

Within the departmental system, three distinct patterns of development have been identified. Departments where there are only undergraduate students, a strong teaching orientation, and only a weak or insignificant research emphasis tend to exhibit a "university orientation." Such units are highly dependent on general funds for their activities, and authority is channeled along traditional lines. The department itself is basically a work organization in which seniority and rank have substantial importance.

Larger universities with more complex organizations and a graduate emphasis may adopt a "departmental orientation." As this transition occurs, the department assumes a greater role in the decisions which affect its destiny. While most funding is provided from central sources, substantial funds may also be available directly to the department as a result of its own fund-raising activities. These programs tend to reward research and publication, creating an avenue that quickly becomes the fast track for promotion and recognition. Such an organization typically has relatively few nationally or internationally known scholars and thus offers younger faculty an opportunity for rapid advancement. In an organization with a departmental orientation, the administrator (i.e., the chairperson or head) is a person of great importance and whose competence and leadership qualities have considerable impact on the success of the program. However, appointment to such a position is normally based on academic credentials which have little to do with the tasks and responsibilities of administration. A successful administrator must operate in a relatively democratic manner, balancing the needs and demands of aggressive young faculty, a few established scholars, and some senior faculty with a more traditional, university orientation.

A final stage of development occurs as a department attains a national reputation for scholarship and research and adopts a "disciplinary orientation." The central figures in such an organization are researchers with established reputations. They may often have limited teaching duties and almost never teach at the undergraduate level. In some instances these faculty may be so influential that they have little or no incentive to acquiesce to dictates of the administrator. In fact, the administrator may even be perceived as a threat to scholarship. If individualism among senior faculty becomes rampant, the department may become virtually ungovernable.

Obviously, academic departments vary broadly in orientation. Many are in transitional states and, as such, have internal conflicts as well as conflicts with the external power structures. It is not surprising that there should be examples of organizational structures that have been created with the objective of overcoming the problems which are viewed as being associated with the departmental structure. Such organizations are identified by a variety of names such as institutes, bureaus, and centers. Within the accounting discipline and other professional fields, these organizations are often called schools. Their common thread is that their formation resulted principally from a dissatisfaction with the departmental system and not because of latent positive forces which created a need for them. Critics of these organizations argue that these schools add needlessly to the complexity of the organizational structure of the university without solving the problems that their creation sought to avoid. Central to an assessment of the need for and value of schools of accounting is the realization that the existence of nondepartmental organizational structures is not unique to either accounting or to professional programs as a group, but can be found throughout the university.

ACCOUNTING EDUCATION RESEARCH

Administrative Structure

The organizational structure of accounting programs has been widely studied in recent years. Investigation centers around the controversy of whether accounting programs should be organized as departments within the college of business or as separate schools. Dressel's work (Dressel, Johnson, and Marcus, 1970) on the evolution of the departmental system supports the proposition that the strongest support for the professional school organization would come from schools whose accounting programs have a departmental orientation. While this question has not been empirically tested, casual review of the list of institutions that are members of the Federation of Schools of Accountancy makes it an appealing research issue.

Much attention has been given to the question of whether schools of accounting can accomplish the educational goals established by the profession. The AICPA (1977) has published formal educational standards for accounting programs and schools of accounting. The curriculum standards propose a five-year program divided into pre-professional and professional segments in a format which is inconsistent with traditional Bachelor's/Master's degree formats. Thus, the standards themselves in a sense endorse the idea of separate schools. A study by Spiceland, Brenner, and Hartman (1980) finds substantial support for the AICPA standards among academics, CPA's, management accountants, and large firm controllers.

As noted earlier, nonaccounting research indicates that the proliferation of institutes, centers, and schools is an outgrowth of dissatisfaction with the departmental system. A question of much significance is whether the pressure for schools of accounting is specifically based upon dissatisfaction and whether the school format may be reasonably expected to address the problems that exist. Sterling (1975) has stated the major arguments for schools of accounting in terms of their educational advantages and their research advantages. His principal argument is that accounting faculty have inadequate control over the curriculum because accounting faculty in a college of business are in the minority. In addition, he argues that there are insufficient incentives to engage in applied research in institutions with a college/department structure for the accounting program. Sterling's propositions have not been subjected to empirical tests, but they certainly warrant investigation. To the extent that nonaccounting faculty have an impact on the promotion/tenure decisions of accounting faculty, there may indeed be disincentives for the pursuit of applied research, particularly where the nonaccounting faculty lack a professional orientation or an appreciation for such a posture.

Some research has been conducted on attitudes toward the school of accounting by faculty, deans, practitioners, and students. Most of this work has focused on determining whether affected groups are supportive of the concept of a separate school. Dressel's work on the nature of university organizations (Dressel, Johnson, and Marcus, 1970) would in general support the a priori contention that business school deans and faculty of departments with either a university or discipline orientation would have negative attitudes toward the idea of a separate school of accounting. This theory would, however, support the contention that faculty in programs with a departmental orientation would be supportive of the separate school idea. Existing research is consistent with these implications. A nonempirical paper by Meckling and Zimmerman (1976) of The University of Rochester is strongly critical of the professional school idea, particularly because it might hinder the publication of interdisciplinary academic research. Later empirical work by Bremser, Brenner, and Dascher (1977a) also finds that deans are unfavorably disposed toward the idea of separate schools, while departmental chairpersons and heads support it. In another paper (1977b), they find substantial support from management accountants for the concept of a professional school. Rayburn and Bonfield (1978) reach similar conclusions and expand the surveyed groups to include nonaccounting faculty (negative attitude), accounting faculty (positive attitude), and accounting students (positive attitude). A recent paper by Siegel (1983) is strongly supportive of the professional school concept from the students' perspective. Siegel surveyed students who were actually enrolled in existing professional schools and compared their responses with those of a control group of students in a traditional program. His findings show that students in professional schools are more committed to the profession, better satisfied with their schools, and have greater confidence in their future achievement potential. In a paper reviewing the historical development of schools of accounting, Bloom, Debessay, and Markell (1986) find that proponents of schools of accounting have based their position on improved professional identity and visibility and greater competency of graduates. Opponents have traditionally argued that separate schools are undesirable from the standpoint of the administrative burden, budgetary problems, and redundancy of courses.

The question of whether organization as a separate school of accounting is of benefit to the individual program has been studied by Eckel and Ross (1985). They constructed a matched pairs sample of schools of accounting and accounting departments and made comparisons of seven dimensions of the programs, including curriculum, budgetary matters, fund-raising, faculty background, and research. Eckel and Ross conclude that, among the institutions in the sample, schools of accounting "receive more external funding, have more autonomy over pedagogy and the hiring of new faculty, and experience less difficulty in the recruitment of faculty and students, than do departments of accounting" (p. 11). Both the Eckel and Ross article and the Bloom article cited above provide the interested researcher with an extensive bibliography of published and unpublished research on this much debated-topic.

Five-year Programs

As mentioned earlier, the interest among accounting educators and researchers in schools of accounting and five year programs is sufficiently interrelated to the point that separating the two is virtually impossible. Interest in the five-year program became evident when the AICPA took the position of favoring five years of university education for CPA certification (Hendrickson, 1971). The underlying reasoning for the recommendation is found in Roy and MacNeill's *Horizons for a Profession* (1967) and the AICPA report titled *Report of the Committee on Education and Experience Requirements for CPAs* (AICPA, 1969), commonly referred to as the Beamer Report. The Roy and MacNeill study and the Beamer Report are particularly important sources of background on the subjects of schools of accounting and five-year programs for those planning research in these important areas.

Holstrum and Wilson (1974) studied the university curricula of 19 universities to determine whether recent changes were consistent with the Beamer Report. While many areas of study were found to be reasonably consistent with the report, several were not—financial accounting, computer applications and information systems, behavioral and quantitative areas, and the number of electives. Further investigation to confirm the merits of the curriculum proposed by the AICPA and to indicate the degree of compliance of current curricula with that model would appear to be particularly appropriate. One could speculate that the widespread adoption of personal computers in the last decade may have impacted both model curricula and those actually being taught at the present time.

The five-year education proposal has been controversial and, as a result, it has been widely studied. As early as 1974, Whitham (1974) surveyed proprietors and managing partners of CPA firms concerning their views toward a five-year university education requirement for certification. The respondents to the survey did not agree with the recommendations of the AICPA, concluding instead that a bachelor's program could provide the educational background required to enter the accounting profession at the time. A careful reading of the recommendations resulting from this study indicates that the orientation leans more heavily toward the education required of entry-level professionals than of career professionals. This emphasis raises the interesting question of the proper role of professional education in accounting: should it prepare one for entry-level responsibilities, or should it provide a framework for an entire professional career?

Brown and Balke (1983) surveyed public accountants and management accountants concerning their views toward the five-year education and schools of accounting. Their findings indicate much greater support for the extended education among public accountants than among those in industry. This study provides extensive lists of reasons for and against five-year accounting programs as well as both public and industrial accountants' responses to each reason.

The subject of five years of pre-professional education and requirements for taking the CPA examination are closely related, as indicated above. Arnold and Geiselhart (1984) surveyed practitioners in three states (New York, Florida, and Massachusetts) concerning their views on the five-year education requirement for CPA's. (Florida is the only one of the three states with a legislated five-year education requirement for CPA certification.) Their findings reveal mixed response. They also indicate that the issue of a five-year requirement cannot be separated from the issue of continuing professional education and suggest that the relevant issue is the structure of all postgraduate (beyond baccalaureate) education, including both pre-entry level and post-entry level (continuing education).

Concerning the problems of implementing a fifth year of education as a requirement to become a CPA, Yost (1986) surveyed student reaction to the requirement in Florida. He concludes that student reaction is being determined by factors other than educational and professional attempts to improve the public accounting profession. Potential CPA's are taking advantage of inconsistent state requirements to circumvent the objective of the five-year requirement, arguing for uniform national requirements.

Another dimension of the five-year educational requirement is specialization, particularly in the fifth year. Tax is the area most frequently cited as involving a sufficient body of specialized knowledge to warrant a fifth year of education, resulting in a specialized Master's degree. At least two surveys of Master's degree programs in tax have been published. Lubell and Broden (1975) surveyed a number of tax programs in the early 1970's, speculating about rapidly increasing growth in this area in the future. Tidwell and Wyndelts (1977) studied 18 AACSB-accredited schools offering Master's degree programs in tax, providing considerable data on students, faculty and course offerings. They offer five specific areas of study that warrant attention, some of which provide the background for research opportunities in accounting identified below.

Izard and McKinney (1983) surveyed accountants in the southeast concerning their perceptions and attitudes about the certification of tax specialists. Their results indicate possible support for a special certification of tax specialists, as well as indications of certification requirements and post-certification requirements.

RESEARCH OPPORTUNITIES IN ACCOUNTING

While much has been written and said about administrative structure for accounting programs and about the desirability and content of five-year accounting programs, significant research opportunities remain. Much of the available material on these subjects is the opinion of the writer and/or is based on the experience at one institution or a small number of institutions. Empirical research which extends these earlier efforts and confirms or refutes assertions that have been made will add significantly to the accounting education literature.

Concerning administrative structure, work remains to be done on the substantive impact on outcomes of accounting education of the gradual move from a departmental structure to schools of accounting. A related question is how the dual characteristics of accounting programs—professional education at the undergraduate and Master's levels and academic preparation at the Master's and doctoral level—is related to academic structure. The research mission of a professional discipline such as accounting is also a subject worthy of study. In general, research is required on the current status of the transition from departments to schools, the impact of that transition on the outcomes of the accounting education process, and the relative desirability of different administrative structures in terms of meeting the broad objectives of accounting education.

The trend toward longer education for students entering accounting practice is slowly emerging. Several dimensions of this trend are worthy of study. Work on the content and alternative structures for five-year programs will contribute to a knowledge of accounting education in general and will be of great value to those schools that have not yet made the transition. Several states have legislated postbaccalaureate requirements to qualify for taking the CPA examination, and the AICPA has advocated an increased education requirement for almost two decades. The problems and impact of legislation on academic programs as well as on students is a subject worthy of consideration. Ultimately, the impact of increased education on the professional success of students and the quality of accounting services available should be addressed in an empirical research setting.

ACCREDITATION OF PROGRAMS

ACADEMIC RESEARCH IN OTHER DISCIPLINES

The Role of Accreditation

The objective of accreditation is to provide evidence of educational quality to interested parties outside the institution. Perhaps the most critical educational issue to arise in the last decade is the issue of quality in our educational institutions. Much anecdotal and some empirical data suggest that a decline in overall quality has occurred in the last 10 to 20 years. There has, for example, been a notable decline in the entrance examination scores of high school students entering college (Warren, 1983a). At the same time, grade-point averages of college students have risen without any particular evidence that the students have learned more than in prior years. Many writers have lamented the quality of current higher education, and a 1981 report by the American Council on Education concluded that "most analysts and observers agree that quality noticeably declined in the past two decades" (Warren, 1983a, p. 2). Close examination of the literature reveals, however, that there is little formal evidence which documents differences in quality between educational institutions today and those of earlier years. Thus, scholars have recently stressed the need for research which definitively measures quality in higher education (Warren, 1983a).

Development of Accreditation

The first accrediting associations were established to accredit institutions as a whole. More recently, other associations have begun to evaluate and accredit specific programs such as business schools and accounting programs. Millard (1983) describes the historical development of these associations in the United States from their formation in the 19th century until the present. He points out that a major problem with accreditation as an indicator of quality is that accreditation standards focus on processes and input factors rather than on results or outcomes. Standards of accreditation for faculty are, for example, generally expressed in terms of such things as percent of faculty with earned doctorates rather than in terms of whether faculty qualifications are adequate to meet the educational objectives of the institution. Another criticism of the accreditation process is the fact that institutions of declining quality are often able to maintain their accredited standing even as their programs slide further and further toward mediocrity (Clemow, 1985). If accreditation associations are to effectively promote quality, the standards for accreditation must effectively measure outcomes which are indicative of quality and not simply measure definitions of inputs to the educational process (Adelman, 1983).

Focus of the Accreditation Process

Warren (1983b) asserts that the classroom is the area where one must focus in order to measure quality in higher education because courses are the basic element of the college learning experience. Such a process would seem to require that courses or groups of courses have specifically stated, externally established standards of learning or achievement as indicators of mastery of that subject. Whether such learning, or knowledge, has been acquired by students could be determined by examinations.

An alternative, more universal system of measuring quality involves the use of comprehensive examinations. The use of externally-prepared comprehensive examinations allows the assessment of student achievement to be independent of the teaching function. O'Neill (1983) observes that in the United States "there is no arms-length relationship . . . between the teaching function and the certifying function. Faculty members not only teach but in effect guarantee, first, that their teaching meets established standards in both content and quality and, second, that the students have learned what the faculty have taught" (p. 71). He suggests that externally-prepared examinations should serve as the basis for accreditation by allowing direct measurement of the extent to which students achieve prescribed standards of knowledge.

Admission and Retention of Students

Much research on the subject of admissions focuses on the role of the SAT/ACT and on graduate admissions tests such as the GRE or GMAT. As we have noted in Chapter 3, the information value of admissions tests scores is somewhat diminished by the fact that high school grades are better predictors of college grades than are admissions tests. Despite this fact, the literature supports the use of admissions tests because they provide additional evidence about the student's verbal and mathematical skills and are more comparable to each other than high school grades (Hanford, 1985). Other benefits include the element of information value to the student and the value of the scores in student advising (Hargadon, 1981).

For some graduate schools and highly selective institutions, an additional step in the admissions process might include an interview. Research indicates that such steps may be useful if they are conducted properly. Interviewers should have formal training in the psychology and dynamics of interviewing and understand the limitations of this process (Myslinski and Jeffrey, 1985).

A topic closely related to the admission process is the student's college selection decision. Competition for students has stimulated research on this topic. Efforts to model the college choice decision have concluded that it is affected by a number of factors, including students' individual characteristics and family backgrounds, as well as characteristics of the institution. Successful student recruiting hinges on targeting effective communication toward the appropriate applicant groups (Chapman, 1981; Litten, 1982). Research on the selection decision of graduate students focuses strongly on intangible factors. Effective recruiting of graduate students requires a department with a good reputation and a positive faculty/student rapport as established by personal interviews during the selection process (Olson and King, 1985).

ACCOUNTING EDUCATION RESEARCH

Accreditation Standards

The AICPA published its recommendations for standards for professional accounting programs in 1977 (AICPA, 1977). These recommendations provide educational standards for seven areas of accounting programs: (1) general standards, (2) admission and retention standards, (3) curriculum standards, (4) accounting faculty standards, (5) financial support and budget standards, (6) physical plant standards, and (7) library and computer standards. In addition, the document also lists standards for performance of graduates which are a mixture of input and output standards. In general, the input standards are stated in terms of output criteria. For example, standard No. 1 on faculty states that the faculty shall possess the experience and qualifications necessary for successful conduct of a professional accounting program. However, most of the discussion of the standards centers on input measures such as percent of faculty with earned doctorates. The standards for students are stated in terms of their performance, but no recommendation is made for evaluation of students other than by faculty-prepared examinations. In the standards for graduates, one standard states that graduates should be capable of passing professional examinations—an output-oriented measure.

The American Assembly of Collegiate Schools of Business (AACSB) has also published standards for accounting programs (AACSB, 1986–87). These standards cover (1) objectives of accounting programs, (2) students, (3) personnel, (4) curriculum, (5) library and computers, (6) financial resources, (7) educational innovation, and (8) maintenance of accreditation. As in the case of the AICPA-suggested standards, the emphasis between input and output measures is mixed, with much of the detailed explanations revolving around input measures. Reference is made to the CPA exam as one measure of the factors to be considered in evaluation of student quality, but no other direct measures of the quality of graduates is suggested.

A recent paper by Campbell and Williamson (1983) implies that accounting administrators are somewhat skeptical about the capacity of these standards to significantly improve accounting education. Additional research is needed to assess the effectiveness of the AACSB standards as well as to determine alternative ways of measuring the quality of accounting programs. The nonaccounting research cited earlier suggests that such efforts are needed. The only direct output measures of the quality of graduates suggested in current standards relate to the CPA exam. Since the CPA exam has only a licensure objective, there is not even prima facie evidence to support its use in some sort of accreditation scheme.

One recent paper does indicate that schools view accreditation by the AACSB as an important priority. Brown and Balke (1983) surveyed AACSB business schools and found that a large number intended to seek separate accreditation of their accounting programs. The survey also provided data on the structure of the accounting curriculums of respondents. Another paper by Rouse, Davis and Friedlob (1986) surveyed the attitudes of administrators toward a revision in the AACSB relevant experience-standard. The revision, which constitutes a departure from a strictly defined measure of input toward a more subjective measure which also emphasizes scholarly output, received a mixed reaction from respondents. The authors do not address the input/output measurement issue specifically.

Admission and Retention Standards

The growth in the popularity of accounting as a major without a corresponding increase in the capacity of accounting programs has promoted interest in the subject of admission and retention standards among accounting educators. Tiller and White (1983) report that the use of admission/retention standards at Indiana University resulted in admitting students with higher grades and SAT math scores as compared with students majoring in other subjects. Dockweiler and Willis (1984) employed discriminant analysis to predict junior and senior GPA of accounting majors. They achieved very high classification accuracy employing only GPA in introductory accounting and overall GPA as predictor variables.

Harrell and Stahl (1983) suggest that nonintellective criteria may be useful in making admission decisions to accounting programs. In particular their study shows that the nonintellective variable, need for achievement, is positively correlated with overall grades and the desire to pursue a career in public accounting. Conversely, the variable need for affiliation, is negatively correlated with these factors.

Eckel and Johnson (1983) have developed a discriminant model which attempts to predict success in the accounting program. The subjects were 96 accounting graduates at Bowling Green State University. A two-variable model consisting of lower-level accounting grades and ACT math score was able to correctly classify 85.2% of the subjects when success was defined as a graduate with an upper-level GPA of at least 2.5.

The Eckel and Johnson study is interesting, but it is limited by its definition of success, which is confined to a single academic variable of questionable value. Success in class and success in professional accomplishment clearly do not represent the same outcome. As we noted in chapter 3, the limited evidence available indicates little if any relationship between college grades and measures of professional success.

Ingram and Petersen (1987) tested a model which incorporates the AICPA aptitude test and the AICPA Level I achievement test in an attempt to predict success in upper-division accounting courses. The authors concluded that the use of these tests did not improve upon the predictive power of a model which employed GPA in the first two years as the only independent variable.

RESEARCH OPPORTUNITIES IN ACCOUNTING

Additional research that seeks to develop accreditation standards for accounting programs in terms of outcomes is clearly needed. The majority of accreditation standards currently in use focus on inputs such as institutional physical assets and faculty qualifications. While assessment of these factors is useful, the quality of a program must finally be judged by the achievements of its graduates. Basic questions involving specification of the outcomes to be measured must first be answered. Determining the nature of these outcomes will require specification of the objectives of accounting programs in terms of educational or professional competence. If the outcome of interest is purely educational, then some type of exit exam might serve as an objective measure of program quality. The use of some type of professional achievement outcome would clearly be more difficult to develop and implement. The CPA exam is also obviously inappropriate for a variety of reasons, not the least of which is that educational institutions have no control over the content and administration of the CPA exam.

Research is also needed to determine ways of measuring faculty quality. Traditional measures of faculty quality such as publications need to be assessed in terms of their contribution to program objectives and the competence of graduates. Other measures of faculty quality that are more directly related to the teaching function should be devised.

FACULTY VITALITY

ACADEMIC RESEARCH IN OTHER DISCIPLINES

Faculty vitality is an indispensable element for excellence in collegiate education. The topic of faculty vitality which is related to other topics such as compensation systems, has been extensively researched. A recent issue of *New Directions for Higher Education* (Baldwin, 1985), provides the interested reader with a review of much of this research as well as a collection of nine articles exploring the many aspects of this topic. The reader may also wish to refer to Chapter 4 of this monograph, to the section on faculty development.

The key to faculty vitality is a reward system that fosters vitality. That system must be flexible. The factors that motivate business professors are not identical in nature and hierarchy to those that motivate philosophy professors (Baldwin and Krotseng, 1985). In addition, the factors that motivate a faculty member clearly change over the course of his or her career (Lawrence, 1985). It is nevertheless possible to specify in general terms the key elements of a reward structure that fosters faculty vitality.

It is not clear that the key element of the reward structure is monetary. Indeed, much research suggests that the intangible satisfactions of an academic career derived from association with students, intellectual exchange, and the freedom which an academic position offers are the most profound factors in attracting and retaining faculty at a university (Baldwin and Krotseng, 1985).

One must not, however, ignore the importance of the financial reward system. Its importance is accentuated by the fact that rewards in the form of recognition, promotion, and privileges result from the same activities which produce increased merit pay. The reward structure of the academic career is unusual in that salary adjustments and promotion decisions in many institutions are not based upon performance in the most visible activity from the viewpoint of students, alumni, and taxpayers. Substantial research, mostly in the form of case studies, has been devoted to determining what type of activity is rewarded in academe. In institutions where research is considered an integral part of a faculty member's duties, it consistently ranks as the most important, if not the only, determinant of promotion and salary increase.

An early paper by Skeels and Fairbanks (1968) involved a multi-institutional study of members of the American Economic Association. The authors concluded that faculty who were frequent publishers were more mobile and more highly rewarded than nonpublishers. In a study of 11 academic departments at the University of Illinois, Katz (1973) employed regression analysis to model academic salaries. The findings indicate that publications were the most important factor in the reward system and that teaching, as measured by student evaluations, was unimportant. In a study of economics professors at the University of Wisconsin, Siegfried and White (1973) found that all aspects of a professor's activities—teaching, research, and service—were significant in predicting salary, but that research output and administrative experience were the principal routes to success. Similar findings were reported by Tuckman, et al. (1977).

A more recent study by Kasten (1984) employed a simulation approach to ascertain faculty attitudes toward the criteria used for tenure and merit pay decisions. His findings indicated that both tenure and merit pay were closely associated with research productivity and that teaching and service had a somewhat smaller effect on the awarding of tenure and merit pay.

Other important tangible elements for faculty vitality include research tools such as laboratories, library, and computer resources, a core of good students, and balanced workloads which keep teaching from becoming an arduous task (Schuster, 1985). From the viewpoint of the faculty member who enjoys teaching, it is difficult to envision a vital, successful academic program in the absence of quality students who use their collegiate experience as a springboard toward achieving their personal goals and professional aspirations.

Significant intangible elements of vitality include a sense of community, intellectual freedom, and the stimulation of colleagues (Schuster, 1985). The importance of colleagues can hardly be overstated. Association with creative and dynamic colleagues brings out the best in individual faculty members, and it is doubtful if any professor could achieve his or her full potential in an environment where this stimulation were absent. This point can also be reinforced on a less positive plane. Any faculty member with a decade or more of experience can probably offer evidence of academic programs which have not achieved their potential because of a lack of collegiality among the faculty.

A final intangible element that fosters faculty vitality deserves separate discussion. That element is leadership, certainly from the president or chancellor and the academic dean, but more importantly, from the department administrator. We have noted elsewhere in this chapter that the credentials for appointment to department administrator are almost exclusively academic, yet these credentials do little to prepare the individual for administrative responsibilities. Such an inconsistency portends disastrous consequences on occasion. Bevan (1985) cites a case whereby a young professor was informed that his tenure had been denied when he passed the administrator in the hallway. The administrator stated that he would explain later when he "had time" (Bevan, p. 19).

In contrast to the individual characterized above, a successful administrator is a person who has the capacity to foster the positive aspects of collegiality, is sensitive to individual concerns, and is understanding of the aspirations and apprehensions of young faculty. The successful administrator remains accessible to the faculty and spends much time interacting with faculty on academic and administrative issues (Bevan, 1985).

ACCOUNTING EDUCATION RESEARCH

The subject of faculty development has not been covered in an accounting context. Limited work covers the subject of faculty recruiting, but this research basically addresses beginning salaries and macro variables related to supply of doctoral graduates as compared with position vacancies (Mehl and Lammers, 1979; American Taxation Association, 1983). In addition, substantial descriptive statistics have been gathered for several years with the support of the American Accounting Association (Williams, et al., 1984–85; 1983–84; 1982–83; 1980–81; 1979–80). A recent paper by Lewis, Lin, and Williams (1984) distills some of these data into statements about recent trends in accounting compensation. In general, accounting faculty members are better paid than university professors as a whole; however, the data indicate that the relative advantage enjoyed by accounting professors may be shrinking. The paper also indicates that accounting faculty of doctoral-granting institutions "enjoyed relatively better economic status than those schools not offering the doctorate."

Much anecdotal evidence suggests the existence in the accounting field of salary compression, a decline in the relative salary premium associated with academic rank and/or experience. The suggested cause of salary compression is the existence of upward pressure on starting salaries of new faculty resulting from a shortage of new doctoral graduates in relation to available opportunities. The absence of similar demand for more experienced faculty, combined with market friction caused by high relocation costs, results in a slower rate of increase for salary of experienced faculty. A question of much interest is whether salary compression affects all faculty groups or whether those faculty with high productivity are insulated from it. Recent research suggests that salary compression is widespread, affecting all faculty ranks. This evidence also indicates that research productivity may not fully insulate a professor from the effects of salary compression (Jacobs and Herring, 1987).

RESEARCH OPPORTUNITIES IN ACCOUNTING

Basic descriptive research on the reward system used in accounting programs is needed to establish whether the issues related to faculty vitality in accounting programs are different from those in other disciplines. In particular, it would be useful to understand where professional activities fall in the hierarchy of factors which maintain faculty vitality.

Also needed is additional research on the reward structure. Research on the salary structure of accounting faculty would determine whether the variables which are predictive of salary in other disciplines are also predictive of accounting salaries. Several aspects of the salary compression issue are unresolved, including the measurement of institutional effects such as program prestige and program structure. Some institutions, for example, may be less affected by the salary compression problem than others. Research is needed to identify and measure the institutional aspects of this important issue.

FINANCING OF PROGRAMS

EDUCATION RESEARCH IN OTHER DISCIPLINES

The subject of financing of programs encompasses the budgetary process, a broad range of topics in the political economy area, descriptive/demographic studies of the sources of funding for higher education, and studies which address issues related to the value of higher education. Only a limited number of these topics appear to be of general interest to or offer potential opportunities for researchers in accounting education. Of general interest to any academician is research related to the value of higher education, and, of more specific interest to accounting educators, is research related to budgeting.

Underlying the entire subject matter of financing of higher education is the issue of educational value. Educators are universally aware of articles in popular magazines and newspapers which suggest that there are too many educational institutions and too many students seeking higher education. These critics further contend that excessive resources are devoted to higher education, that many graduates are unable to obtain employment upon graduation, and that the higher education system has produced an overeducated citizenry. Extensive work by Bowen (1977) leads to the inescapable conclusion that these popular criticisms have little merit. Much of the quality of life in the United States is a result of decades of emphasis on education. Bowen's research indicates that the nonmonetary benefits of education are so significant a factor in an overall assessment of educational value that important decisions affecting the future of higher education should be primarily based on these considerations as opposed to monetary issues. Such a posture clearly is consistent with the view that overemphasis on vocational skills within higher education is an undesirable potential. Bowen's arguments do not demean the importance of technical disciplines, but they do serve as a reminder that the merits of higher education should not be judged primarily from a vocational perspective.

Of particular interest to accounting educators are recent research efforts related to the budgetary process. Accounting programs are among the vocationally-oriented disciplines that have increased in popularity in the last 20 years because of an increased emphasis on the monetary rewards of higher education. This popularity has produced growth in those programs, which is in part desirable, but growth has not come without problems, which include a potential oversupply of graduates resulting in lower starting salaries and the failure of some students to be placed. In addition, resource allocation and reallocation within the institutional budgetary process has not been commensurate with individual program growth and decline. For accounting programs in particular, increased enrollment in business administration generally has created substantial cost and quality problems associated with the service mission of teaching elementary principles courses.

Revolutionary new approaches to the educational budgetary process are being adopted in several states (Albright, 1985). These approaches involve shifting away from enrollment-driven formulas toward budgetary processes that consider quality. These new systems include reward structures emphasizing teaching which have been implemented in elementary and secondary schools and which offer the potential for use in higher education. The use of multiyear planning horizons in the budgetary process is another innovation that offers the promise of greater stability in the financial structure of higher education. Emphasis on quality has also been enhanced in several states via the creation of centers of excellence and professorships endowed by appropriations. Other potential reforms of budgetary systems include the establishment of goals stated in terms of measurable outcomes such as performance on the national teacher examinations or pass rates on licensure examinations. While such criteria can be overused and misused, they potentially have a place in the process of program quality assessment.

Finally, ways must be devised of dealing with the failure of budgetary systems to deal with changing enrollment patterns within the university. Enrollment limitation schemes based on GPA and other variables do not have unlimited capacity to solve the problems associated with excess demand. Maximum educational quality for the resource dollar also requires greater flexibility to reallocate funds from programs with excess capacity to those with excess demand.

ACCOUNTING EDUCATION RESEARCH

No significant research on the budgetary/financing process has been published in accounting journals.

RESEARCH OPPORTUNITIES IN ACCOUNTING

The controversy surrounding the value of a vocational emphasis in higher education poses direct questions about the content of accounting curricula. In a broader context, the curriculum issues also involve the five-year program issue. Specifically, one question of interest deals with the issue of whether the undergraduate business program should include fewer technical courses and more liberal arts courses. If accounting programs were designed as five-year programs, such a shift in undergraduate emphasis would be more feasible.

There are also some budgetary questions which may be of interest to accounting education. Most accounting programs have a very strong professional orientation, and external funding is strongly dependent on maintaining ties with the profession. An important way of developing and nurturing these ties is by continuing to produce graduates of a quality commensurate with the needs of employers. Thus, the teaching mission of an accounting program is a crucial element for success. Better ways of incorporating the teaching mission into the budgetary process and of compensating good teaching should be a priority of accounting programs.

ACADEMIC PROGRAM RATINGS

ACADEMIC RESEARCH IN OTHER DISCIPLINES

The subject of academic program ratings has received considerable attention in the academic literature. Perhaps the most frequently cited studies are those of the American Council on Education published in 1964 (Cartter, 1964) and 1970 (Roose and Andersen, 1970) in which recognized scholars rated excellence in 30 disciplines at U.S. universities from the point of view of selecting a doctoral program. These studies have been used in the educational community as important evaluations of programs; they have also provided data for other research designed to determine those specific factors such as size and research productivity of faculty that are associated with program ratings.

The desire for academic program ratings can be associated with a number of objectives, such as resource allocation among institutions and choice of institutions for study (particularly doctoral study). A great deal of concern has been expressed about the use of reputational ratings in making judgments about program quality. Among the problems associated with program ratings are the following (Hartnett, Clark and Baird, 1978):

1. The ratings are unfair to doctoral programs that do not place primary emphasis on research and on preparing students to do research.
2. There is a strong halo effect in that the ratings of a program may be unduly affected by the prestige, size or reputation of the university of which the program is a part.
3. There is a time lag in that ratings are usually based on impressions of what a program was in the past rather than on its current strengths and weaknesses.
4. Rating information seldom makes for a better understanding of a specific program's strengths and weaknesses and is not useful for program improvement.

Despite these problems, a great deal has been learned about program ratings that may be useful in assessing the quality of one program in comparison with others. Several studies in the nonaccounting literature that have investigated certain aspects of program ratings are discussed in the following paragraphs.

Elton and Rodgers (1973) studied the question of what constitutes quality in graduate education, suggesting that the Cartter study published by the American Council on Education may have resulted in a halo effect related to size variables. Data were collected from public sources for each department of mathematics, physics, chemistry and geology that were rated in the Cartter study as "extremely attractive," "attractive," "acceptable plus" and for a random sample of "less-than-acceptable-plus" departments. The size variables considered were (1) number of areas of specialization within a department; (2) number of faculty; (3) number of Ph.D. degrees awarded between 1960–1964; (4) number of full-time students; (5) number of first-year students; and (6) ratio of part-time to full-time students. The six size variables were used as predictor variables in four separate stepwise multiple discriminant analyses to demonstrate that the Cartter institutional ratings of departments in physical sciences can be predicted using data in the public domain that are related primarily to size. The researchers conclude with the statement that judgment program ratings such as the Cartter study are confounded with measures of size, and more suitable measures of quality are needed.

Beyer and Snipper (1974) examined the relationship of the rated quality of university departments to other possible quality indicators in two physical and two social sciences. The reputations of individual faculty members were found to be more closely associated with departmental reputation in the physical sciences than in the social sciences. Discriminant analysis of financial data and other objective indicators were 95–100 percent successful in disciminating the Cartter report ratings of quality for a stratified random sample of 20 departments in each of four scientific fields. The same variables were not the best predictors for all fields, however. The findings are discussed in terms of Kuhn's ideas of paradigm development, indicating that the structure of knowledge within a field has implications for attempted measures of quality. For example, in low paradigm fields like sociology, there is little relationship between objective indicators like the number of faculty or the level of funding and the subjective Cartter ratings of quality.

Solomon and Walters (1975) studied the relationship between prestige and productivity in graduate sociology departments, focusing primarily on the causal relationship between the two. The analysis, based on 45 departments, led the authors to the conclusion that current prestige of graduate sociology departments is essentially a function of prior prestige rather than of staff productivity.

Hartnett, Clark and Baird (1978) accumulated peer ratings of the quality of doctoral program faculties in chemistry, history and psychology. The ratings were then compared with those of the American Council on Education of six and 11 years earlier. The researchers conclude that ratings proved to be highly stable over the 11-year period, particularly for chemistry and history. Some ratings were also obtained for subspecialties within the three disciplines studied. While it is clear that variations in quality among subspecialties do exist and are important for individual program evaluations, in the authors' opinions it is unlikely that such subspecialty ratings would be feasible or useful in national surveys of the reputations of doctoral programs. Finally, the authors indicate that ratings were found to be highly related to a number of research-related variables such as size, productivity, and percentage of alumni holding academic positions at Ph.D.-granting universities, but were unrelated or only very weakly related to such variables as student-reported quality of teaching, the degree of faculty concern for students, or the degree of departmental effort toward the career development of junior members of the faculty.

Schwebel (1982) addressed a different dimension in faculty ratings when comparing the research productivity of education faculty and faculty in other fields. He first demonstrated that the average publication record of articles by education faculty both in their entire careers and in the prior two years had been markedly lower than that of agriculture or biological science faculty and slightly lower than social science faculty. Several reasons are cited for this difference, including the fact that many education faculty members spent considerable portions of their careers as practitioners rather than in academe. Historically, the nature of the mission of the education faculty has resulted in their preoccupation with day-to-day demands rather than on research, and faculty workloads in education exceeded those of faculty members in other disciplines.

ACCOUNTING EDUCATION RESEARCH

Several attempts have been made to rank academic accounting programs. These studies can generally be separated into two types—rankings based on surveys of judgmental perceptions of quality, and rankings based on objective measures of faculty and/or doctoral graduate productivity. Figure 6 includes a brief summary of seven such studies in terms of the nature of the ranking and the source of the information used to accomplish the ranking. The first two studies are judgmental surveys of quality; the remaining five are rankings based on objective measures of faculty and/or doctoral graduate productivity.

One striking feature of these studies is that many recognized the efforts of prior studies and attempted to improve on the methodology previously used. For example, some expand the number of journals used to rank faculties in previous studies; others attempted to standardize the quality of journals used to rank faculties; others attempted to relate research productivity to the size and/or age of the faculty or doctoral program.

Several other studies are important for the serious researcher in the area of accounting program ranking, although they do not result in program rankings themselves. Benjamin and Brenner (1974) surveyed accounting faculty members and department administrators concerning their quality rankings of 24 accounting and business-related journals. The study indicates a quality ranking of the 24 publications. Further, the researchers conclude that no significant differences exist between the rankings of faculty and de-

FIGURE 6
RANKINGS OF ACADEMIC ACCOUNTING PROGRAMS

Study	Year	Nature of Ranking	Source
Estes *Journal of Accountancy*	(1970)	Overall program quality	Survey of six groups: deans, accounting heads, full professors, other teachers, practitioners, accounting professional leaders
Carpenter, Crumbley, Strawser *Journal of Accountancy*	(1974)	Quality of faculty; effectiveness of graduate programs	Survey of accounting faculty
Bazley, Nickolai *Accounting Review*	(1975)	Faculty research productivity based on article count in four journals	Published article count
Andrews, McKenzie *Accounting Review*	(1978)	Faculty research productivity based on article count in four journals, adjusted for perceived journal quality and faculty size	Published article count and analysis
Windal *Accounting Review*	(1981)	Faculty research productivity based on article count in twelve journals and average output per faculty member	Published article count and analysis
Brown, Gardner *Accounting Review*	(1985)	Faculty and doctoral graduates based on citation analysis in four journals	Citation count
Jacobs, Hartgraves, Beard *Accounting Review*	(1986)	Doctoral graduates based on publication in eight journals adjusted for number of doctoral graduates and age of doctoral program	Publication count and analysis

partment administrators, and no significant differences were noted in responses compared on the basis of the number of articles or the number of books written by the respondents. Weber and Stevenson (1981) refined the quality-ranking approach of Benjamin and Brenner by considering subspecialties within accounting. They also speculated on the impact of their results on several of the ranking studies summarized in Figure 6. These two studies appear to be particularly relevant for future research efforts that attempt to rank accounting programs based on published research of faculty members or doctoral graduates, providing evidence on the perceived quality of a variety of accounting journals.

Finally, Crum (1981) provides information concerning doctoral programs in U.S. universities as part of an ongoing project concerning the supply of new doctorates. Several items of information concerning doctoral output are presented, including listings of those schools producing relatively few and relatively large numbers of doctorates and projections for doctoral program output for years beyond 1981.

RESEARCH OPPORTUNITIES IN ACCOUNTING

Future research in the area of academic program ratings is suggested in three broad areas: current program ratings, factors affecting program ratings, and the use of program ratings.

Assuming some value is associated with academic program ratings, a continuous research effort to update program ratings seems appropriate. To date many of these ratings have focused on the success of doctoral graduates of institutions. Extensions of those efforts, which look at additional measures of quality in terms of outputs, appears justifiable. Also, the study of relative quality for undergraduate and Master's programs, based on observed outcomes, is desirable.

The education and related literature is rich with material on factors affecting program ratings. Greater emphasis in the future of accounting education research should be placed on the determination of factors that affect accounting program ratings at all levels.

Finally, the use of program ratings is worthy of further study. Universities appear to require academic programs to formulate standards of comparison for a variety of purposes, including internal resource allocations, faculty evaluation, implementation of new programs and program changes, etc. Research in the area of the use of program ratings would be very beneficial to universities in their efforts to formulate valid standards of comparison for these and other purposes.

CONTINUING PROFESSIONAL EDUCATION

EDUCATION RESEARCH IN OTHER DISCIPLINES

The subject of continuing professional education (CPE) has been widely discussed in the educational literature as well as in the literature of specific professions that require or recommend individual CPE programs. Published research ranges from broad considerations of the need for and nature of CPE to narrow studies concerning the detailed CPE needs of individual professional groups.

Three books are described below which provide the serious researcher in the area of CPE a rich background for the study of specific research questions in this area. Houle's *Continuing Learning in the Professions* (1980) provides an extensive bibliography and an organized discussion of many previous research efforts. Among the topics discussed are the crisis in the professions leading to an awareness of the need for CPE, goals of lifelong education, designing and evaluating programs or learning and assuring quality in continuing education.

Two volumes published by the Division of Academic and Professional Programs of the University of Washington include a variety of papers on CPE. *The Assessment and Development of Professionals: Theory and Practice* (LeBreton, 1976) includes papers which examine various problems and solutions in professional planning and development. The second volume, *The Evaluation of Continuing Education for Professional: A Systems View* (Murphy, 1979), focuses on applied research in evaluation methodologies which may be appropriate at every stage of professional program development. Both include papers authored by scholars and practitioners in continuing education and raise numerous research questions which may be fruitful areas for further pursuit.

Another important background source for researchers in CPE in Lowenthal's (1981) discussion of voluntary and mandatory continuing education for professionals. The arguments for and against mandatory CPE are carefully discussed, based on an analysis of several professions, including accounting. The issue of retesting for renewal of practice licenses is also addressed. An extensive bibliography is presented, including references to studies in many fields, including medicine, nursing, law and dentistry.

Knox (1982) studied university-based CPE efforts in five fields—medicine, pharmacy, social work, education and law. From data based on interviews and case descriptions, Knox determined that university CPE programs varied greatly in their vitality as reflected in program expansion and innovation. Three major characteristics associated with vitality were educational leadership, obtaining support and involvement of practitioners.

Applied studies of specific CPE questions in individual occupational fields and professions are numerous in the literature. Two that are indicative of the many studies that have been published are those of Field, and Lloyd and Abrahamson.

Field (1980) surveyed life and health insurance agents in the state of Washington concerning their attitudes toward required agent education. Several conclusions were reached, including the following:

1. Until the benefits of prelicense and/or continuing education can be proved or disproved to exceed their costs, any continuing education program should be finite or limited instead of continuing over the life of the license.
2. A person who teaches an approved course of instruction should qualify for the same number of classroom hours as are granted to an individual who successfully completes the instruction.
3. Any continuing education course (as opposed to a prelicense education course) should require a final examination and the issuance of a grade (including pass-fail).
4. Follow-up studies and additional research is needed in the area of prelicense and continuing education. Research is particularly needed on the benefits, if any, of such education and their relationship to cost.

Lloyd and Abrahamson (1979) prepared an extensive literature survey to assess the effectiveness of continuing medical education (CME). They state that the desired outcome of CME can be defined in terms of at least three possible end-products: physician competence, physician performance, and patient health status. Based on an evaluation of 22 previous studies in the area of physician competence, the authors conclude that CME has been reasonably effective in this area. Based on an evaluation of 26 studies in the area of physician performance, the authors are less optimistic about the effectiveness of CME, indicating that fewer than half of the studies indicated improved physician performance. Based on only four studies in the area of patient health status, the authors essentially reach no conclusion, because half of the studies demonstrated significant improvement in patient health status following CME, and the other half reported no significant improvement. This article raises several interesting methodological questions concerning the studies cited, discusses several areas for future research, and includes an extensive bibliography of the specific studies cited in the general area of CME.

ACCOUNTING EDUCATION RESEARCH

Several studies have investigated the general attitude of accounting practitioners toward CPE. Brenner and Strawser (1972) surveyed CPAs to determine their views on required CPE and the extent of their participation in CPE programs. Several general conclusions can be drawn from this study: (1) The majority of respondents in public practice, as well as those not in public practice, favored mandatory CPE; (2) The majority favored a requirement to demonstrate CPE standard compliance every three years; (3) The majority felt that the CPE recommendation of the AICPA Council was reasonable; and (4) Little support was demonstrated for periodic re-examination of CPA's. Respondents to the Brenner and Strawser survey indicated that nonpracticing CPA's were less involved in formal CPE offerings than were practicing CPA's. A majority of respondents would not have met an average 40 hours-per-year requirement, although at the time of this study the requirement had only recently been proposed and was not in effect in many states. Those attending formal CPE programs took programs from the AICPA, state societies of CPA's, individual firms, colleges, the NAA, and other providers.

Smith, Tidwell and Lembke (1972) studied the participation in CPE by practicing CPA's in four midwestern states when CPE was still voluntary. They found that on the average practicing CPA's were taking more CPE courses than were suggested by the AICPA Council, although approximately one-fourth of practicing CPA's did not satisfy the AICPA proposal. This study attempted to identify significant relationships between the level of CPE participation and specific characteristics: age, education, years of experience, job level, firm size, office size, community size, memberships, and professional reading activities.

The issue of mandatory vs. voluntary CPE is discussed by May (1975). He describes the rapid advancement from no CPE requirements to national recognition of the need for CPE and suggests that a legislated program is generally more desirable than a formal voluntary program.

A survey by the California Department of Consumer Affairs (1983) covered a variety of professions and other licensed occupations in California. California CPA's were found to have taken 50 percent more continuing education hours per year than most other professionals, spent less money on courses taken and were more satisfied with the results than other professional groups. The majority of respondents expressed satisfaction with the current mandatory CPE program, were satisfied with course locations, rated as excellent the choices of courses available, and preferred courses offered by professional associations.

Drury (1980) surveyed professional accountants in Canada, investigating their general attitudes toward a variety of CPE issues. Specifically, he attempted to determine what professional accountants in Quebec were doing to satisfy CPE requirements, what support or obstacles they were encountering, and what their attitudes were toward voluntary or mandatory CPE. Reasons cited for CPE involvement were professional requirements, personal satisfaction, and job advancement. Many respondents indicated that they did not use formal CPE courses but rather were engaged in informal reading and other CPE activities. Employer support was generally found to be satisfactory. A majority of the respondents supported voluntary CPE, were not seriously opposed to mandatory CPE and were opposed to government-controlled CPE.

Anderson and Arlinghaus (1984) surveyed corporate executives who had a direct relationship to the tax function in Fortune 500 companies. Most companies were found to encourage their staff personnel to be involved in CPE activities but did not require their involvement. Most paid part or all of the cost of CPE courses. The following ranking of the effectiveness of sources of CPE resulted from this study: other, college courses, AICPA courses, Practicing Law Institute, state CPA society, in-house courses, and the National Association of Accountants courses. The "other" category included courses offered by such organizations as the Tax Executives Institute and the World Trade Institute.

In a study of tax professionals in Ohio, Salzarulo and Arlinghaus (1985) surveyed Big Eight accounting firms. While the major thrust of this study was the formal education (i.e., degrees earned) rather than continuing education, approximately one-third of respondents felt that their employers would be supportive of their entering an evening tax-related advanced degree program. The majority spent a significant amount of time in tax training programs, mostly sponsored by their own firms. The level of satisfaction with these programs was high, and the programs were generally considered to be of high quality.

Fish, Gipple and Katz (1985) discuss the elusive nature of assessing CPE quality and the importance of assessing CPE needs. Educational need is defined as the gap between an individual's level of competence and the higher level of competency needed for effective performance as defined by the individual, the organization, or society. A needs triangle is described, consisting of determining likely sources of identifying CPE needs, probable sources of CPE, and information-gathering techniques. While this article does not involve empirical research, it provides a framework for assessing CPE quality and CPE needs, a potentially fertile area of further accounting education research.

Seiler and Label (1974) studied the impact of changes in university accounting curricula on professional staff training efforts. While the study does not involve CPE per se, it does raise some interesting questions concerning the relationship of staff training programs of CPA firms and the university curriculum recently completed by new entrants into the profession. Three conclusions are reached concerning changing university curricula and staff training programs:

1. A smaller portion of the accountant's formal educational program is being devoted to technical accounting subjects.
2. The approach taken in formal accounting courses is becoming more conceptual and less procedurally oriented.
3. The amount of professional experience of a given faculty will directly affect the curriculum of that institution. While these conclusions are reached in the context of firm training programs, the same may be true for CPE in a broader sense and may have relevance for future CPE research efforts.

RESEARCH OPPORTUNITIES IN ACCOUNTING

Continuing professional education (CPE) has been a part of the accounting profession for many years, but it has been the subject of limited study in the accounting education literature. A logical starting point in future research is the current status of CPE requirements, particularly for CPA certification purposes. Research should ultimately be done concerning the impact of CPE on accounting education and practice. Some who advance certain positions concerning accounting education (e.g., five-year programs) call for a simultaneous consideration of CPE as part of a student's career-long education. The relationship of pre-professional education and CPE is a fruitful area of pursuit. Also, the impact of CPA on practice, including the updating of practitioners' knowledge and the quality of accounting practice are worthy of study.

The delivery of CPE and the role that educators play or should play is an interesting topic for consideration. A related question is the role that involvement in CPE plays or should play in the evaluation of faculty.

CHAPTER 6 BIBLIOGRAPHY

AACSB, *Accreditation Council Policies, Procedures, and Standards* (AACSB, 1986–87).

AICPA, *Final Report: Board on Standards for Programs and Schools of Professional Accountancy* (New York: AICPA, 1977).

———, *Report of the Committee on Education and Experience Requirements for CPAs* (New York: AICPA, 1969).

———, *Schools of Accountancy: A Look at the Issues* (New York: AICPA, 1975).

Adelman, C., "The Major Seventh: Standards as a Leading Tone in Higher Education," *New Directions for Higher Education* (September 1983), pp. 39–54.

Albright, B., "Quality Incentives in the Budget," *New Directions for Higher Education*, No. 52 (September 1985), pp. 15–30.

American Taxation Association Committee on Educational Standards for Tax Faculty, "Demand for Tax Faculty Members—A Static or Changing Need?" *The Journal of The American Taxation Association* (Spring 1983), pp. 52–55.

Anderson, D. T., and B. P. Arlinghaus, "The Recruiting, Training, and Professional Involvement of Tax Personnel in Large Corporations," *Tax Executive* (April 1984), pp. 169–195.

Andrews, W. T., and P. B. McKenzie, "Leading Accounting Departments Revisited," *The Accounting Review* (January 1978), pp. 135–138.

Arnold, D. F., and T. J. Geiselhart, "Practitioners' View on Five-Year Educational Requirement," *The Accounting Review* (April 1984), pp. 314–324.

Baldwin, R. G., ed., "Incentives for Faculty Vitality," *New Directions for Higher Education*, No. 51 (September 1985).

———, and M. V. Krotseng, "Incentives in the Academy: Issues and Options," *New Directions for Higher Education*, No. 51 (September 1985), pp. 5–20.

Bazley, J. D., and L. A. Nickolai, "Comparison of Published Accounting Research and Qualities of Accounting Faculty and Doctoral Programs," *The Accounting Review* (July 1975), pp. 605–610.

Benjamin, J. J., and V. C. Brenner, "Perceptions of Journal Quality," *The Accounting Review* (April 1974), pp. 360–362.

Bevan, J. M., "Who has the Role of Building Incentives?" *New Directions for Higher Education*, No. 51 (September 1985), pp. 45–58.

Beyer, J. M., and R. Snipper, "Objective Versus Subjective Indicators of Quality in Graduate Education," *Sociology of Education* (Fall 1974), pp. 541–557.

Bloom, R., A. Debessay, and W. Markell, "The Development of Schools of Accounting and the Underlying Issues," *Journal of Accounting Education* (Spring 1986), pp. 7–29.

Bowen, H. R., *Investment in Learning: The Individual and Social Value of American Higher Education* (San Francisco: Jossey-Bass Publishers, 1977).

Bremser, W. G., V. C. Brenner, and P. E. Dascher, "Schools of Professional Accountancy: The Management's Accountant's View," *Management Accounting* (September 1977a), pp. 14–16, 23.

———, "The Feasibility of Professional Schools: An Empirical Study." *The Accounting Review* (April 1977b), pp. 465–473.

Brenner, V. C., and R. H. Stawser, "CPAs' Views on Required Continuing Education," *Journal of Accountancy* (January 1972), pp. 86–89.

Brown, J. F., Jr., and T. E. Balke, "Accounting Curriculum Comparison by Degree Program of Schools Intending to Seek AACSB Accreditation," *Issues in Accounting Education* (1983), pp. 50–59.

———, and ———, "Do Accountants Need More Education?" *Management Accounting* (November 1982), pp. 26–29.

Brown, L. D., and J. C. Gardner, "Applying Citation Analysis to Evaluate the Research Contributions of Accounting Faculty and Doctoral Programs," *The Accounting Review* (April 1985), pp. 262–277.

California Department of Consumer Affairs, "Study Shows CPAs Attitude Toward CPE in California," *Journal of Accountancy* (September 1983), pp. 12, 14.

Campbell, D. R., and R. W. Williamson, "Accreditation of Accounting Programs: Administrators' Perception of Proposed Standards," *Issues in Acounting Education* (1983), pp. 60–70.

Carpenter, C. G., D. L. Crumbley, and R. H. Strawser, "A New Ranking of Accounting Faculties and Doctoral Programs," *Journal of Accountancy* (June 1974), pp. 90–94.

Cartter, A. M., *An Assessment of Quality in Graduate Education* (Washington: American Council on Education, 1966).

Chapman, D. W., "A Model of Student College Choice," *Journal of Higher Education* (September/October 1981), pp. 490–505.

Clemow, B., "Collegiate Accreditation," *The College Board Review* (Winter 1985–86), pp. 19–21, 31–34.

Crum, W. F., "1980 Survey of Doctoral Programs in Accounting in the United States," *The Accounting Review* (July 1981), pp. 634–641.

Dockweiler, R. C., and C. G. Willis, "On the Use of Entry Requirements for Undergraduate Accounting Majors," *The Accounting Review* (July 1984), pp. 496–504.

Dressel, P. L., F. C. Johnson, and P. M. Marcus, *The Confidence Crisis: An Analysis of University Departments* (San Francisco: Jossey-Bass Publishers, 1970).

———, and S. B. Pratt, *The World of Higher Education* (San Franciso: Jossey-Bass Publishers, 1971).

Drury, C. H., "Continuing Professional Education for Accountants: A Survey of Activities," *Cost and Management* (January-February 1980), pp. 8–11.

Eckel, N., and W. A. Johnson, "A Model for Screening and Classifying Potential Accounting Majors," *Journal of Accounting Education* (Fall 1983), pp. 57–65.

———, and T. Ross, "Schools Versus Departments of Accounting: Is There Really a Difference?" *Journal of Accounting Education* (Spring 1985), pp. 1–14.

Eells, W. C., and E. V. Hollis, *Administration of Higher Education: An Annotated Bibliography* Bulletin No. 7 (Washington: U.S. Government Printing Office, 1960).

Elton, C. F., and S. A. Rodgers, "The Departmental Rating Game: Measure of Quantity or Quality?" *Higher Education* (1973), pp. 439–446.

Estes, R. W., "A Ranking of Accounting Programs," *Journal of Accountancy* (July 1970), pp. 86–90.

Field, I. M., "Required Continuing Agent Education—Panacea or Palliative?" *Best's Review* (March 1980), pp. 26–28, 82, 84, 88–89.

Fish, G. L., L. D. Gipple, and J. E. Katz, "Assessing CPE Needs," *Journal of Accountancy* (July 1985), pp. 79–83.

Hanford, G. H., "Further Comment: Yes the SAT Does Help Colleges," *Harvard Educational Review* (August 1985), pp. 324–331.

Hargadon, F., "Tests and College Admissions," *American Psychologist* (October 1981), pp. 1112–1119.

Harrell, A. M., and M. J. Stahl, "Need for Achievement, Need for Affiliation, and the Academic Performance and Career Intentions of Accounting Students," *Journal of Accounting Education* (Fall 1983), pp. 149–154.

Hartnett, R. T., M. J. Clark, and L. L. Barid, "Reputational Ratings of Doctoral Programs," *Science* (March 1978), pp. 1310–1314.

Hendrickson, H. S., "The Changing Content of the CPA Examination," *Journal of Accountancy* (July 1971), pp. 60–67.

Heron, R. P., and D. Friesen, "Growth and Development of College Administrative Structures," *Research in Higher Education* (1973), pp. 333–346.

Holstrum, G. L., and D. A. Wilson, "Recent Changes in U.S. Accounting Curriculums: A Move Toward the Beamer Recommendations?" *Journal of Accountancy* (April 1974), pp. 90–94.

Houle, C. O., *Continuing Learning in the Professions* (San Francisco: Jossey-Bass Publishers, 1980).

Ingram, R. W., and R. J. Petersen, "An Evaluation of AICPA Tests for Predicting the Performance of Accounting Majors," *The Accounting Review* (January 1987), pp. 215–223.

Izard, C. D., and J. D. McKinney, "The Certification of Tax Specialists: Some Empirical Results," *The Journal of the American Taxation Association* (Fall 1983), pp. 40–48.

Jacobs, F. A., A. L. Hartgraves, and L. H. Beard, "Publication Productivity of Doctoral Alumni: A Time-Adjusted Model," *The Accounting Review* (January 1986), pp. 179–187.

―――, and H. C. Herring, III, "Salary Compression in the Academic Marketplace: Some Empirical Evidence," *Issues in Accounting Education* (Fall 1987), pp. 237–250.

Kasten, K. L., "Tenure and Merit Pay as Rewards for Research, Teaching, and Service at a Research University," *Journal of Higher Education* (July/August 1984), pp. 500–514.

Katz, D. A, "Faculty Salaries, Promotions, and Productivity at a Large University," *The American Economic Review* (June 1973), pp. 469–477.

Knox, A. B., "Organizational Dynamics in University Continuing Professional Education," *Adult Education* (1982), pp. 117–129.

Lawrence, J. H., "Developmental Needs as Intrinsic Incentives," *New Directions for Higher Education*, No. 51 (September 1985), pp. 59–68.

LeBreton, P. P. (Ed.), *The Assessment and Development of Professionals: Theory and Practice* (Seattle: University of Washington, 1976).

Lewis, M. T., W. T. Lin, and D. Z. Williams, "The Economic Status of Accounting Educators: An Empirical Study," *Advances in Accounting* (1984), pp. 127–144.

Litten, L. H., "Different Strokes in the Applicant Pool: Some Refinement in a Model of Student College Choice," *Journal of Higher Education*, (July/August 1982), pp. 383–402.

Lloyd, J. S., and S. Abrahamson, "Effectiveness of Continuing Medical Education," *Evaluation and the Health Professions* (September 1979), pp. 251–280.

Lowenthal, W., "Continuing Education for Professionals—Voluntary or Mandatory?" *Journal of Higher Education* (September/October 1982), pp. 519–538.

Lubell, M. S., and B. C. Broden, "The Masters Degree in Taxation: An Academic Survey," *The Accounting Review* (January 1975), pp. 170–176.

May, G. S., "Continuing Professional Education—Required or Voluntary?" *Journal of Accountancy* (August 1975), pp. 110–113.

Meckling, W. H., and J. L. Zimmerman, "Schools of Accountancy—Accomplish Little," *The CPA Journal* (October 1976), pp. 25–29.

Mehl, A. G., and L. E. Lammers, "A Report and Analysis of the Accountancy Faculty Recruiting Surveys of 1975–1978," *The Accounting Review* (July 1979), pp. 609–617.

Millard, R. M., "Accreditation," *New Directions for Higher Education* (September 1983), pp. 9–28.

Murphy, K. J., ed., *The Evaluation of Continuing Education for Professionals: A Systems View* (University of Washington, 1979).

Myslinski, N. R., and R. I. Jeffrey, "The Dental Admissions Interview," *College and University* (Winter 1985), pp. 160–179.

Olson, C., and M. A. King, "A Preliminary Analysis of the Decision Process of Graduate Students in College Choice," *College and University* (Summer 1985), pp. 304–315.

O'Neill, J. P., "Examinations and Quality Control," *New Directions for Higher Education* (September 1983), pp. 69–79.

Rayburn, F. R., and E. H. Bonfield, "Schools of Accountancy: Attitudes and Attitude Structure," *The Accounting Review* (July 1978), pp. 752–756.

Roose, K. D., and C. J. Andersen, *A Rating of Graduate Programs* (Washington: American Council on Education, 1970).

Rouse, R., J. R. Davis, and G. T. Friedlob, "The Relevant Experience Criterion for Accounting Accreditation by the AACSB—A Current Assessment," *Journal of Accounting Education* (Spring 1986), pp. 147–160.

Roy, R. H., and J. H. MacNeill, *Horizons for a Profession* (New York: AICPA, 1967).

Salzarulo, W. P., and Arlinghaus, B. P., "Developments in the Education of Tax Professionals in Ohio," *The Ohio CPA Journal* (Summer 1985), 15–19.

Schuster, J. H., "Faculty Vitality: Observations from the Field," *New Directions for Higher Education*, No. 51 (September 1985), pp. 21–32.

Schwebel, M., "Research Productivity of Education Faculty: A Comparative Study," *Educational Studies* (Summer 1982), pp. 224–239.

Seiler, R. E, and W. A. Label, "Impact of Curricular Changes Upon Professional Staff Training Efforts," *The Accounting Review* (October 1974), pp. 854–859.

Siegel, G., "National Study on Professional Accounting Education: Initial Results on Departmental/Professional School Differences," *Issues in Accounting Education* (1983), pp. 9–18.

Siegfried, J., and K. White, "Financial Rewards to Research and Teaching: A Case Study of Academic Economists," *The American Economic Review* (May 1973), pp. 309–315.

Skeels, J. W., and R. P. Fairbanks, "Publish or Perish: An Analysis of the Mobility of Publishing and Non-Publishing Economists," *The Southern Economic Journal* (July 1968) pp. 17–25.

Smith, J. H., V. H. Tidwell, and V. C. Lembke., "An Analysis of Participation in Continuing Education," *Journal of Accountancy* (January 1972), pp. 40–45.

Solomon, W. E., and A. T. Walters. "The Relationship Between Productivity and Prestige of Graduate Sociology Departments: Fact or Artifact." *The American Sociologist* (November 1975), pp. 229–236.

Spiceland, J. D., V. C. Brenner, and B. P. Hartman, "Standards for Programs and Schools of Accounting: Accounting Group Perceptions," *The Accounting Review* (January 1980), pp. 134–143.

Sterling, R., "Professional Schools of Accountancy: Some Academic Questions," in *Schools of Accountancy: a Look at the Issues* (New York: AICPA, 1975), 51–66.

Tidwell, V. H., and R. W. Wyndelts, "Graduate Tax Education in AACSB Schools: Where We Stand Today," *The Accounting Review* (October 1977), pp. 963–970.

Tiller, M. G., and C. White, "Are Accounting Majors Really Better? Evaluating Admission and Retention Standards for Undergraduate Accounting Programs?" *Journal of Accounting Education* (Spring 1983), pp. 19–34.

Tuckman, H. P., J. H. Gapinski, and R. P. Hagemann, "Faculty Skills and the Salary Structure in Academe: A Market Perspective," *The American Economic Review* (September 1977), pp. 692–702.

Warren, J. R., "Editor's Notes," *New Directions for Higher Education* (September 1983a), pp. 1–7.

———. "Quality in the Classroom," *New Directions for Higher Education* (September 1983b), pp. 55–67.

Weber, R. P. and W. C. Stevenson, "Evaluations of Accounting Journal and Department Quality," *The Accounting Review* (July 1981), pp. 596–612.

Whitman, R. B., Five Years of Education Not Required," *Journal of Accountancy* (September 1974), pp. 93–96.

Williams, D. Z. et al., *Accounting Data Base: 1984–1985* (Also 1983–84; 1982–83; 1980–81; 1979–80); All published by the Center for Accounting Research, University of Southern California).

Windal, F. W., "Publishing for a Varied Public: An Empirical Study." *The Accounting Review* (July 1981), pp. 653–658.

Yost, G. C., "The Fifth Year: Reaction in Florida," *Journal of Accounting Education* (Spring 1986), pp. 45–54.

CHAPTER 7

Outcomes

In this monograph, we structured discussions of the major research domains in higher education around a simple input-process-output model that was introduced in Chapter 1 and elaborated upon in Chapters 3 through 6. Faculty and students are viewed as inputs into an educational process that is largely shaped by administrators and other constituents. In Chapters 3 and 4, we examined the inputs—students and faculty; in Chapter 5, the educational process. In Chapter 6, we discussed the context of education as influenced by administration and constituents. In the model, outputs are designated only as "outcomes," with no further explication. A diagram presenting the primary components of the framework is presented in Figure 7.

Our discussion of outcomes in this chapter is different from that of the preceding chapters, largely because the education literature on the issues is only beginning to develop. Our review led us through national-level committee reports, public speeches by government officials at all levels, and several important articles in the professional and popular press calling for improvement of higher education through evaluation of its accomplishments. At the same time, we noted that the movement toward accountability of elementary and secondary educational institutions that swept through state legislatures in the early 1980's is now shifting toward higher education.

Meanwhile, most of the empirical research evidence about outcome specification and measurement is found in articles that are concerned more with how to change outcomes than with examination of their theoretical or practical meaning. The result is that we do not know enough about outcomes of higher education. Research that enhances our understanding of outcomes can make a profoundly important contribution to accounting education, higher education, and the accounting profession. Therefore, in this chapter we discuss outcomes as a research frontier. What outcomes are, and what they could be, are the real-world issues that will motivate education research in numerous research domains.

The first section of this chapter is a discussion of outcomes, focusing on the importance, and difficulty, of identifying and evaluating outcomes in higher education. The second section introduces outcome specification, and the concluding section focuses on outcome specification in accounting education.

IDENTIFYING AND EVALUATING OUTCOMES

Outcomes are the things that are accomplished by, in, or through higher education. In the higher education literature, the term is often preceded by an adjective that identifies some type of outcome, such as the affective and cognitive outcomes of instruction as observed in students (e.g., Perkins and Abbott, 1982); or the institutional outcomes of political, economic, and social forces, as reflected in changing faculty workloads (e.g., Slaughter, 1985). Higher education aims at achieving a variety of valued outcomes and avoiding dysfunctional or less desirable ones. A comprehensive list of outcomes, or even ways of talking about outcomes, seems impossible to compile, although several lengthy ones exist (e.g., Heiss (1975) presents over 300 student outcome measures). We may think of outcomes from a variety of real-world decision perspectives, ranging from that of the legislator who wants to know what benefits are to be derived from a proposed budget increase for higher education, to a student who wants to know what is worth learning in order to achieve personal goals and aspirations. We have chosen to discuss outcomes from three perspectives: societal, institutional, and individual.

Societal outcomes of higher education represent the broadest level of our classification. These outcomes are those that are valued because they are thought to promote the general welfare of our society and its citizens. They include enduring education objectives such as those embodied in Dewey's conception of education as a civilizing influence in human society (Dewey, 1916), and the ideals commonly inscribed in Latin on uni-

FIGURE 7
ACCOUNTING EDUCATION RESEARCH FRAMEWORK

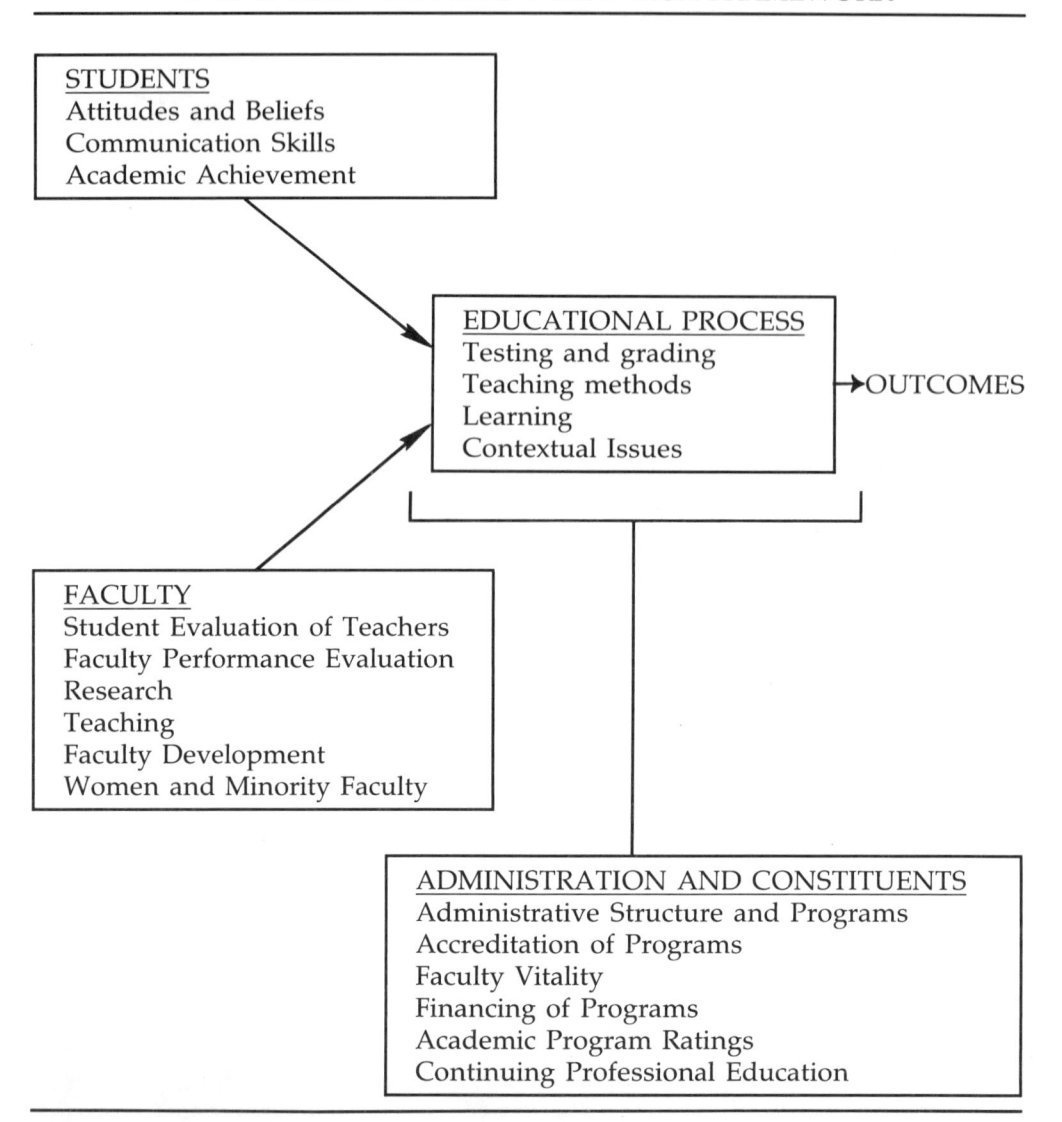

STUDENTS
Attitudes and Beliefs
Communication Skills
Academic Achievement

EDUCATIONAL PROCESS
Testing and grading
Teaching methods
Learning
Contextual Issues
→ OUTCOMES

FACULTY
Student Evaluation of Teachers
Faculty Performance Evaluation
Research
Teaching
Faculty Development
Women and Minority Faculty

ADMINISTRATION AND CONSTITUENTS
Administrative Structure and Programs
Accreditation of Programs
Faculty Vitality
Financing of Programs
Academic Program Ratings
Continuing Professional Education

versity insignia. Because they directly reflect fundamental societal values, they are difficult to define and evaluate and virtually impossible to measure.

Societal outcomes that are often mentioned reflect diverse ideologies of authors working from the perspectives of a variety of academic disciplines. Two articles, Rossides (1984) and *The Governors' Report on Education* (1986), illustrate the importance of the issues as well as the fundamental differences in perspectives. The Governors' Report presents a summary of education's successes and failures and a call for improvement through outcome evaluation and cooperative effort between government and education. Rossides, arguing from an extreme sociological position, presents higher education as a tool of an elite, repressive upper class in a capitalistic society and suggests that the valued outcomes of higher education are clever machinations of the ruling class. Some of the societal outcomes of higher education that are often mentioned in the public forum and in the literature (e.g., Association of American Colleges, 1985; National Institute of Education, 1984; Bennett, 1984; Rossides, 1984) are the enhancement of the following.

- Economic growth, control, and efficiency
- Social stability
- Cultural vitality
- International credibility
- Social, racial, and sexual equity
- Military strength
- General prosperity

Less ambitious societal outcomes that are often linked to higher education are unemployment reduction, productivity increases, workforce training, wealth redistribution, and maintenance of societal and social norms. Many of these are broad, widely accepted societal objectives. Others are more controversial, and none is the sole responsibility of higher education. Turnbull (1985), noting some of the practical problems associated with understanding higher education's outcomes, warns that ". . . it is essential to realize that the purposes of higher education are a matter of fundamental debate." The debates over education's societal purposes are carried out within and between divergent parties, each with its own unique perspective, values, and objectives, and each with its own configuration of desired outcomes of higher education.

Institutional outcomes are those that have implications for the many organized aggregates of individual interests (institutions) involved in higher education. These institutions include the traditional list: colleges and universities; academic disciplines, programs, and departments, etc.; as well as state legislatures, funding agencies, professional organizations, student and faculty groups, and many others. Desired institutional outcomes, like societal outcomes are quite diverse, reflecting the values and objectives of many different parties. Of these outcomes, those that are found in most university statements of "mission" are the most widely discussed (e.g., Astin, 1982; Turnbull, 1985; Slaughter, 1985; Hoyt and Spangler, 1979). They include the following:

- Maintenance and generation of knowledge
- Education of successive generations of students
- Provision of service benefitting society
- Development of faculty research and teaching potential
- Improvement of teaching and learning in higher education
- Retention of high quality students, faculty, and administrators
- Development of resources to achieve primary objectives through teaching, research, and service

Schools, departments, and programs within colleges and universities may directly pursue some of these outcomes and contribute to the achievement of others. They also typically pursue a variety of more specific outcomes in response to the objectives of several constituent groups, such as state legislatures, accreditation boards, professional organizations, and academic disciplines, as well as faculty and student organizations.

Institutional outcome assessment in higher education has historically included such measures as the number of degrees awarded, the student retention rate, the proportion of undergraduates continuing their educations through graduate school, and the win-loss ratio of athletic teams, as well as measures of the economic, physical, and intellectual resources commanded by the institution. More mundane measures include the extent of library usage, student participation in campus cultural and social activities, and the consumption rates of various campus services. All these measures gauge important institutional outcomes, but they are rather distant from those that comprise higher education's mission statements. They are equally distant from the individuals through whom institutional missions are directed and achieved—students, faculty, and administrators. Recently, institutional outcome assessment has shifted in emphasis from traditional measures toward evaluation of the individual outcomes of those through whom higher education achieves its primary goals—students and faculty (Astin, 1982; Ewell, 1985).

The *individual* outcomes that are sought by students, faculty, and administrators in higher education defy enumeration. For the most part, they entail a more or less well-defined notion of personal growth or achievement. Examples are effective teaching and meaningful research by faculty; purposeful leadership by administrators; and knowledge acquisition and skills development by students. Some of the student outcomes that are frequently cited in the higher education literature (Pace, 1984; Ewell, 1985; Trainor, 1986) are the following:

- Knowledge acquisition
- Cognitive and affective development
- Development of skills and competencies
- Enhancement of values awareness and socialization

Student outcomes are usually presented in language broad enough to admit numerous interpretations. For the last decade, the appropriateness, specification, and measurement of these outcomes have been at the center of widespread debate and reforms that have continued in primary and secondary education. The issues have been extensively publicized in the political arena at the national and state levels, acted upon by many state legislatures, and decided in our judicial system. Most of the public discussions about student outcomes progress to a central question: What specific knowledge, skills, competencies, developmental levels, etc. should students be expected to attain through higher education?

Measures of individual student outcomes have been around for years in higher education (Pace, 1984). Most appear only in the research literature, as summarized in the preceding chapters. These include the many measures of student development that researchers use to judge the effectiveness of alternative instructional, curricular, and institutional alternatives. A few are widely used in administrative decision-making and in a variety of other ways. Of the latter measures, student grades and standardized admissions test scores are the best-known and most widely-used. Student grades, even though mistrusted by many faculty, seem to many students and recruiters to be among the most important outcomes of the educational process. Within each academic community, a student's grades (or grade point average) are also important—both to the compilers of Dean's Lists, scholarship committees, and other registers of accomplishment, and to the students they represent. Since grades are the primary evaluative dimension of a student's academic record, they are, in turn, often the only tangible summary of an endeavor that demands years of students' lives. In higher education, educators generally agree that course grades are primarily measures of knowledge acquired; they do not agree that grades are always valid, reliable measures of whatever it is that students were supposed to have gained in a given course. The meaning and validity of grades vary considerably within academic programs, and too much between programs for their widespread use as outcomes in institutional assessment.

Like grades, standardized aptitude and achievement test scores may play a very significant role in students' lives by directing and limiting individual student's choices. They are designed to measure individual student characteristics, to help students choose among academic programs, and to aid faculties and administrators in selecting the students most suited to their programs. For example, prospective students are evaluated, to some extent, based on their scores on the ACT, SAT, GRE, GMAT, LSAT, MCAT, etc. Unlike student grades, admissions test scores are also used as a basis for evaluating institutions of higher learning (Pace 1984; Ewell, 1985). Universities, colleges, and programs use them to signal admissions selectivity to prospective students, faculty, recruiters, and others as well as to evaluate the achievement of a primary institutional outcome, the "educating" of students. Secondary schools are evaluated by their senior students' scores on undergraduate admissions exams, and undergraduate programs are evaluated by their senior students' scores on graduate admissions exams. The assumption, borne out by some empirical evidence, is that these scores capture some of the knowledge imparted through academic progress.

Other tests are designed specifically to aid in institutional evaluation through student outcome assessment (e.g., ACT-COMP and the UGRE; Pace, 1979; Hurdle, 1981). Most of the better-known tests assess student general knowledge attainment; many evaluate specific skills (such as communication skills) or competencies (such as mathematical reasoning). Hundreds of instruments are published, and available, for the assessment of student personality traits, aptitudes, values, interests, and attitudes (Heiss, 1975). The most recent and potentially interesting of these instruments is the AACSB's Core Curriculum Assessment Program (CCAP), which is designed to assess educational outcomes for higher education business programs in several disciplines (AACSB, 1987). The number and diverse measurement objectives of these measures attest to the many student outcomes that are sought in higher education. They also suggest the improbability of discovering a single, comprehensive outcome measure that adequately captures student outcomes for all students, or for all institutions.

Aggregated individual faculty outcomes are also used to evaluate the achievement of institutional outcomes. For example, the number and quality of an institution's faculty publications are viewed as indicants of the "knowledge advancement" achieved by an institution for use by state legislators, funding agencies, prospective faculty and students, and others. Many other faculty outcome measures, most having to do with teaching and service, are used as a basis for evaluating individual faculty members, and in aggregate, as indicants of various institutional outcomes (Astin, 1982; Slaughter, 1985). As with student outcomes, a comprehensive faculty outcome measure, robust enough for all faculty and institutions, does not exist.

Outcomes are obviously complex, reflecting the many objectives and goals of higher education's actors and institutions. They exist at multiple levels, for diverse purposes, with varying degrees of clarity and importance. For the most part, the measures that are available, whether used for individual or institutional outcome assessment, tend to be rather narrow, at least in comparison to the outcomes sought in higher education. Regardless of their restricted scope, and sometimes questionable validity, measures of education's outcomes are important because they are used as a basis for significant decisions by and about students, faculty, administrators, and other constituents of higher education. As reliance on outcome measures increases, so do the debates over their validity and usefulness, and the level of concern over the fundamental purposes and outcomes of higher education. Higher education is asked to account not only for how well it achieves its purposes, but also to explain why those purposes are worth pursuing.

Most of the evidence brought to bear in the public arena, by both critics and advocates, is drawn from among the measures that are already available as decision-making tools and formal evaluation criteria. More evidence on most of the issues is available in the published research of higher education and in journals devoted to education in many academic disciplines, including accounting. For many years, education researchers have studied outcomes as the criteria by which their innovations, alternatives, theories, and hypotheses have been evaluated. Many of higher education's outcomes are the researcher's dependent variables. In accounting, for example, researchers have used student grades, exam scores, student evaluations of teaching, CPA examination performance, psychological inventories, and various attitude measures as criteria (dependent variables) to evaluate alternative instructional methods and program structures (see Chapters 3 and 6, in particular).

Many of the very real problems with institutional assessment are research methods problems involving the measurement and control of the many variables that may influence outcomes. Among the more frequently cited are the evaluation of outcomes without controlling for "inputs" (notably student quality), and measurement mis-specification (e.g., evaluated outcomes which do not measure the primary objectives of the institution). These and other research methods concerns are discussed in Chapter 2. Other concerns center on the practical impact of the use of the assessments. For example, measured (or measurable) outcomes might supplant less accessible outcomes as institutional objectives; incomplete assessment for external parties may contribute to inefficiencies, etc. Astin (1982) and others (e.g., Ewell, 1985; Turnbull, 1985) provide more complete discussions of these and related issues. One area of agreement among most parties is that, regardless of its limitations, outcome assessment, based largely on aggregated individual outcomes, is an important part of higher education's future. Another is that outcome specification and assessment, and the introspection that accompanies them, are prerequisites for self-improvement in higher education.

OUTCOME SPECIFICATION IN HIGHER EDUCATION

In recent years, educators in several academic disciplines have called for the re-evaluation and/or affirmation of educational outcomes. The questions they want to ask seem simple enough. William W. Turnbull, Distinguished Scholar in Residence at Educational Testing Services, observed that ". . . people keep asking the deceptively simple question, 'Are they learning anything in college these days?'" (Turnbull, 1985, p. 24). The answers to this question and many equally publicized "simple" questions are put forth eloquently in the broad rhetoric of college and university administrators. They are seldom as elegant as education's critics ("Why can't Johnny read?") and rarely as straightforward in discussing their accomplishments [cf. the National Commission on Excellence in Education's warning that the U.S. educational system had "put the nation at risk" (May, 1983)]. The public dialogue, whether or not it clarifies the issues, has renewed higher education's examination of its fundamental missions and outcomes.

Outcome specification—identifying and assigning responsibility for specific outcomes in higher education—is not an easy task. The institutions that bear the responsibility are not static; they continue to expand, change, and specialize. New disciplines continue to appear, both within and separate from the traditional ones. Even among the relatively "new" disciplines, increasing specialization and change is apparent. "Business" was the subject matter of economics; then schools of commerce; now schools of management, business, business administration, industrial management, economics, and so on. The traditional business disciplines of accounting, economics, management, marketing, production, and finance are no longer the only departments in our business schools. Closer to home, increasing specialization is apparent along functional lines (e.g., financial, managerial, auditing, tax, governmental, systems, etc.) and in terms of other dimensions (note the expanding list of faculty designations in Hasselback's *Accounting Faculty Directory* since its inception in 1977, and the increasing "sectionalizing" of the American Accounting Association). Most other disciplines have become increasingly focused into specialized areas also. Many educators are concerned that increasing academic compartmentalization, created partially in response to an ever-changing technological, social, and economic environment, leaves us ill-prepared for the task of outcome specification at general levels.

The well-known debates over the desired depth and breadth of learning are illustrative of the difficulty of specifying many important outcomes in higher education today. The concerns shared by most educators are that, as disciplines proliferate, the required core curriculum shrinks; and that the elective core courses are becoming increasingly specialized, and less likely to include many fundamentally important outcomes (e.g., Costin, 1982; Peterson, 1985; Bennett, 1984; Trainor, 1986). In the past, the core curriculum was comprised of required coursework that could introduce students to all, or most, of the academic disciplines. One of its purposes was to provide a body of common knowledge and educational experiences that could serve as a foundation for further learning.

Today's typical core curriculum requires students to choose from among an expansive array of courses from numerous disciplines. Besides raising the obvious concerns over the students' choice criteria, the efficiency of the educational process, and the breadth vs. depth debate, the core's increasing electivity creates considerable diversity in students in terms of the knowledge they bring with them to their chosen academic majors, and in terms of the "education" they acquire at our institutions. Many educators argue that we do not know who is responsible for, or who should attempt to address, the inadequacies in the general learning of our students. William Bennett, Secretary of Education, while pointing to some of the significant shortcomings in our graduating classes, observed that "if the faculty as a whole is not corporately responsible for the curriculum as a whole, but only for their particular specializations, the undergraduate degree is reduced to a series of individual judgments on discrete and unrelated educational experiences" (Bennett, 1984).

We do not know where, or whether, many valued educational outcomes are being achieved, largely because they are not part of the substantive knowledge that defines most disciplines. These include some rather fundamental skills such as learning skills (effective study; information acquisition, analysis, and synthesis; problem-structuring and solving; etc.), many practical outcomes (communication and leadership skills development, socialization), and higher-order outcomes, such as cognitive development (e.g., critical thinking, abstract reasoning, probabilistic thinking, creativity, and values awareness). To the extent that these and other student outcomes are important, accounting educators and researchers must understand them. As in most disciplines, we need to know more about what and how our students learn and what role we play in the process, in order to know what to teach and how to teach it.

OUTCOME SPECIFICATION IN ACCOUNTING EDUCATION

Our perspective as educators and researchers must broaden so that we may learn more about what we ought to be achieving in education, but it must also retain its strong professional orientation. There is clearly a need for discipline specific educational research in accounting. Many other academic disciplines have a well-developed body of educational literature that is largely oriented toward understanding the specific educational needs of a particular discipline. There is no single unique dimension of accounting that distinguishes it from other disciplines. However, the field is unique in the configuration of elements that are brought together in its educational programs. We have discussed some of the dimensions that combine to differentiate accounting from other disciplines throughout this monograph. The substantive knowledge of accounting is diverse (e.g., tax vs. systems) and multi-disciplinary (e.g., managerial accounting). We have reason to believe that accounting students are different from students in other disciplines (see Chapter 3) and that accounting faculty are involved in a more complex set of activities than are faculty in other disciplines (see Chapter 4).

Academic accounting's most important distinguishing feature, however, is that it serves the accounting profession. In Chapter 1, we noted that the legal, technological, and business environment facing the profession is increasingly dynamic and challenging. At the same time, the call for accountability and re-evaluation of outcomes in higher education is creating an atmosphere that is conducive to improvement through self-assessment. Throughout this monograph, we have pointed to educational outcomes that we believe are important to the accounting profession (e.g., the need for better student communication skills; student professionalization and values awareness; the importance of substantive accounting research, etc.). We believe that outcome specification and assessment is one of the most important tasks facing the academic and practicing professions. Accounting education research, by attending to outcome specification, measurement, and assessment, can help forge the links among higher education, accounting education, and the future of the profession. In pursuing accounting education research, we need to understand, both as educators and as accountants, the linkages between what we do, how we do it, and why.

More than most academic disciplines, accounting has benefitted from the active interest and support of its profession. Indeed, accounting's academics and practitioners have been at the task of specifying outcomes for many years. Langenderfer (1987) provides an interesting account of the history of accounting education policy for the last 100 years by focusing on the important relationships between the profession and academic accounting. In the last 20 years, several distinguished committees, boards, commissions, and task forces, representing the accounting profession, academia, and others, have been convened to examine the role of accounting education in the continuing development of the profession. Their reports include the following:

- *Horizons for a Profession* (Roy and MacNeill, 1967)
- *Report of the Committee on Education and Experience Requirements for CPAs* (1969) (the Beamer committee)
- *Education Requirements for Entry Into the Accounting Profession* (1978) (the Albers task force)

- *The Report of the Board on Standards for Programs and Schools of Professional Accounting* (1977)
- *Researching the Accounting Curriculum: Strategies for Change* (1975)
- *The Commission on Auditors' Responsibilities: Report, Conclusions, and Recommendations* (1978)

Horizons set forth a tentative common body of knowledge for accounting and accounting education. It has been endorsed by the AICPA through the Beamer committee and Albers task force committee reports, and its recommendations studied and implemented through several subsequent AAA and AICPA committees and reports. Much of the accumulated wisdom of these deliberations is found in the significant insights of the AAA Committee on the "Future Structure, Content, and Scope of Accounting Education."

The Committee Report (1986), like *Horizons* 20 years ago, provides a starting point for the specification of accounting's outcomes. The committee, chaired by Norton Bedford, included recognized leaders from accounting academia and professional practice. The committee's specific recommendations were ". . . intended to serve as broad guidelines and to provide direction for those who initiate changes in accounting education." (AAA Committee on the Future Structure, Content, and Scope of Accounting Education, 1986, p. 169). The report's discussions and recommendations identified or implied numerous educational outcomes at the societal, institutional, and individual levels, presented in terms of the desired scope, content, and structure of accounting education. The desired accounting *student outcomes* included the following:

1. A strong, broad *general education* that induces students to develop:
   - Capacities for inquiry, abstract logical thinking, and critical analysis; literacy, which includes writing, reading, speaking, and listening; understanding numerical data; historical consciousness; an appreciation of science; the study of values; the experience of art; international and multicultural experiences; and study in depth
   - An awareness of the evolutionary nature of society, knowledge of history, different cultures, literature, and the social sciences
   - An awareness of the potential for technological change through a knowledge of the natural sciences
   - The capacity to use an expanded knowledge base
   - The capability to be creative, sensitive, and aware of the needs of society and individuals
   - An awareness of opportunities for the profession to contribute to the continuing development of civilization, through knowledge of the arts and philosophy
   - Some minimum level of knowledge in mathematics, statistics, computer systems, and economics
2. A *general professional education* that encourages students to attain the knowledge required for entry into an accounting career and for subsequent career success through lifelong learning, and the capacity to apply this knowledge in creative and innovative ways, in accordance with high standards of professional ethics through the following:
   - The attainment of broad introductory knowledge and skills spanning the entire spectrum of the accounting discipline
   - Understanding of the nature, design, and uses of information systems
   - Knowledge of the accounting profession, its history and responsibilities, and their legal and moral implications
   - Knowledge of the relationships among decision problems and information in organizations

- Knowledge about financial information and public reporting
- Effective communication and interpersonal skills
- Personal capacities, including:
  - Ambition and persistence
  - Appreciation of ethical standards and conduct
  - Empathy
  - Creative thinking and problem solving abilities
  - Understanding of cultural and international issues
  - Logical reasoning
  - Sensitivity to social responsibilities
  - Leadership potential
3. A *specialized professional accounting education* that leads the student to gain:
   - The ability to function at the entry level as a qualified professional in performing a valuable service for society in a specialized area
   - An advanced, clearly usable level of accounting knowledge and skills
   - A conceptual and theoretical knowledge to facilitate change as needed and to provide an ability to develop creative applications of the rules and procedures used in the specialization
   - The ability to extend the specialization through research, planning, and design into new areas of application
   - A heightened awareness of the expanding needs of society

The committee report provides a host of educational outcomes that are logically derived from its thoughtful estimation of the future of the accounting profession. A continuing task, shared by academics and professionals, is the specification of other desired outcomes—from the perspectives of faculty, administrators, legislators, and others. Having identified outcomes that are valued in accounting, the researcher's tasks are to develop measures for those that can be reasonably measured, and then use them to evaluate outcome achievement. Examples of measures and evaluation techniques that may be used abound in the education literature. In the preceding chapters, we identified numerous measures of outcomes in higher education—measures of student learning, achievement, and development; of faculty teaching effectiveness and research productivity; and of many other individual and institutional outcomes. These measures are the criteria by which education researchers judge the effectiveness of curricular, instructional, and institutional alternatives and innovations. By working with the accounting profession, accounting education researchers can begin to devise outcome measures and evaluation techniques that are more clearly linked to valued outcomes than is possible in many other disciplines.

In Appendix A, we have listed outcome specification and measurement as important research objectives within each of this monograph's research domains. Some general outcomes in need of attention are effective teaching, research productivity, and student learning; more specific outcomes include student professionalization and values awareness. For each of these, and many others, we need to know why the outcome is important, how to measure or otherwise assess it, and how to achieve it. Ideally, the research would begin with the specification of an outcome for some decision purpose or model, followed by identification or creation of valid outcome measures, systematic observation, and active experimentation. Research aimed at outcome measurement and evaluation might begin by focusing on how and why specific outcomes are important in the practice of accounting, or in the achievement of professional objectives. Consider the importance ascribed to communication skills development by the accounting profession in recent years (Chapter 3). Research in the area might progress by identifying or developing measures of communications effectiveness (e.g., oral communication skills) that capture the skill levels required in the profession. Ideally, measures would be validated against observable criteria by showing, for example, that oral communication skills of staff accountants, as gauged by our measure, are positively associated with client satisfaction and cooperativeness, and negatively associated with client attrition. Then, the validated instrument may be used to evaluate the effectiveness of present and potential educational treatments thought to influence oral communication skills. In the past, much research has focused only on this last step, without considering the meaning and validity of the desired outcome and its measurement. Outcome specification, measurement, and evaluation are crucial activities to accountants, researchers, and all concerned with the profession's future.

As in every area of higher education, we in accounting must think about outcomes in terms of the uniqueness of our discipline and the goals of our institutions and society. We are all part of an institutional structure—higher education—that is in a state of widespread controversy over its fundamental purposes. Higher education's call for communication among various interested parties, sensitivity to each discipline's uniqueness, and exploration of our common grounds is driven by numerous considerations. One is that many of our desired outcomes are the same as those of other disciplines. Our research in accounting education can certainly benefit from the decades of work reported in the education literature, and introduced in the preceding chapters. However, many of our outcomes are unique, or at least valued differently in accounting than in various other disciplines. We believe that a compelling reason for encouraging accounting education research is that, as in most academic disciplines, we do not know enough about education and its outcomes to achieve our potential. In accounting, we need to know more about education, and the role of education in "an expanding profession" (AAA, 1986). We must gain a better understanding of outcomes and the phenomena that affect them, so that policies and agendas may be properly directed and evaluated, in both accounting education and the accounting profession.

CHAPTER 7 BIBLIOGRAPHY

American Accounting Association Committee on the Future Structure, Content, and Scope of Accounting Education, "Future Accounting Education: Preparing for the Expanding Profession," *Issues in Accounting Education* (Spring 1986), pp. 168–195.

AACSB (American Assembly of Collegiate Schools of Business), M. R. Blood, letter and brochure: "Core Curriculum Assessment Program (CCAP)" (August 1987).

Association of American Colleges Committee on the Project on Redefining the Meaning and Purpose of Baccalaurate Degrees, *Integrity in the Curriculum* (February 1985).

Astin, A. W., "Why not Try Some New Ways of Measuring Quality?" *Educational Record* (Spring 1982), pp. 10–15.

Bennett, W. J., *To Reclaim a Legacy*, Study Group on the State of Learning in the Humanities in Higher Education, National Endowment for the Humanities (November 1984).

Commission on Auditors' Responsibilities: Report, Conclusions, and Recommendations (New York: AICPA, 1978).

Costin, F., "Some Thoughts on General Education and the Teaching of Undergraduate Psychology," *Teaching of Psychology* (February 1982), pp. 26–28.

Dewey, J., *Democracy and Education* (Macmillan Publishing, 1916).

Education Requirements for Entry Into the Accounting Profession (New York: AICPA, 1978).

Ewell, P. "Assessment: What's it All About?" *Change* (Nov/Dec 1985), pp. 32–36.

"Governors' Report on Education: Text of the Section on College Quality," *Chronicle of Higher Education* (Sep. 3, 1986), pp. 79–80.

Heiss, A. *Evaluation of Institutions of Postsecondary Education: An Annotated List of Instruments* (Washington, D.C.: Council on Postsecondary Accreditation, 1975).

Hoyt, D. P. and R. K. Spangler, "The Measurement of Administrative Effectiveness of the Academic Department Head," *Research in Higher Education* (1979), pp. 291–303.

Hurdle, L. S., "Re-Appraising General Education for Higher Education in the 1980s," *Journal of Negro Education* (1981), pp. 191–195.

Langenderfer, H. Q., "Accounting Education's History—A 100-year Search for Identity," *Journal of Accountancy* (May, 1987), pp. 302–331.

National Institute of Education, *Involvement in Learning.* (Study Group on the Condition of Excellence in American Higher Education, October 1984).

Pace, C. R., *Measuring Outcomes of College,* (San Francisco: Jossey-Bass, 1979).

Pace, C. R., "Historical Perspectives on Student Outcomes: Assessment with Implications for the Future," *NASPA Journal* (Fall 1984), pp. 10–18.

Perkins, D. and R. Abbott, "Validity of Student Ratings for Two Affective Outcomes of Introductory Psychology," *Educational and Psychological Measurement* (1982), pp. 317–323.

Peterson, M. W., "Emerging Developments in Postsecondary Organization Theory and Research: Fragmentation or Integration," *Educational Researcher* (March 1985), pp. 5–12.

Report of the Board on Standards for Programs and Schools of Professional Accounting (New York: AICPA, 1977).

Report of the Committee on Education and Experience Requirements for CPAs (New York: AICPA, 1969).

Researching the Accounting Curriculum: Strategies for Change, ed. W. L. Ferrara (Sarasota, FL: American Accounting Association, 1975).

Rossides, D. W., "What is the Purpose of Education?" *Change* (April 1984), pp. 14–46.

Roy, R. H. and J. H. MacNeill, *Horizons for a Profession* (New York: AICPA, 1967).

Slaughter, S. "From Serving Students to Serving the Economy: Changing Expectations of Faculty Role Performance," *Higher Education* (1985), pp. 41–56.

Trainor, S. L., "The Link: Addressing the Problems of Higher Education Through the Core Curriculum," *Innovative Higher Education* (Spr/Sum 1986), pp. 94–101.

Turnbull, W. W. "Are They Learning Anything in College?" *Change* (Nov/Dec 1985), pp. 23–26.

APPENDIX A

Summary of Accounting Education Research Opportunities

CHAPTER 3—RESEARCH RELATED TO STUDENTS

Research Domain	Project Number	Researchable Topic
Student Attitudes and Beliefs		
Male-female comparisons	3–1	Catalog changes over time in the numbers of male and female students majoring in accounting
	3–2	Examine differences in career attitudes among male and female accounting majors
	3–3	Examine the relative drop-out rates from accounting programs among male and female students
Environmental factors	3–4	Examine the impact of university selectivity on student attitudes
	3–5	Examine the impact of accounting program selectivity on student attitudes
	3–6	Identify and examine various environmental factors that affect accounting students' attitudes toward their major
	3–7	Examine student attitudes that result in their changing majors to and from accounting
	3–8	Determine the extent to which accounting majors enter the university with an intent to major in accounting and the important factors in this decision
Other	3–9	Examine accounting students' attitudes toward four- and five-year education options
	3–10	Identify faculty characteristics which correlate positively with student attitudes toward faculty
	3–11	Examine the relationship of accounting students' self concepts and their attitudes toward faculty
	3–12	Examine accounting students' preconceived attitudes toward faculty and the impact on students' academic performance

Communication Skills

Communication apprehension among accounting students

3–13 Determine the extent of communication apprehension (written and oral) among accounting students

3–14 Determine the impact of communication apprehension on the choice of accounting as a major

3–15 Determine if accounting students write in more ambiguous, less intense, terms than other students

3–16 Determine the impact of apprehension on sending vs. receiving messages

3–17 Determine the image of accounting in terms of required communication skills for career success

3–18 Determine the impact on student performance of misplacement (i.e., high apprehensives in a field requiring high skill)

3–19 Determine if accounting students intentionally avoid situations requiring use of their underdeveloped communication skills

Communication skills and professional success

3–20 Examine the importance of oral and written communication skills on career success in different aspects of accounting (e.g., public vs. industry vs. government, large vs. small organizations, urban vs. rural locations, etc.)

3–21 Determine the impact on career success of misplacement (i.e., high apprehensives in positions requiring well developed skills)

3–22 Examine the extent of agreement among students, educators, practitioners concerning communication skills required for career success

3–23 Compare the importance of communication skills for success in accounting and other professional fields

3–24 Identify the disparity, if any, between required communication skills for career advancement and those possessed by four- and five-year graduates

Image of accounting profession

3–25 Determine if accounting is viewed as a field where highly developed communication skills are not required

3–26 Examine how accounting might change its image concerning required communication skills for professional success

Communication skills instruction

3–27 Determine how communication skills are currently being taught to accounting students

	3–28	Determine the extent to which communication requirements exist in accounting courses and how they are evaluated
	3–29	Determine if communication problems of accounting professors, if any, are transferred to students
	3–30	Examine the success of writing improvement programs offered in accounting at some universities
	3–31	Determine whether assessment of accounting students' writing skills by communication experts results in greater improvements than if evaluated only by accounting faculty
	3–32	Examine differences in communication requirements in four- and five-year programs
	3–33	Compare success of communications courses vs. integration of communication requirements in accounting courses
	3–34	Compare the desired delivery system for high- and low-communication apprehensive accounting students
	3–35	Examine the ability of accounting educators to evaluate written and oral communication requirements in accounting classes
Academic Achievement	3–36	Examine the relationship between specific aspects of accounting education (e.g., length of education, specific courses taken) and professional examination success
	3–37	Examine the impact of minority faculty members on attracting minority students
	3–38	Examine the intellectual and non-intellectual correlates of achievements in accounting
	3–39	Identify qualities in students that are predictive of success in accounting
	3–40	Determine the appropriate education level for success on the CPA and other professional examinations
	3–41	Examine the problem of attracting sufficient minority students into accounting
	3–42	Examine the problems of professional placement and advancement of women, minorities and older students

CHAPTER 4—RESEARCH RELATED TO FACULTY

Research Domain	Project Number	Researchable Topic
Student Evaluation of Teachers (SET)		
Validity and reliability	4–1	Assess generalizability of previous research findings to accounting
	4–2	Examine differential validity and reliability of specific SET questionnaire items or factors for accounting vs. non-accounting instructors and instruction
	4–3	Identify and evaluate alternative measures of effective teaching in accounting
	4–4	Examine specific instructor behaviors and characteristics associated with effective teaching in accounting, and in specific accounting courses
	4–5	Identify and evaluate additional measures of student academic achievement in accounting
	4–6	Identify and evaluate additional measures of student educational goal achievement (e.g., increased professionalism, communication skills improvement, cognitive development, learning motivation)
	4–7	Identify and evaluate other institutional outcomes of effective teaching, such as alumni loyalty, recruiter interest, and attractiveness to prospective students
Utility of SET	4–8	Describe the ways that SET are currently used in accounting programs
	4–9	Determine the relative weight assigned in performance evaluation at different types of institutions, for different groups of faculty and for different courses
	4–10	Identify and evaluate alternative modes of SET feedback for formative evaluation
	4–11	Identify and examine the potential impact of nuisance and background variables on the utility of SET
	4–12	Identify and compare alternative norm groups for comparative evaluation of accounting faculty

APPENDIX A

Faculty
Performance
Evaluation (FPE)

    Use of FPE

        4–13   Assess generalizability of previous research to accounting

        4–14   Describe the ways that FPE is currently administered in accounting programs

        4–15   Explore the potential impact of the shortage of accounting faculty on FPE

        4–16   Describe and evaluate the relative importance of research, teaching and service in different types of institutions and accounting programs

    Improvement of FPE

        4–17   Identify and evaluate alternative means of assessing research productivity

        4–18   Identify and evaluate alternative means of assessing teaching effectiveness

        4–19   Identify and evaluate alternative means of assessing service activities

        4–20   Examine the effectiveness of alternative FPE programs

        4–21   Identify the constituents served and objectives pursued by accounting faculty

Faculty Research
Activities

    Utility of research

        4–22   Explore the relationships among research, teaching and service by accounting faculty

        4–23   Identify the constituents served and objectives pursued by accounting research

        4–24   Identify and evaluate the rewards that attach to research productivity

    Improvement of research

        4–25   Identify and examine the factors that inhibit and enhance faculty research productivity

        4–26   Identify and compare the characteristics of more vs. less productive researchers

        4–27   Identify and examine the education/training objectives of accounting Ph.D.s as researchers

    Evaluation of research

        4–28   Identify and examine ways to evaluate research quality

        4–29   Identify and assess the relative importance of the outcomes of research activity

Faculty Teaching
Activities

   Determinants of effective teaching

	4–30	Assess generalizability of previous research to accounting
	4–31	Describe how teaching effectiveness is weighted in salary, promotion, and tenure decisions at various types of institutions
	4–32	Identify and evaluate specific teaching behaviors that yield positive educational outcomes
	4–33	Identify and examine the situational, individual difference, and educational process determinants of effective teaching
	4–34	Examine and evaluate alternative measures of effective teaching outcomes (e.g., CPA examination performance, career advancement, etc.)
	4–35	Identify and examine the education/training objectives of accounting Ph.D.s as teachers

   Evaluation of teaching

	4–36	Describe and compare the evaluation techniques used at different types of institutions, for different academic programs, and for different faculty groups
	4–37	Compare alternative teaching evaluation techniques for summative vs. formative evaluation
	4–38	Identify and evaluate the rewards that attach to teaching effectiveness

Faculty Development

   Demography and productivity

	4–39	Examine career productivity patterns of different groups of accounting faculty
	4–40	Describe faculty demographic trends in accounting
	4–41	Explore relationships between faculty demography in accounting and faculty development models and programs
	4–42	Identify and examine the determinants of accounting faculty career productivity and activity patterns
	4–43	Identify and examine career patterns in terms of promotion and tenure attainment, and other visible developmental career stages

   Programs and improvement

	4–44	Evaluate the impact of current faculty development programs (e.g., sabbaticals, internships, visiting professorships) on faculty performance

APPENDIX A

4–45		Examine the effects of accreditation criteria on faculty development
4–46		Identify and examine the impact of the accounting profession on faculty development
4–47		Identify and examine intervention techniques (e.g., faculty re-tooling, reduced teaching loads in support of research activities) that might induce positive faculty development outcomes
4–48		Describe and evaluate the trends in the status of women and minority faculty in accounting with respect to salary, promotion and tenure equity
4–49		Describe and evaluate the representation of women and minorities among accounting faculty and doctoral programs
4–50		Identify and describe changes in colleague and administrator attitudes toward women and minority faculty
4–51		Describe and evaluate the trends in appointment of women and minorities to administrative and leadership positions in accounting education
4–52		Identify and examine the institutional, background, and other variables that affect the assessment of equity
4–53		Identify and evaluate alternative programs for achieving equity

CHAPTER 5—RESEARCH RELATED TO THE EDUCATIONAL PROCESS

Research Domain	Project Number	Researchable Topics
Testing and Grading	5–1	Prepare a profile of typical accounting examinations for various types and levels of courses
	5–2	Examine and assess the extent to which accounting examinations contain criterion validity (i.e., do they accurately measure achievement or mastery of the subject?)
	5–3	Examine and assess the extent to which accounting examinations contain content validity (i.e., are they a representative sample of the subject matter about which conclusions are to be drawn?)
	5–4	Examine and assess the extent to which accounting examinations contain construct validity (i.e., are the

		traits which an examination purports to measure actually measured by the examination?)
	5–5	Examine and assess the extent to which anxiety enhances or impedes progress on accounting examinations at different levels
	5–6	Examine the extent to which selected variables, such as study habits, study organization, and test taking skills, impact student performance on accounting examinations
	5–7	Examine ways test anxiety that impedes performance can be reduced on accounting examinations
	5–8	Examine the extent to which the timing of examinations within the semester or quarter affect student performance
	5–9	Examine the extent to which examination-taking strategies vary between good and poor accounting students
	5–10	Examine the extent to which accounting students retain material over the long run and propose ways to increase this retention
	5–11	Examine and assess the extent to which accounting examinations emphasize simple recall vs. the testing of complex cognitive skills
	5–12	Examine the extent to which accounting examination feedback to students enhances learning
	5–13	Evaluate the criterion, content and construct validity of the CPA and other professional examinations
Teaching Methods	5–14	Examine the ability levels of accounting students and assess how these relate to the effectiveness of various teaching methods
	5–15	Compare the success in terms of student achievement of innovative teaching methods and traditional teaching methods
	5–16	Compare the impact of homework in accounting classes with and without feedback on student achievement
	5–17	Examine and critique the role of the lecture method in accounting courses
	5–18	Examine the impact of microcomputer integration (e.g., computer assisted instruction (CAI), spreadsheet applications) on student achievement in accounting courses

APPENDIX A

	5–19	Catalog the extent of computer integration currently in place in accounting curricula and identify the different approaches being applied
	5–20	Measure the cost effectiveness of CAI in principles of accounting courses
	5–21	Determine the extent to which aptitude and treatment interactions exist in CAI classes in accounting subjects
	5–22	Identify the subject areas in which CAI is most likely to be useful to accounting students
	5–23	Assess the impact of computer integration on the computer science course requirements in accounting curricula
	5–24	Develop standardized examinations capable of being used in teaching method experiments in accounting courses
	5–25	Measure the commonalities between the various teaching methods used in accounting courses
	5–26	Assess the impact of textbook selection on teaching methods
Learning	5–27	Examine and critique the learning approaches (e.g., holist vs. serialist) preferred by accounting students and faculty
	5–28	Determine the way in which accounting subjects are learned and associate this process with available teaching approaches
	5–29	Identify those aspects of accounting which are unique and should direct teaching/learning activities in specific directions
	5–30	Identify cognitive skills that are associated with accounting aptitude
	5–31	Identify the types of study habits which are successful in accounting courses for different types of students
	5–32	Specify the individual cognitive characteristics which are associated with accounting aptitude
	5–33	Develop licensing examination techniques which require the use of higher cognitive skills than are currently tested
Contextual Issues	5–34	Examine the extent to which individual contextual variables (e.g., class size, physical environment, time of day) impact student learning in accounting

	5–35	Associate the effectiveness of alternative teaching methods with individual contextual variables
	5–36	Determine the extent to which individual contextual variables impact accounting majors and nonmajors in accounting classes
	5–37	Examine how accounting can best be taught in large classes
	5–38	Examine the cost/benefit implications of various contextual alternatives (e.g., class size)
	5–39	Determine whether computer integration can facilitate the use of larger classes

CHAPTER 6—RESEARCH RELATED TO ADMINISTRATION AND CONSTITUENTS

Research Domain	Project Number	Researchable Topic
Administrative Structure and Five-Year Programs		
Administrative structure	6–1	Examine the association between orientation (university, departmental and disciplinary) and program reputation and quality
	6–2	Examine the role of the administrator in different departmental orientations and schools of accounting
	6–3	Examine the relation of external financial support and different department orientations and schools of accounting
	6–4	Examine the relationship of program emphasis (e.g., undergraduate, masters and Ph.D.) in different department orientations and schools of accounting
	6–5	Examine the unique role of the administrator within different department orientations and schools of accounting
	6–6	Identify those factors of dissatisfaction with the departmental structure that led to the emergence of schools of accounting and whether those factors have been improved
	6–7	Determine the extent of program quality increase that has resulted from schools of accounting
	6–8	Examine instances where schools of accounting have

APPENDIX A

		been removed from schools of business in terms of program quality improvements
	6–9	Examine the relative incentives for quality teaching and research (both theoretical and applied) in departments with different orientations and schools of accounting
	6–10	Identify the impact of schools on accounting on curriculum autonomy
	6–11	Identify the impact of schools of accounting on promotion/tenure autonomy
	6–12	Identify the impact of schools of accounting on research standards (both quantitative and qualitative)
Content of five-year programs	6–13	Identify the merits and deficiencies of the AICPA model curriculum
	6–14	Determine the extent of compliance of current five-year programs with the AICPA model program (or alternative model programs)
	6–15	Examine the role of formal education in terms of developing entry-level skills vs. career preparation
Alternative structures for five-year programs	6–16	Examine the nature and merits of alternative program structures (e.g., 3/2, 2/3, 4/1)
	6–17	Examine the nature and extent of specialization available within five-year programs
	6–18	Examine the issue of student commitment and alternative program structures, including attrition rates
Legislation of five-year education requirement	6–19	Identify those factors influencing successful legislation
	6–20	Identify the reaction of key groups (e.g., students, practitioners, educators) to legislation
	6–21	Identify the problems of implementing five-year education legislation
	6–22	Examine the impact of five-year legislation on the quality of academic programs
Impact of five-year programs on students	6–23	Examine the factors affecting students' choices concerning five-year vs. four-year alternatives
	6–24	Examine and compare five-year programs with and without advanced degrees
Accreditation of Accounting Programs	6–25	Examine evidence of quality increase or decrease in accounting programs in recent years

	6–26	Develop a set of standards by which programs can assess their quality relative to other programs
	6–27	Catalog the methods used by programs to admit and retain students in accounting programs with controlled enrollments
	6–28	Recommend superior factors for student admission and retention
	6–29	Examine the extent to which AACSB accounting accreditation standards have improved overall program quality
	6–30	Examine the impact of AACSB accounting accreditation on the outcomes of programs
	6–31	Examine the usefulness of comprehensive examinations as output measures of overall program quality
	6–32	Identify student input factors that result in improved student outcome measures
	6–33	Identify faculty input factors that result in improved student outcome measures
	6–34	Identify educational process input factors that result in improved student outcome measures
Faculty Vitality	6–35	Describe reward systems employed for accounting faculty in comparison with other disciplines
	6–36	Identify predictors of accounting faculty salaries
	6–37	Examine the existence and severity of salary compression in accounting in comparison with other disciplines
	6–38	Examine the association of compensation and vitality of accounting faculty
	6–39	Examine the association of factors contributing to faculty vitality and different departmental orientations (university, departmental and disciplinary) and schools of accounting
	6–40	Examine the association of factors contributing to faculty vitality and different career stages (e.g., assistant, associate and full professor)
	6–41	Examine the relationship of faculty vitality and environmental factors, such as research productivity, quality of colleagues, administrative leadership, etc.
Financing of Programs	6–42	Examine the flexibility/inflexibility of resource reallocation within universities in response to changing student demands

APPENDIX A

	6–43	Examine the financing of uncontrolled student demand for accounting service courses
	6–44	Examine the role of technical education vs. general education in four- and five-year accounting programs
	6–45	Examine the importance of the teaching, research and service missions of accounting programs in continued external financial support
	6–46	Examine the extent to which external contributions add qualitative dimensions to accounting programs
Academic Program Reviews		
Current program ratings	6–47	Determine the relative ratings of programs by practitioners and educators (both professors and administrators)
	6–48	Determine the interrelationships among undergraduate, masters and doctoral program ratings
	6–49	Determine the relative rating of programs for entering practice and entering higher education
Factors affecting accounting program ratings	6–50	Determine the impact of size (e.g., number of students, faculty, etc.) on program ratings
	6–51	Determine the impact of current and past faculty productivity on program ratings
	6–52	Determine the impact of specializations within accounting (e.g., tax) on program ratings
	6–53	Determine the impact of past reputation on program ratings
	6–54	Determine the impact of non-academic factors (e.g., geographic location, athletic success) on program ratings
	6–55	Determine the relative impact of teaching and research variables on program ratings
Use of accounting program ratings	6–56	Identify the ways program ratings are used to implement program improvements
	6–57	Determine the impact of program ratings on internal resource allocations
	6–58	Determine the impact of program ratings on student university choice for undergraduate, masters and doctoral programs
Continuing Professional Education (CPE)		
Current status of CPE	6–59	Identify objectives of CPE

	6–60	Compare accounting CPE with CPE of other professions
	6–61	Catalog current CPE requirements per jurisdiction, highlighting major differences
	6–62	Identify those factors affecting the lack of legislated CPE in those jurisdictions without such legislation
	6–63	Compare the sources of CPE and their relative quality
	6–64	Evaluate the relative success of mandatory and voluntary CPE programs
	6–65	Evaluate CPE as an alternative to periodic reexamination
	6–66	Evaluate the need for CPE for CPAs not in public practice (i.e., education, industry, government)
Impact of CPE on accounting education and practice	6–67	Evaluate the impact of CPE on (1) practitioner competence, (2) practitioner performance, and (3) quality of accounting practice
	6–68	Distinguish between preprofessional education and CPE
Delivery of CPE	6–69	Determine the roles of educators and practitioners in the delivery of CPE
	6–70	Identify factors affecting the quality of CPE (e.g., instructor, location, materials, etc.)
	6–71	Determine the role of universities in delivering CPE for practitioners
	6–72	Examine the impact of CPE instruction as a desired faculty activity

Appendix B
Description of the Database

As part of this project, a database was developed of all publications considered in the writing of this monograph. This database contains approximately 2726 records. In addition to the database, a set of programs has been written to allow "menu-driven" access to the database, and a manual has been developed to facilitate use of the database. The database and programs require use of dBASE III Plus software.

This appendix discusses 1) information contained in the database, 2) data sources, 3) program capabilities, 4) a summary of some of the database information, and 5) database structure and requirements. Further information on these and other topics is provided in the manual, which also includes a user's guide.

Database Contents
The database contains the following information:
1. Article (book) title
2. Author
3. Citation information
4. Year published
5. Abstract (762 characters maximum)
6. Appropriate keywords (14 maximum)

Data Sources
The records were obtained through the following sources:
1) ERIC in the Dialog Information Services, Inc. by using the keywords "higher education" and "educational research." Among these, only the records for materials published subsequent to 1972 were included in the database. The ERIC searches continued until December 1986. Hence, the articles obtained directly from ERIC concluded in September 1986.

2) The authors own search in the literature.

Keywords and abstracts were obtained either through ERIC, or the authors' own readings. For citations appearing in the manuscript, headings were used as keywords.

Program Capabilities
The "menu-driven" programs allow a variety of searching and maintenance operations, including the ability to develop a set of similar words for searching at the same time through the use of a synonym dictionary.

Specifically, the programs allow the user to search the database for the following:
   a. a specific word
   b. specific word and synonyms

A search can be made on any combination of the following:

1. Title
2. Abstract
3. Keywords

The results of the search can be treated as follows:

1. Viewed on the monitor one record at a time with optional printing.
2. Immediately printed
3. Stored to disk
4. Stored to disk and immediately printed

The programs also allow file maintenance on the main database and other databases created using a search stored to disk and on the synonym file.

Summary of Information Contained in Database

1. Number of Records in Database   2,726
   Number of Unique Keywords in
      Keyword Fields   2,343
   Number of Keyword Citations
      in Keyword Fields   16,336

2. Abstract Size

	Number of Records	Percent of Records
No abstract	450	16.5%
Abstract size in Characters		
<255	729	26.7
255–508	1,274	46.8
509–762	273	10.0

3. Journal Information

Journal	Number of Citations
The Accounting Review	147
Teaching of Psychology	113
Research in Higher Education	105
Journal of Research in Science Teaching	70
Journal of Accountancy	70
Journal of Economic Education	70
Journal of Accounting Education	69
Journal of Higher Education	44
Journal of Research in Mathematics Education	42
Journalism Educator	42
Journal of Medical Education	41
Science Education	38
Sociology of Education	36
Journal of College Science Teaching	34
Journal of Chemical Education	34

APPENDIX B

Journal	Number of Citations
Research in Teaching of English	34
Engineering Education	33
Improving College and University Teaching	31

Distributions of Journal Citations:

Number of Citations for one Journal	Number of Journals
147	1
113	1
105	1
70	3
69	1
44	1
42	2
41	1
38	1
36	1
34	3
33	1
31	1
29	1
28	1
27	2
26	2
25	1
21	1
20	1
19	2
17	3
16	1
15	3
14	3
13	2
12	4
11	3
10	7
9	6
8	6
7	8
6	9
5	22
4	25
3	47
2	70
1	180

Year of Publication:

Year of Publication	Number of Records	Percent
59 & prior	13	0.5%
60–69	30	1.1
70	20	0.7
71	24	0.9
72	86	3.2
73	116	4.3
74	176	6.5
75	282	10.3
76	241	8.8
77	189	6.9
78	201	7.4
79	195	7.2
80	152	5.6
81	112	4.1
82	131	4.8
83	196	7.2
84	223	8.2
85	235	8.6
86	101	3.7
87	3	0.1

4. Keywords
Most Frequently Cited Keywords:

Keyword	Number of Citations
teaching methods	305
science education	294
accounting education	292
student attitudes	209
academic achievement	203
college science	190
college students	174
elementary secondary education	144
surveys	127
teacher education	122
student evaluation of teachers	112
instruction	102
foreign countries	99
research methodology	98
psychology	96
preservice teacher education	95
teacher effectiveness	95
college mathematics	84
teacher attitudes	82
secondary education	80
college faculty	79

APPENDIX B

Keyword	Number of Citations
mathematics education	74
student characteristics	72
writing (composition)	70
evaluation	69
student evaluation	68
chemistry	66
research	66
comparative education	63
graduate study	63
learning	62

Number of Citations for one word	Number of Keywords	Percent
305	1	
294	1	
292	1	
209	1	
203	1	
190	1	
174	1	
144	1	
127	1	
122	1	
112	1	
102	1	
99	1	
98	1	
96	1	
95	2	0.1%
84	1	
82	1	
80	1	
79	1	
74	1	
72	1	
70	1	
69	1	
68	1	
66	2	0.1
63	2	0.1
62	1	
59	3	0.1
58	2	0.1
57	1	
56	1	
55	1	
54	2	0.1
53	1	

Number of Citations for one word	Number of Keywords	Percent
50	4	0.2
49	6	0.3
48	2	0.1
46	1	
45	2	0.1
44	2	0.1
42	3	0.1
41	3	0.1
40	3	0.1
39	5	0.2
38	1	
36	4	0.2
35	3	0.1
34	4	0.2
33	7	0.3
32	6	0.3
31	7	0.3
30	1	
29	4	0.2
28	7	0.3
27	4	0.2
26	7	0.3
25	8	0.3
24	8	0.3
23	5	0.2
22	8	0.3
21	6	0.3
20	8	0.3
19	8	0.3
18	14	0.6
17	13	0.6
16	11	0.5
15	22	0.9
14	21	0.9
13	24	1.0
12	30	1.3
11	23	1.0
10	32	1.4
9	43	1.8
8	52	2.2
7	67	2.9
6	79	3.3
5	114	4.9
4	164	7.0
3	216	9.2
2	383	16.4
1	856	36.5
	2,343	

APPENDIX B

Records Having
Number of Keywords

	Number of Records	Percent
1	2,726	100.0%
2	2,567	94.2
3	2,266	83.1
4	2,049	75.2
5	1,849	67.8
6	1,603	58.8
7	1,271	46.6
8	876	32.1
9	455	16.7
10	279	10.2
11	181	6.6
12	111	4.1
13	69	2.5
14	34	1.2
	16,336	

Database Structure

The database's structure is:

Database: Information	Quantity	Field: Type	Width
1. Article (Book) Title	1	Character	150
2. Author	1	Character	45
3. Citation Information	1	Character	55
4. Year Published	1	Numeric	2
5. Abstract	3	Character	254
6. Keywords	14	Character	30

Because of dBASE's structure, the three abstract fields are required. However, the programs provided treat the three abstract fields as if a single field.

The synonym dictionary has the capability of having a main word (30-character maximum) and 15 similar words (each having a 30-character maximum).

System Requirements

In order to run the AAA Educational Database, you must have the following tools:

Hardware
1. An IBM PC, PC/2, AT or XT or other 100 percent IBM PC compatible computer[1]
2. A hard disk with approximately 3.9 meg available

Software:
3. PC DOS release 2.0 or higher, or MS DOS release 2.1 or higher[1]
4. dBASE III PLUS

---

[1] This is required by dBASE III PLUS